HERCULES

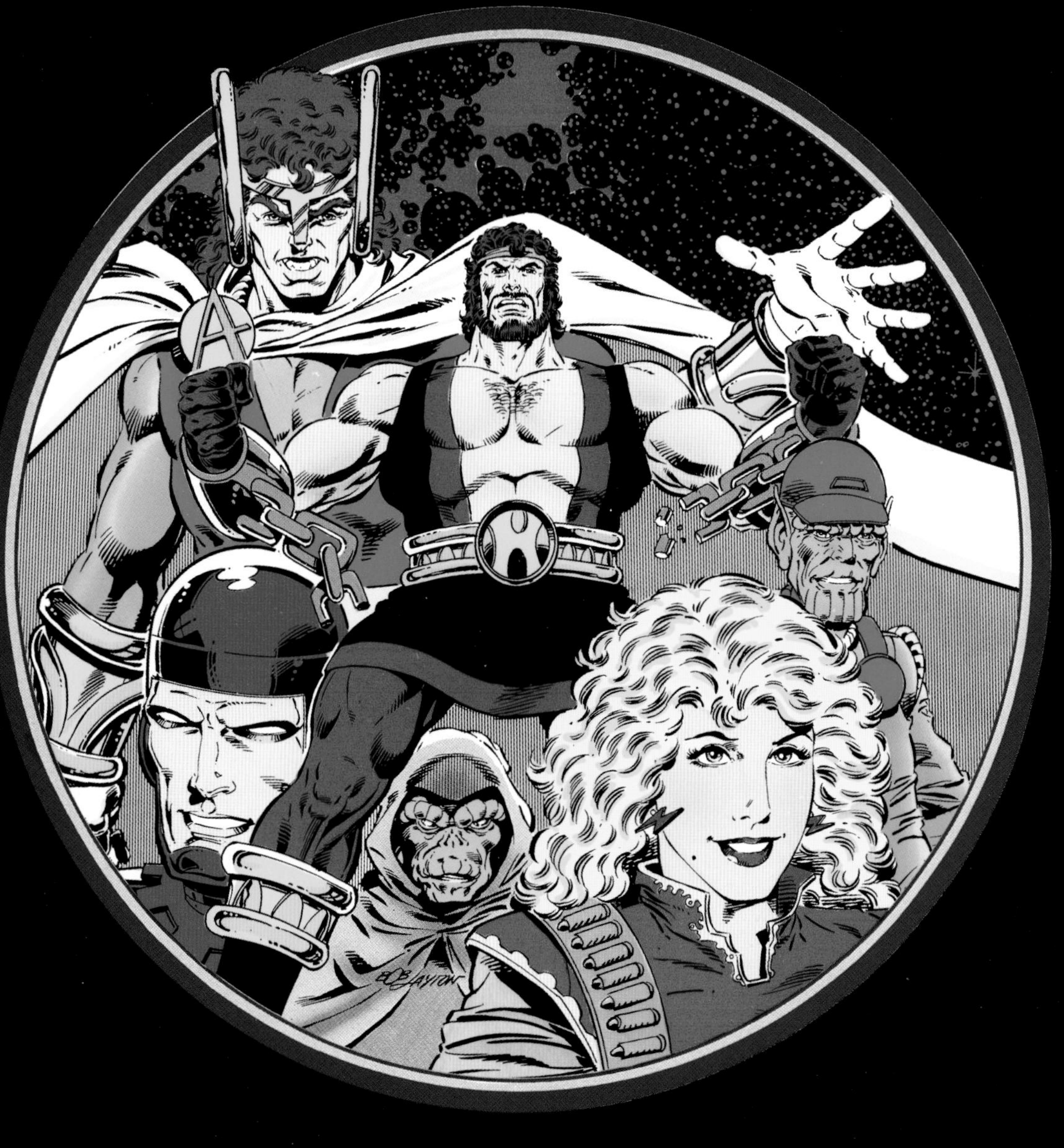

FULL CIRCLE

HERCULES

WRITER & ARTIST
BOB LAYTON

COLORISTS
ANDY YANCHUS,
GEORGE ROUSSOS
& BRAD VANCATA

LETTERERS
JACK MORELLI
& JOHN WORKMAN

EDITORS
GREGORY WRIGHT
& TERRY KAVANAGH

COVER ARTIST
BOB LAYTON

COVER COLORS
TOM CHU

JENNIFER GRÜNWALD

SENIOR EDITOR, SPECIAL PROJECTS
JEFF YOUNGQUIST

RESEARCH
STUART VANDAL

PRODUCTION
JERRON QUALITY COLOR

COLOR RECONSTRUCTION
DIGIKORE

BOOK DESIGNER
SPRING HOTELING

SENIOR VICE PRESIDENT OF SALES
DAVID GABRIEL

EDITOR IN CHIEF
JOE QUESADA

PUBLISHER
DAN BUCKLEY

EXECUTIVE PRODUCER
ALAN FINE

SPECIAL THANKS TO POND SCUM

CIRCLE

ULES: FULL CIRCLE. Contains material originally published in magazine form as MARVEL TALES #197, MARVEL GRAPHIC NOVEL #37, MARVEL COMICS PRESENTS #39-41, and MARVEL #4 and #65. First printing 2009. ISBN# 978-0-7851-3957-7. Published by MARVEL PUBLISHING, INC., a subsidiary of MARVEL ENTERTAINMENT, INC. OFFICE OF PUBLICATION: 417 venue, New York, NY 10016. Copyright © 1983, 1987, 1988, 1990 and 2009 Marvel Characters, Inc. All rights reserved. $19.99 per copy in the U.S. (GST #R127032852); Canadian ment #40668537. All characters featured in this issue and the distinctive names and likenesses thereof, and all related indicia are trademarks of Marvel Characters, Inc. No similarity en any of the names, characters, persons, and/or institutions in this magazine with those of any living or dead person or institution is intended, and any such similarity which may exist ely coincidental. **Printed in China**. ALAN FINE, EVP - Office Of The Chief Executive Marvel Entertainment, Inc. & CMO Marvel Characters B.V.; DAN BUCKLEY, Chief Executive Officer ublisher - Print, Animation & Digital Media; JIM SOKOLOWSKI, Chief Operating Officer; DAVID GABRIEL, SVP of Publishing Sales & Circulation; DAVID BOGART, SVP of Business Affairs & Management; MICHAEL PASCIULLO, VP Merchandising & Communications; JIM O'KEEFE, VP of Operations & Logistics; DAN CARR, Executive Director of Publishing Technology; JUSTIN BRIE, Director of Publishing & Editorial Operations; SUSAN CRESPI, Editorial Operations Manager; ALEX MORALES, Publishing Operations Manager; STAN LEE, Chairman Emeritus. For ation regarding advertising in Marvel Comics or on Marvel.com, please contact Mitch Dane, Advertising Director, at mdane@marvel.com. For Marvel subscription inquiries, please call 17-9158. **Manufactured between 8/12/09 and 9/16/09 by KING YIP (DONGGUAN) PRINTING & PACKAGING FACTORY LTD., DONGGUAN, GUANGDONG, CHINA.**

7654321

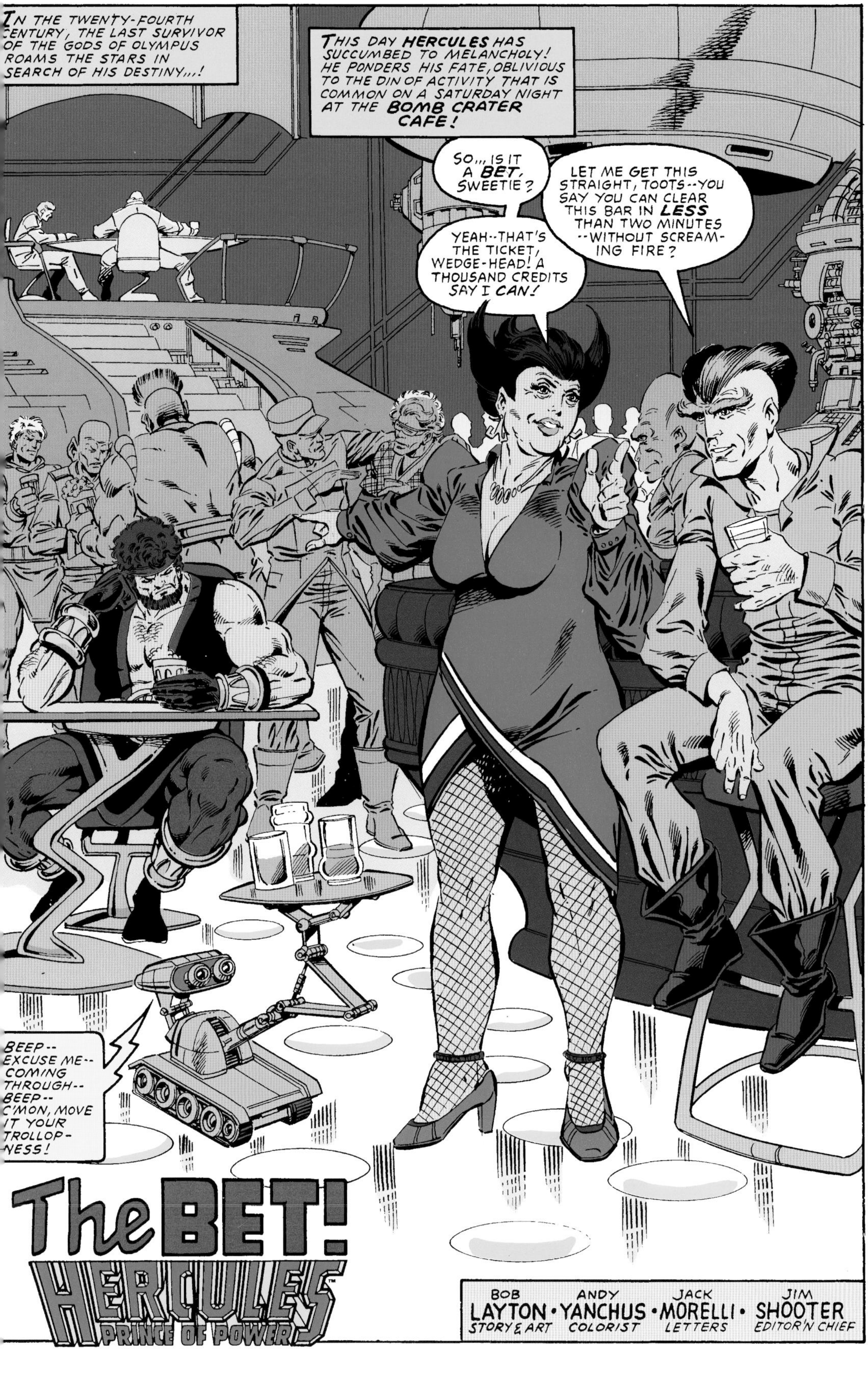
IN THE TWENTY-FOURTH CENTURY, THE LAST SURVIVOR OF THE GODS OF OLYMPUS ROAMS THE STARS IN SEARCH OF HIS DESTINY...!
THIS DAY HERCULES HAS SUCCUMBED TO MELANCHOLY! HE PONDERS HIS FATE, OBLIVIOUS TO THE DIN OF ACTIVITY THAT IS COMMON ON A SATURDAY NIGHT AT THE BOMB CRATER CAFE!
SO... IS IT A BET, SWEETIE?
YEAH--THAT'S THE TICKET, WEDGE-HEAD! A THOUSAND CREDITS SAY I CAN!
LET ME GET THIS STRAIGHT, TOOTS--YOU SAY YOU CAN CLEAR THIS BAR IN LESS THAN TWO MINUTES --WITHOUT SCREAMING FIRE?
BEEP-- EXCUSE ME-- COMING THROUGH-- BEEP-- C'MON, MOVE IT YOUR TROLLOPNESS!
The BET!
HERCULES
PRINCE OF POWER
BOB LAYTON STORY & ART • ANDY YANCHUS COLORIST • JACK MORELLI LETTERS • JIM SHOOTER EDITOR'N CHIEF

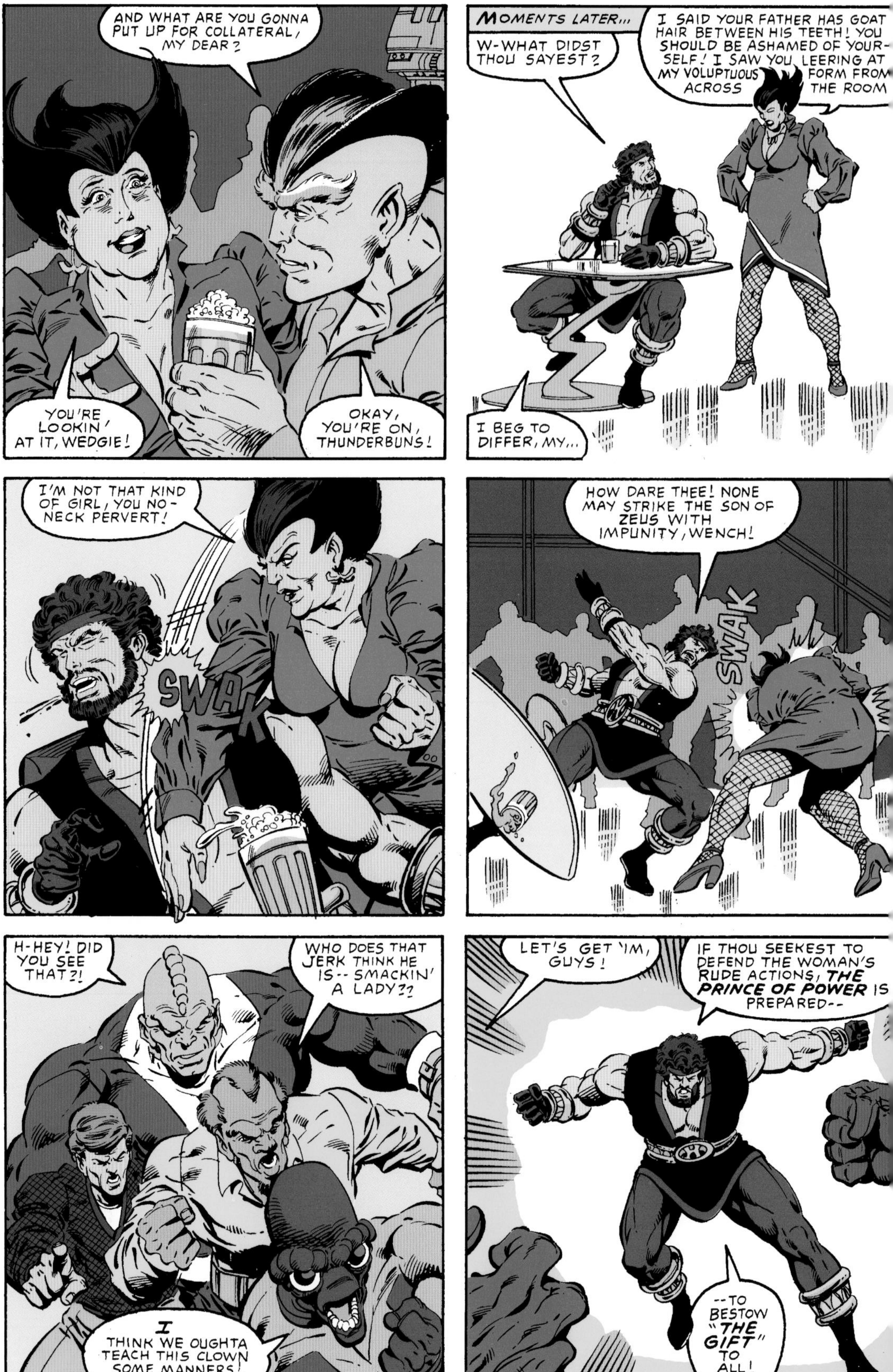
AND WHAT ARE YOU GONNA PUT UP FOR COLLATERAL, MY DEAR?
YOU'RE LOOKIN' AT IT, WEDGIE!
OKAY, YOU'RE ON, THUNDERBUNS!
MOMENTS LATER...
W-WHAT DIDST THOU SAYEST?
I SAID YOUR FATHER HAS GOAT HAIR BETWEEN HIS TEETH! YOU SHOULD BE ASHAMED OF YOURSELF! I SAW YOU LEERING AT MY VOLUPTUOUS FORM FROM ACROSS THE ROOM
I BEG TO DIFFER, MY...
I'M NOT THAT KIND OF GIRL, YOU NO-NECK PERVERT!
SWAK
HOW DARE THEE! NONE MAY STRIKE THE SON OF ZEUS WITH IMPUNITY, WENCH!
SWAK
H-HEY! DID YOU SEE THAT?!
WHO DOES THAT JERK THINK HE IS -- SMACKIN' A LADY??
I THINK WE OUGHTA TEACH THIS CLOWN SOME MANNERS!
LET'S GET 'IM, GUYS!
IF THOU SEEKEST TO DEFEND THE WOMAN'S RUDE ACTIONS, THE PRINCE OF POWER IS PREPARED--
--TO BESTOW "THE GIFT" TO ALL!

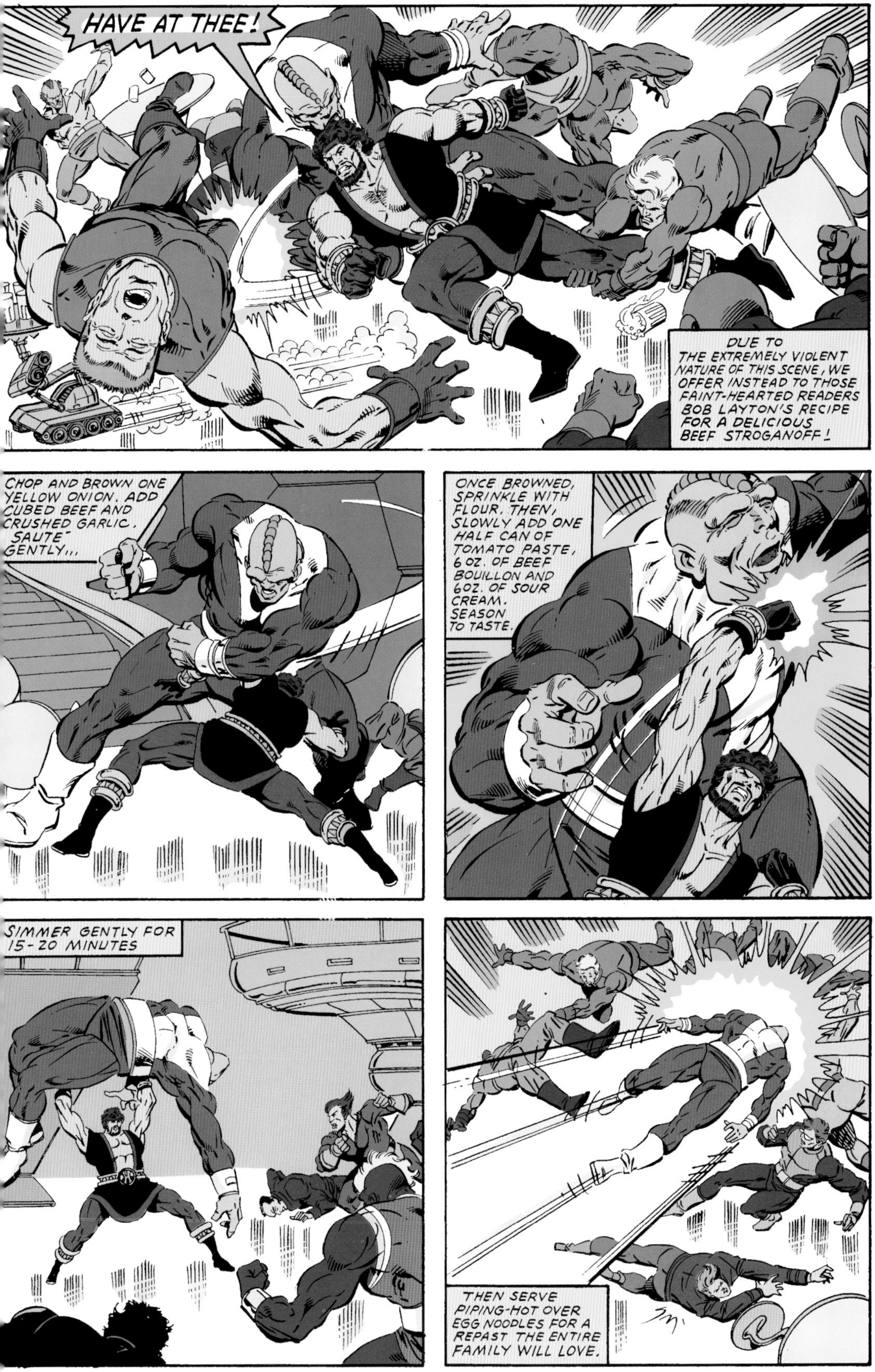
HAVE AT THEE!
DUE TO THE EXTREMELY VIOLENT NATURE OF THIS SCENE, WE OFFER INSTEAD TO THOSE FAINT-HEARTED READERS BOB LAYTON'S RECIPE FOR A DELICIOUS BEEF STROGANOFF!
CHOP AND BROWN ONE YELLOW ONION. ADD CUBED BEEF AND CRUSHED GARLIC. SAUTE' GENTLY...
ONCE BROWNED, SPRINKLE WITH FLOUR. THEN, SLOWLY ADD ONE HALF CAN OF TOMATO PASTE, 6 OZ. OF BEEF BOUILLON AND 6OZ. OF SOUR CREAM. SEASON TO TASTE.
SIMMER GENTLY FOR 15-20 MINUTES
THEN SERVE PIPING-HOT OVER EGG NOODLES FOR A REPAST THE ENTIRE FAMILY WILL LOVE.

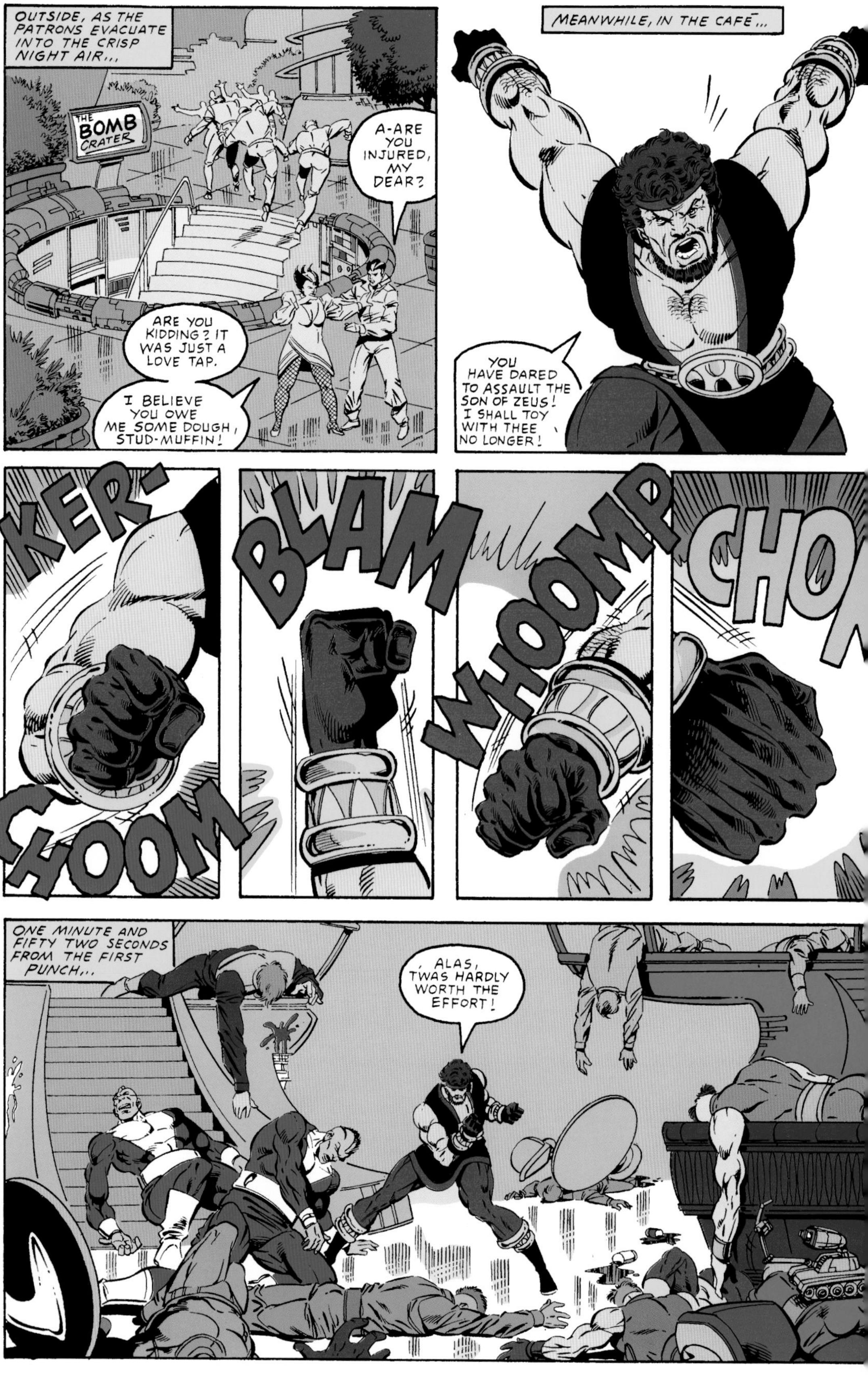
OUTSIDE, AS THE PATRONS EVACUATE INTO THE CRISP NIGHT AIR...
THE BOMB CRATER
A-ARE YOU INJURED, MY DEAR?
ARE YOU KIDDING? IT WAS JUST A LOVE TAP.
I BELIEVE YOU OWE ME SOME DOUGH, STUD-MUFFIN!
MEANWHILE, IN THE CAFÉ...
YOU HAVE DARED TO ASSAULT THE SON OF ZEUS! I SHALL TOY WITH THEE NO LONGER!
KER-CHOOM
BLAM
WHOOMP
CHO
ONE MINUTE AND FIFTY TWO SECONDS FROM THE FIRST PUNCH...
ALAS, 'TWAS HARDLY WORTH THE EFFORT!

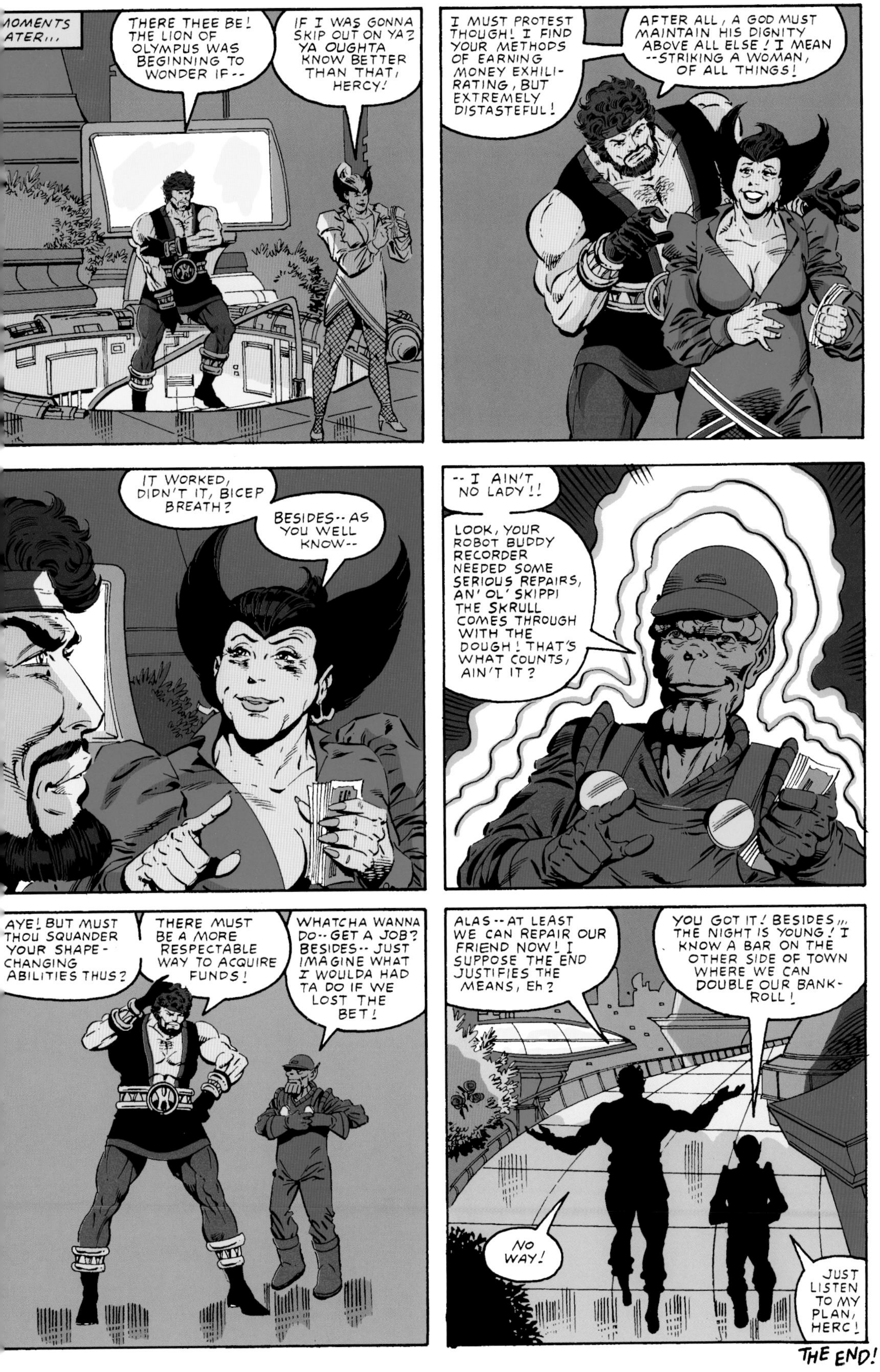
MOMENTS LATER...
THERE THEE BE! THE LION OF OLYMPUS WAS BEGINNING TO WONDER IF --
IF I WAS GONNA SKIP OUT ON YA? YA OUGHTA KNOW BETTER THAN THAT, HERCY!
I MUST PROTEST THOUGH! I FIND YOUR METHODS OF EARNING MONEY EXHILIRATING, BUT EXTREMELY DISTASTEFUL!
AFTER ALL, A GOD MUST MAINTAIN HIS DIGNITY ABOVE ALL ELSE! I MEAN --STRIKING A WOMAN, OF ALL THINGS!
IT WORKED, DIDN'T IT, BICEP BREATH?
BESIDES-- AS YOU WELL KNOW--
-- I AIN'T NO LADY!!
LOOK, YOUR ROBOT BUDDY RECORDER NEEDED SOME SERIOUS REPAIRS, AN' OL' SKIPPI THE SKRULL COMES THROUGH WITH THE DOUGH! THAT'S WHAT COUNTS, AIN'T IT?
AYE! BUT MUST THOU SQUANDER YOUR SHAPE-CHANGING ABILITIES THUS?
THERE MUST BE A MORE RESPECTABLE WAY TO ACQUIRE FUNDS!
WHATCHA WANNA DO-- GET A JOB? BESIDES-- JUST IMAGINE WHAT I WOULDA HAD TA DO IF WE LOST THE BET!
ALAS-- AT LEAST WE CAN REPAIR OUR FRIEND NOW! I SUPPOSE THE END JUSTIFIES THE MEANS, Eh?
YOU GOT IT! BESIDES,,, THE NIGHT IS YOUNG! I KNOW A BAR ON THE OTHER SIDE OF TOWN WHERE WE CAN DOUBLE OUR BANK-ROLL!
NO WAY!
JUST LISTEN TO MY PLAN, HERC!
THE END!

A MARVEL® GRAPHIC NOVEL

HERCULES™
PRINCE OF POWER

FULL CIRCLE

by BOB LAYTON

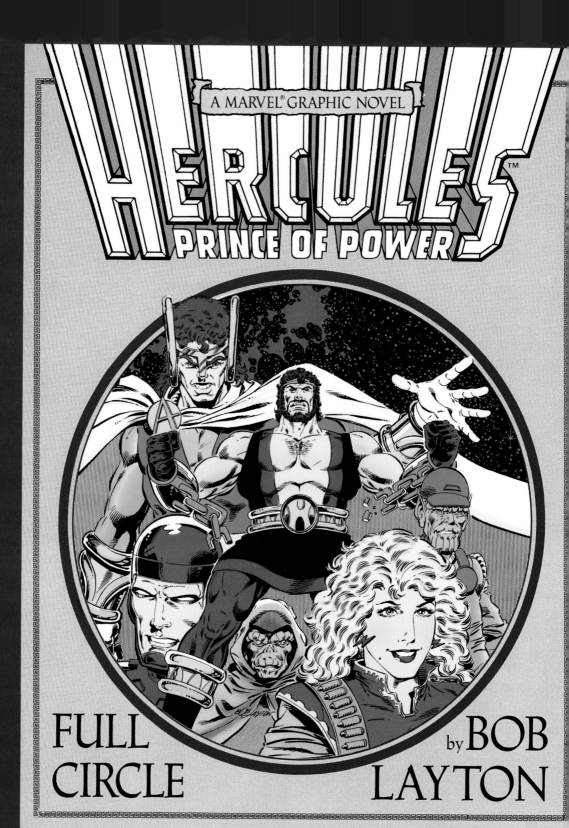

A • MARVEL® • GRAPHIC • NOVEL

HERCULES
PRINCE OF POWER

Published by
THE MARVEL ENTERTAINMENT GROUP, INC.
387 PARK AVENUE SOUTH
NEW YORK, NY 10016

ISBN: 0-87135-397-0

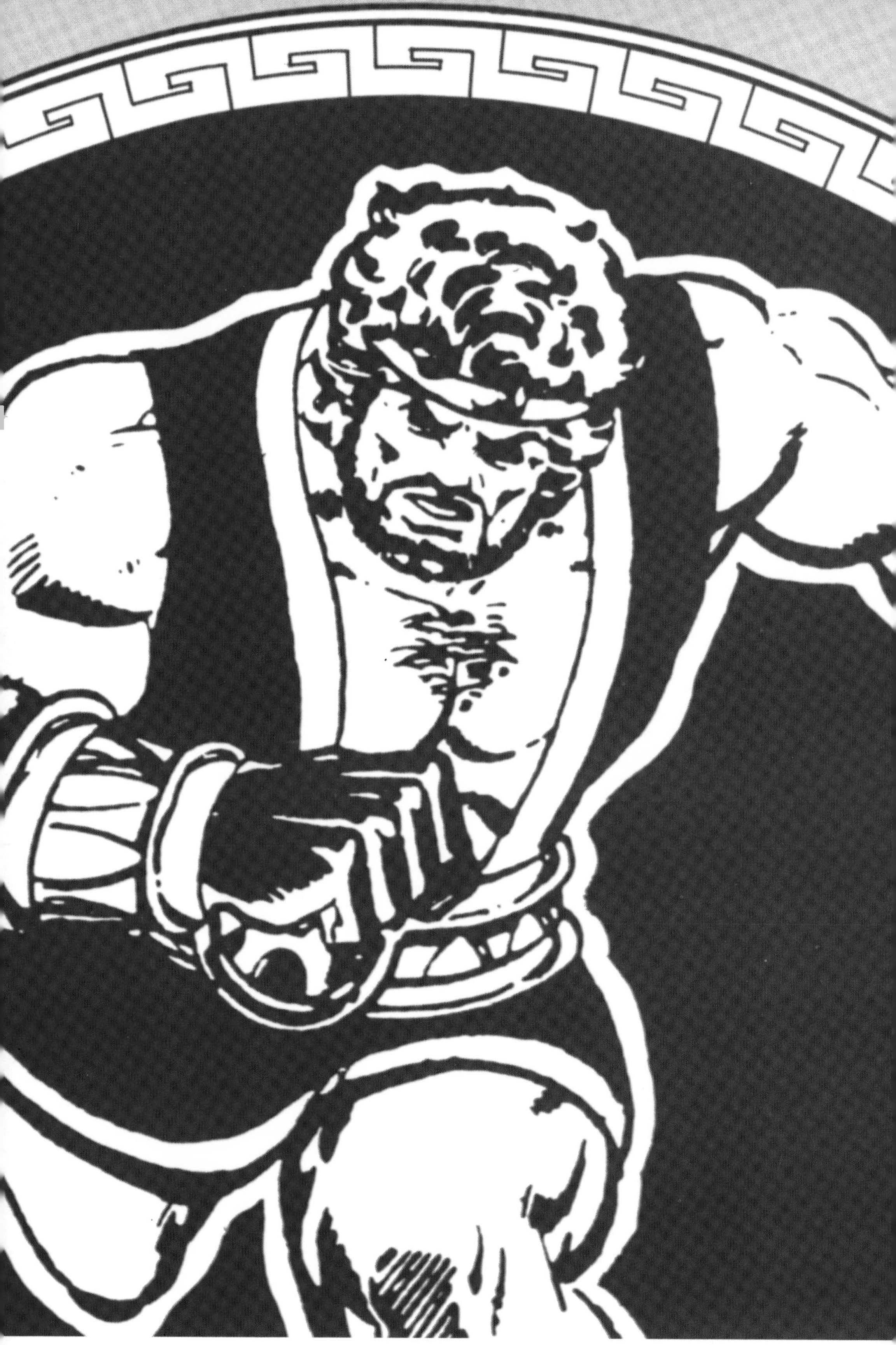

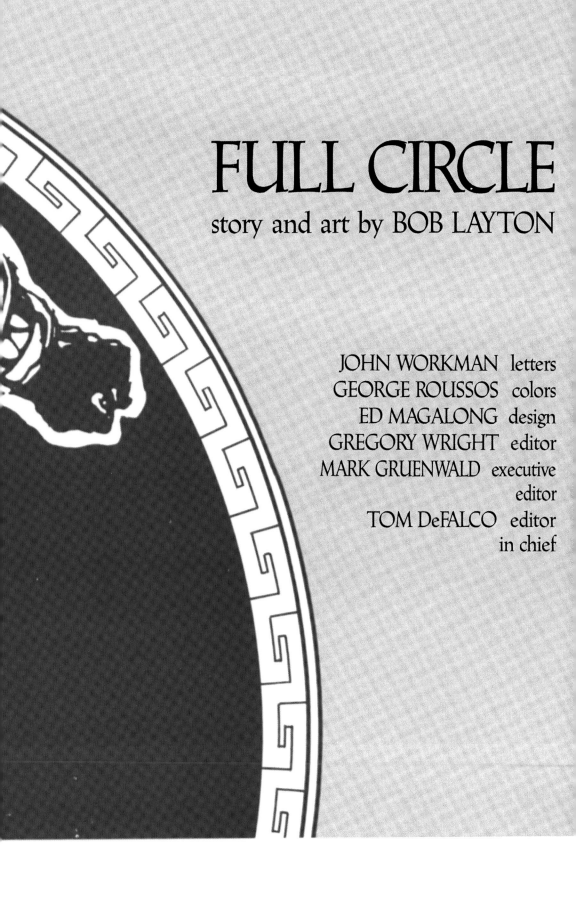

FULL CIRCLE

story and art by BOB LAYTON

JOHN WORKMAN letters
GEORGE ROUSSOS colors
ED MAGALONG design
GREGORY WRIGHT editor
MARK GRUENWALD executive
editor
TOM DeFALCO editor
in chief

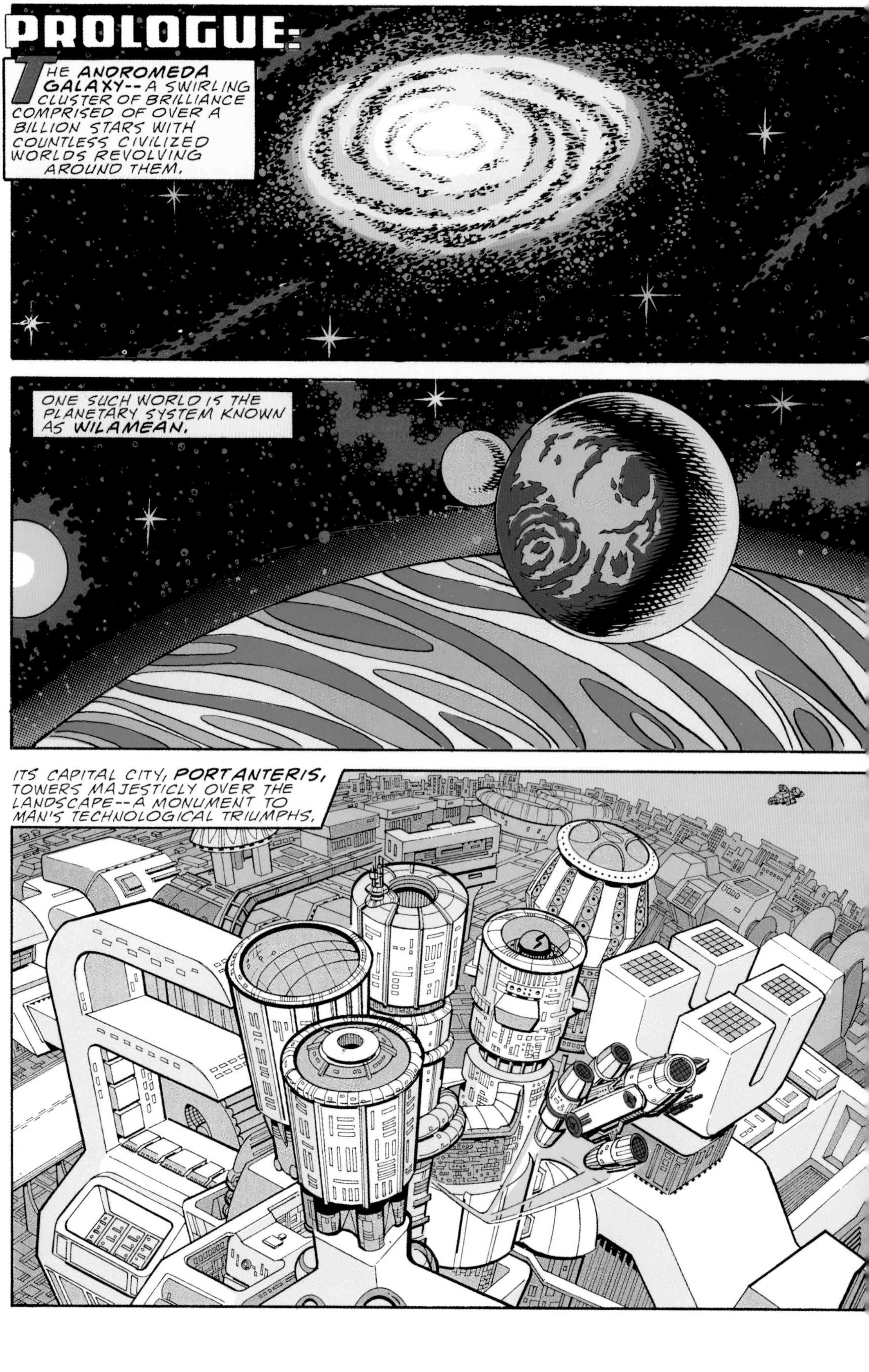
PROLOGUE:
THE ANDROMEDA GALAXY--A SWIRLING CLUSTER OF BRILLIANCE COMPRISED OF OVER A BILLION STARS WITH COUNTLESS CIVILIZED WORLDS REVOLVING AROUND THEM.
ONE SUCH WORLD IS THE PLANETARY SYSTEM KNOWN AS WILAMEAN.
ITS CAPITAL CITY, PORTANTERIS, TOWERS MAJESTICLY OVER THE LANDSCAPE--A MONUMENT TO MAN'S TECHNOLOGICAL TRIUMPHS.

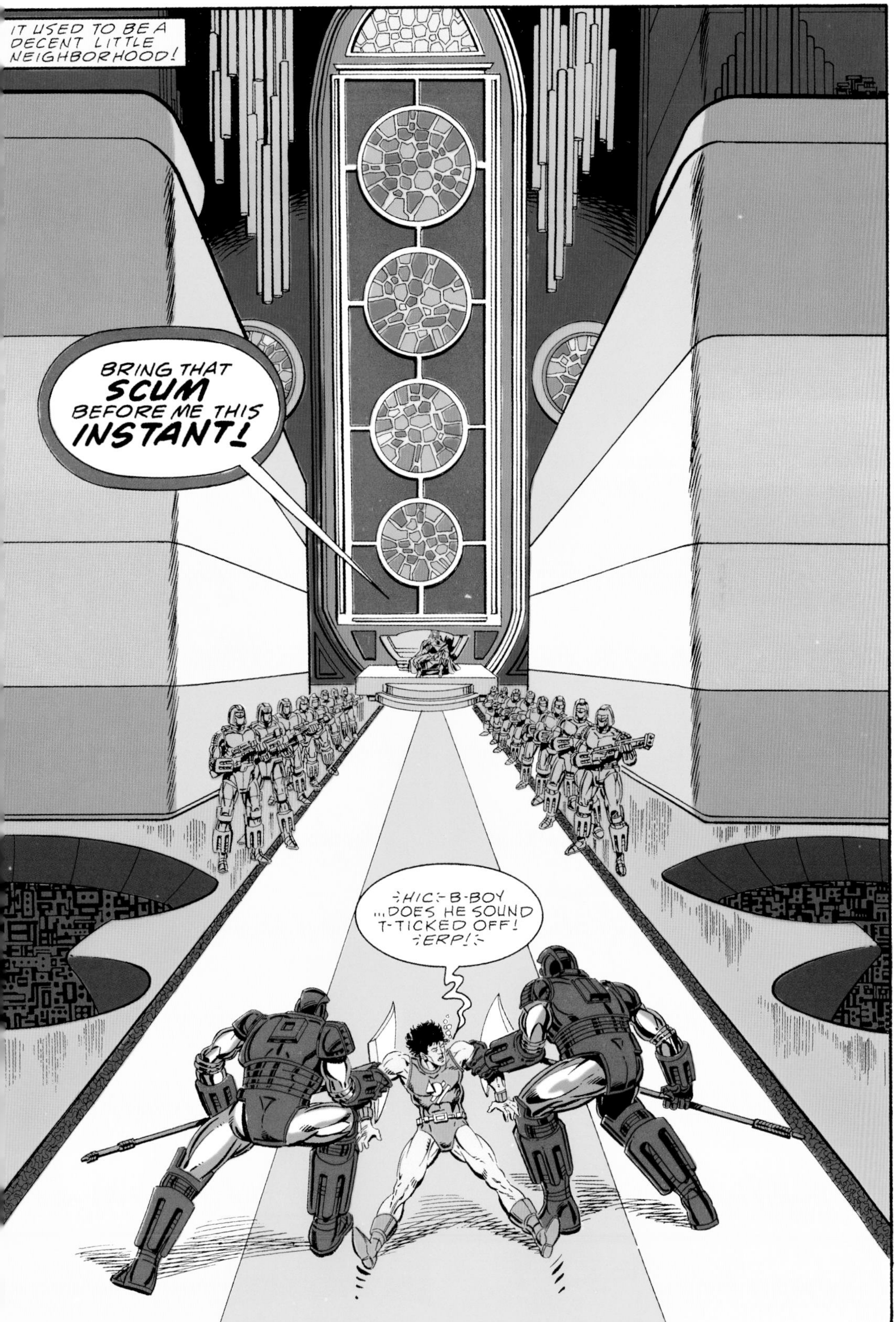
IT USED TO BE A DECENT LITTLE NEIGHBORHOOD!
BRING THAT SCUM BEFORE ME THIS INSTANT!
-HIC- B-BOY ...DOES HE SOUND T-TICKED OFF! -ERP!-

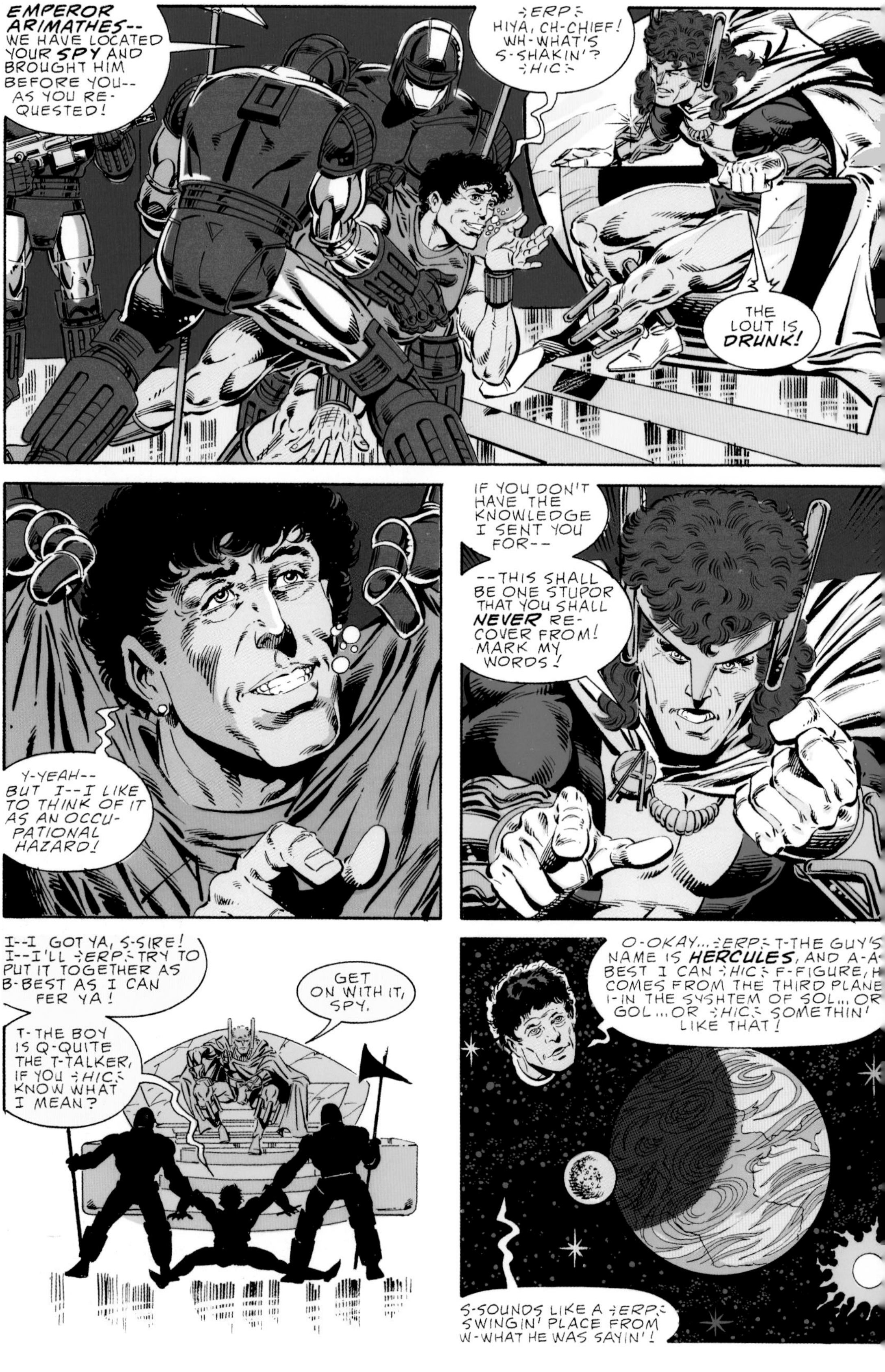
EMPEROR ARIMATHES-- WE HAVE LOCATED YOUR SPY AND BROUGHT HIM BEFORE YOU-- AS YOU REQUESTED!
-ERP- HIYA, CH-CHIEF! WH-WHAT'S S-SHAKIN'? -HIC-
THE LOUT IS DRUNK!
Y-YEAH-- BUT I--I LIKE TO THINK OF IT AS AN OCCUPATIONAL HAZARD!
IF YOU DON'T HAVE THE KNOWLEDGE I SENT YOU FOR--
--THIS SHALL BE ONE STUPOR THAT YOU SHALL NEVER RECOVER FROM! MARK MY WORDS!
I--I GOT YA, S-SIRE! I--I'LL -ERP- TRY TO PUT IT TOGETHER AS B-BEST AS I CAN FER YA!
T-THE BOY IS Q-QUITE THE T-TALKER, IF YOU -HIC- KNOW WHAT I MEAN?
GET ON WITH IT, SPY.
O-OKAY... -ERP- T-THE GUY'S NAME IS HERCULES, AND A-A BEST I CAN -HIC- F-FIGURE, H COMES FROM THE THIRD PLANE I-IN THE SYSHTEM OF SOL... OR GOL... OR -HIC- SOMETHIN' LIKE THAT!
S-SOUNDS LIKE A -ERP- SWINGIN' PLACE FROM W-WHAT HE WAS SAYIN'!

-HERC AND A WHOLE PACK O' -LAWS L-LIVED ⸬HIC⸬ ATOP 'IS MOUNTAIN ⸬HIC⸬ CALLED 'YMPUS, THOUSANDS OF Y-YEARS AGO! ⸬HIC⸬

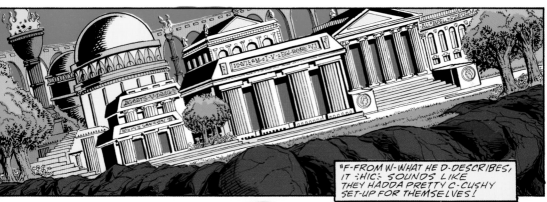

"F-FROM W-WHAT HE D-DESCRIBES, IT ⸬HIC⸬ SOUNDS LIKE THEY HADDA PRETTY C-CUSHY SET-UP FOR THEMSELVES!

S B-BEST AS I CAN FIGURE, THEY PASSED THE TIME BY ⸬RP⸬ EITHER SCREWIN' 'ROUND OR BEATIN' THE 'RAP OUTTA EACH OTHER!

17

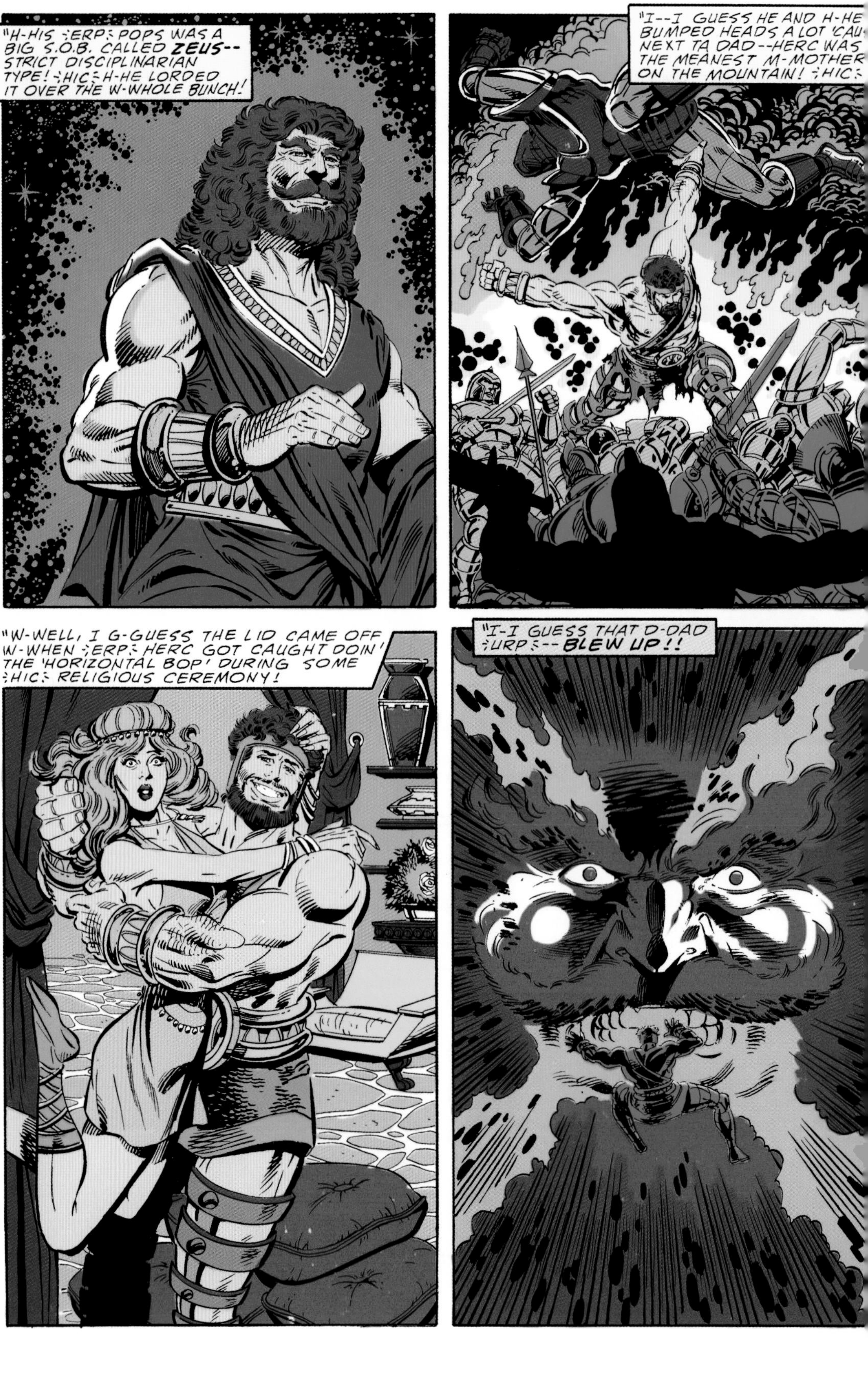
"H-HIS ;ERP; POPS WAS A BIG S.O.B. CALLED ZEUS-- STRICT DISCIPLINARIAN TYPE! ;HIC; H-HE LORDED IT OVER THE W-WHOLE BUNCH!
"I--I GUESS HE AND H-HE BUMPED HEADS A LOT 'CAU NEXT TA DAD--HERC WAS THE MEANEST M-MOTHER ON THE MOUNTAIN! ;HIC;
"W-WELL, I G-GUESS THE LID CAME OFF W-WHEN ;ERP; HERC GOT CAUGHT DOIN' THE 'HORIZONTAL BOP' DURING SOME ;HIC; RELIGIOUS CEREMONY!
"I-I GUESS THAT D-DAD ;URP;--BLEW UP!!

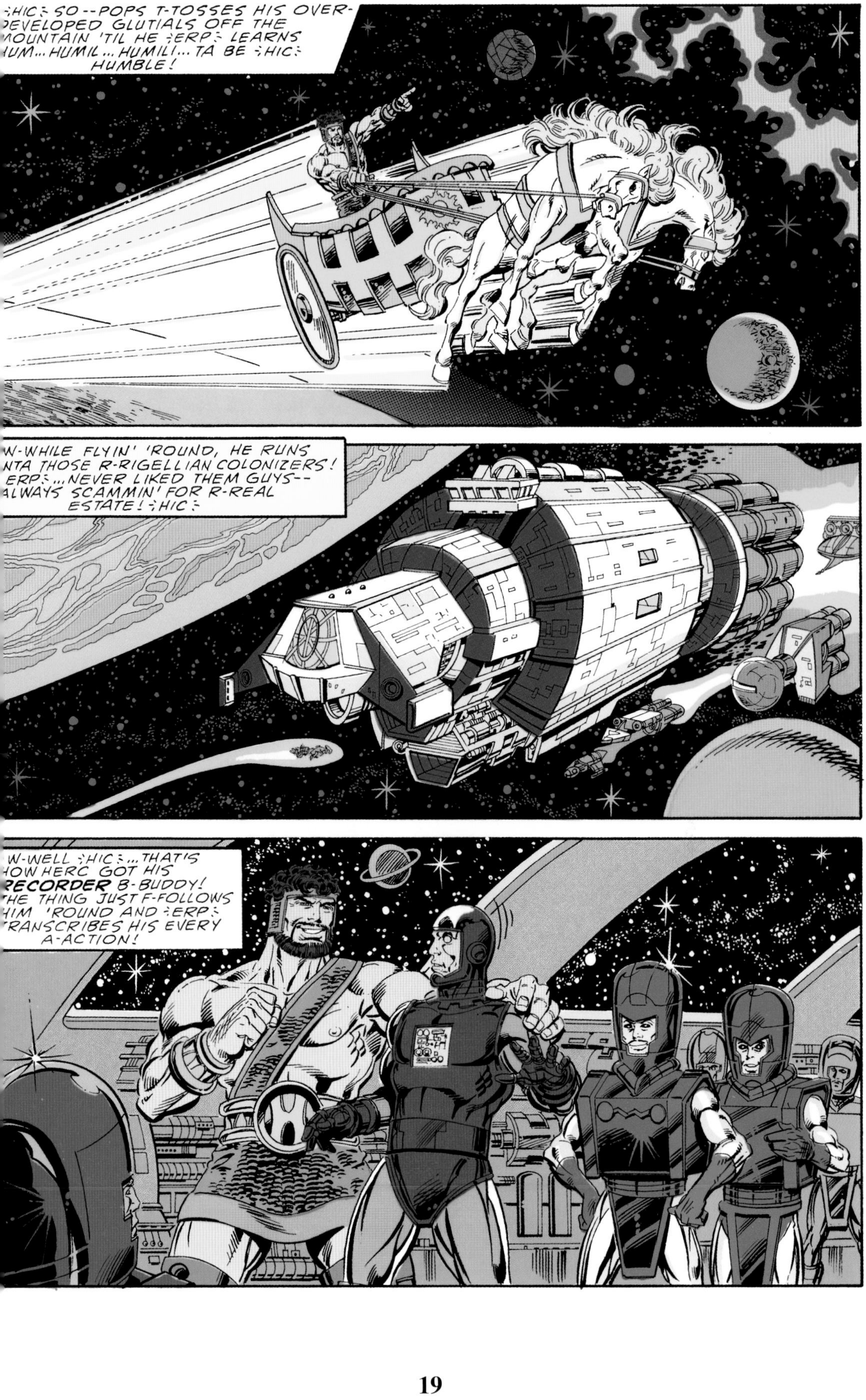
HIC: SO--POPS T-TOSSES HIS OVER-DEVELOPED GLUTIALS OFF THE MOUNTAIN 'TIL HE :ERP: LEARNS HUM... HUMIL... HUMILI... TA BE :HIC: HUMBLE!
W-WHILE FLYIN' 'ROUND, HE RUNS INTA THOSE R-RIGELLIAN COLONIZERS! :ERP: ...NEVER LIKED THEM GUYS-- ALWAYS SCAMMIN' FOR R-REAL ESTATE! :HIC:
W-WELL :HIC: ...THAT'S HOW HERC GOT HIS **RECORDER** B-BUDDY! THE THING JUST F-FOLLOWS HIM 'ROUND AND :ERP: TRANSCRIBES HIS EVERY A-ACTION!

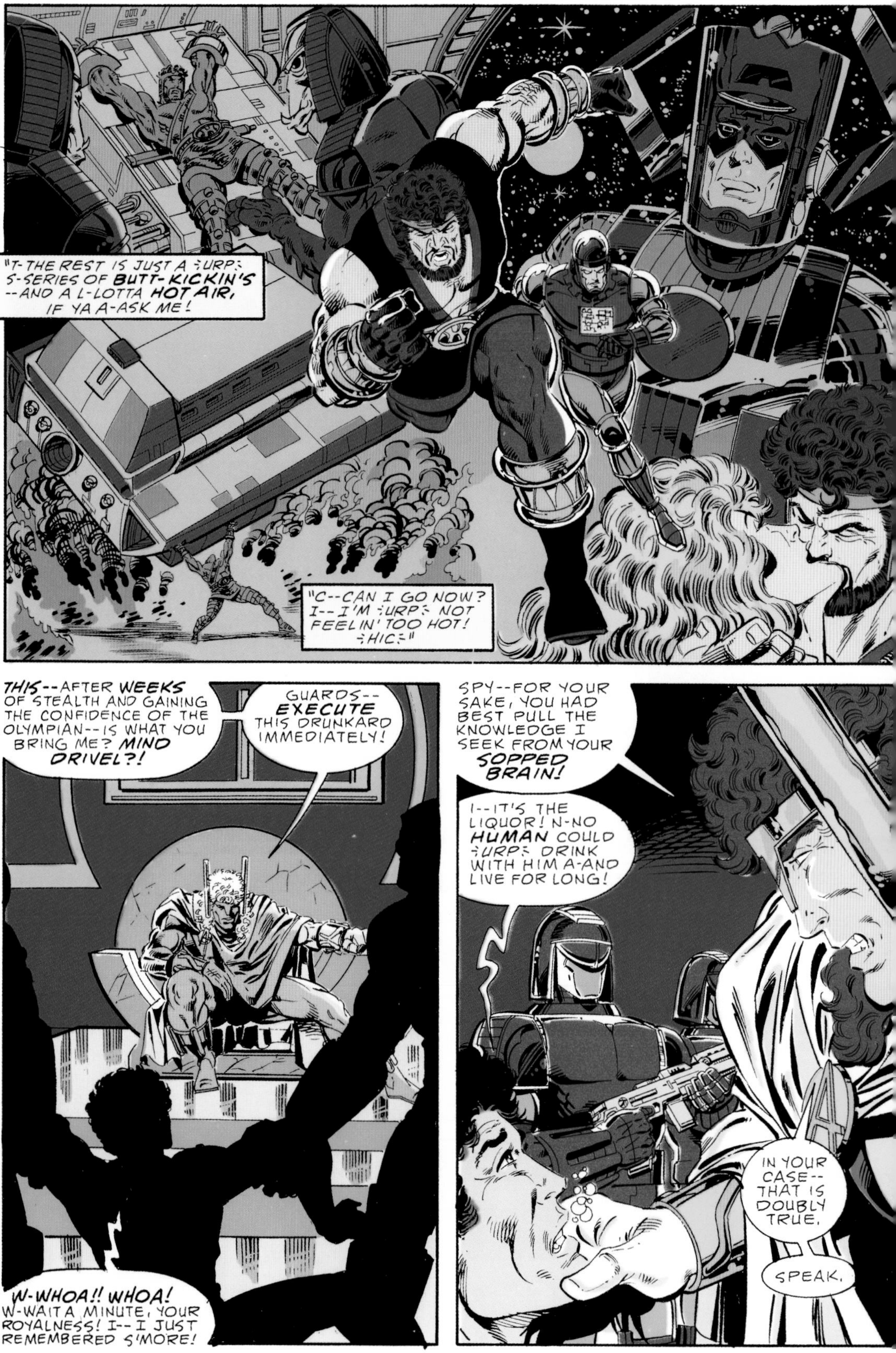
"T-THE REST IS JUST A URP S-SERIES OF BUTT-KICKIN'S --AND A L-LOTTA HOT AIR, IF YA A-ASK ME!
"C--CAN I GO NOW? I--I'M URP NOT FEELIN' TOO HOT! HIC"
THIS--AFTER WEEKS OF STEALTH AND GAINING THE CONFIDENCE OF THE OLYMPIAN--IS WHAT YOU BRING ME? MIND DRIVEL?!
GUARDS--EXECUTE THIS DRUNKARD IMMEDIATELY!
W-WHOA!! WHOA! W-WAIT A MINUTE, YOUR ROYALNESS! I--I JUST REMEMBERED S'MORE!
SPY--FOR YOUR SAKE, YOU HAD BEST PULL THE KNOWLEDGE I SEEK FROM YOUR SOPPED BRAIN!
I--IT'S THE LIQUOR! N-NO HUMAN COULD URP DRINK WITH HIM A-AND LIVE FOR LONG!
IN YOUR CASE--THAT IS DOUBLY TRUE.
SPEAK.

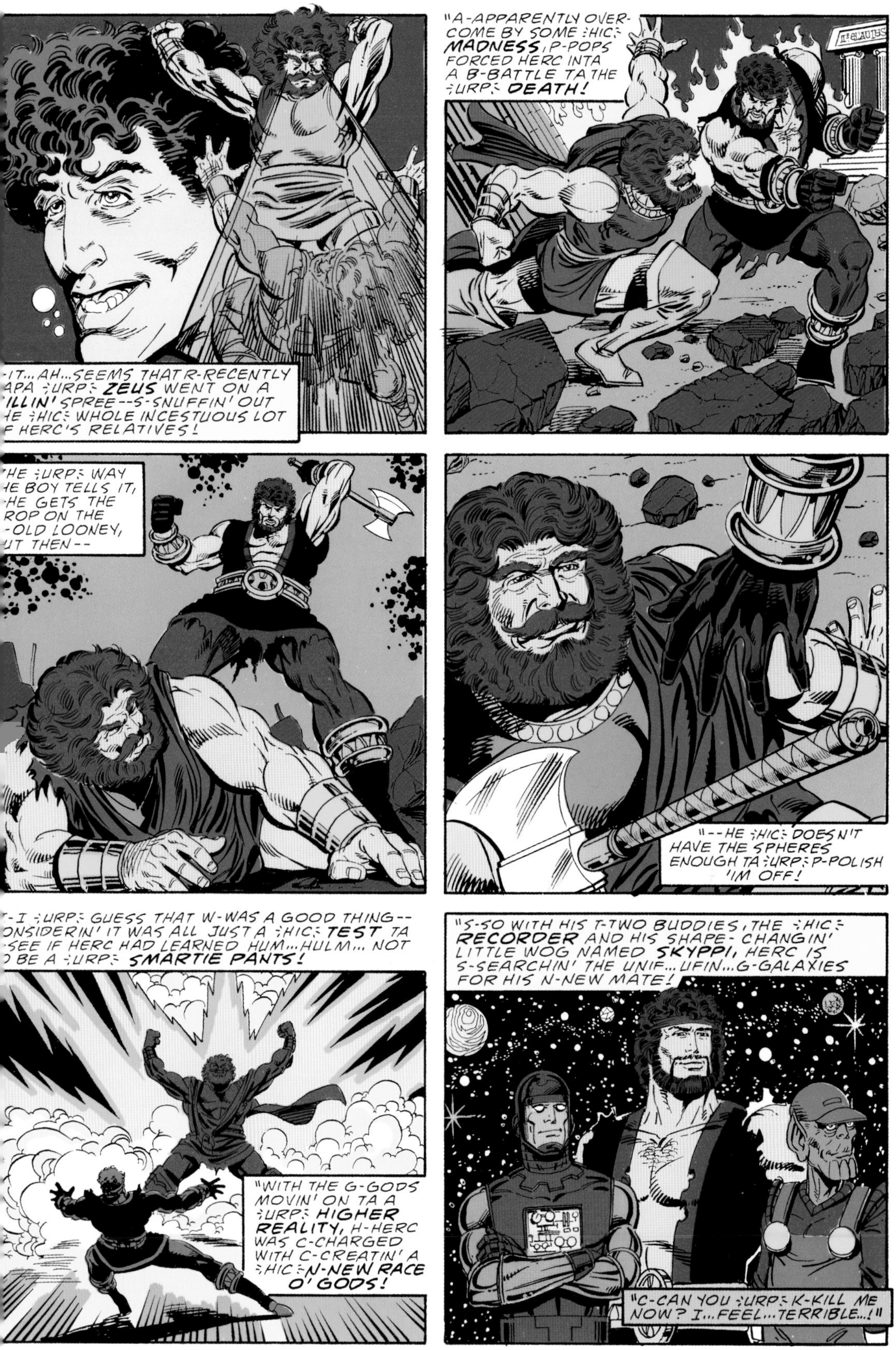
-IT...AH...SEEMS THAT R-RECENTLY APA :URP: ZEUS WENT ON A ILLIN' SPREE--S-SNUFFIN' OUT HE :HIC: WHOLE INCESTUOUS LOT F HERC'S RELATIVES!
"A-APPARENTLY OVER-COME BY SOME :HIC: MADNESS, P-POPS FORCED HERC INTA A B-BATTLE TA THE :URP: DEATH!
HE :URP: WAY HE BOY TELLS IT, HE GETS THE ROP ON THE -OLD LOONEY, UT THEN--
"--HE :HIC: DOESN'T HAVE THE SPHERES ENOUGH TA :URP: P-POLISH 'IM OFF!
-I :URP: GUESS THAT W-WAS A GOOD THING--ONSIDERIN' IT WAS ALL JUST A :HIC: TEST TA SEE IF HERC HAD LEARNED HUM...HULM... NOT O BE A :URP: SMARTIE PANTS!
"WITH THE G-GODS MOVIN' ON TA A :URP: HIGHER REALITY, H-HERC WAS C-CHARGED WITH C-CREATIN' A :HIC: N-NEW RACE O' GODS!
"S-SO WITH HIS T-TWO BUDDIES, THE :HIC: RECORDER AND HIS SHAPE-CHANGIN' LITTLE WOG NAMED SKYPPI, HERC IS S-SEARCHIN' THE UNIF...UFIN...G-GALAXIES FOR HIS N-NEW MATE!
"C-CAN YOU :URP: K-KILL ME NOW? I...FEEL...TERRIBLE...!"

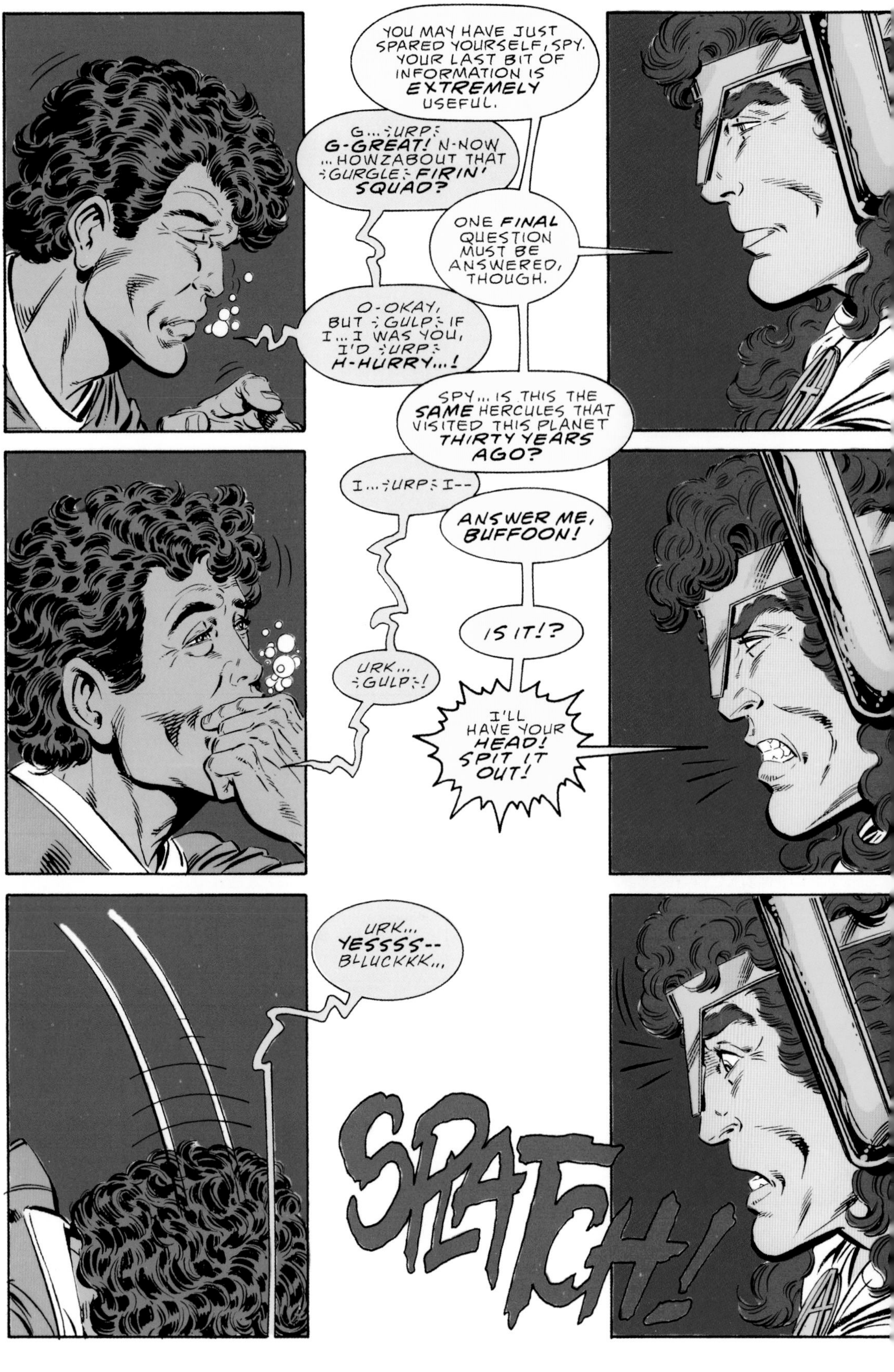

YOU MAY HAVE JUST SPARED YOURSELF, SPY. YOUR LAST BIT OF INFORMATION IS EXTREMELY USEFUL.
G...:URP: G-GREAT! N-NOW ...HOWZABOUT THAT :GURGLE: FIRIN' SQUAD?
ONE FINAL QUESTION MUST BE ANSWERED, THOUGH.
O-OKAY, BUT :GULP: IF I... I WAS YOU, I'D :URP: H-HURRY...!
SPY... IS THIS THE SAME HERCULES THAT VISITED THIS PLANET THIRTY YEARS AGO?
I...:URP: I--
ANSWER ME, BUFFOON!
IS IT!?
URK... :GULP:!
I'LL HAVE YOUR HEAD! SPIT IT OUT!
URK... YESSSS-- BLLUCKKK...
SPLATCH!

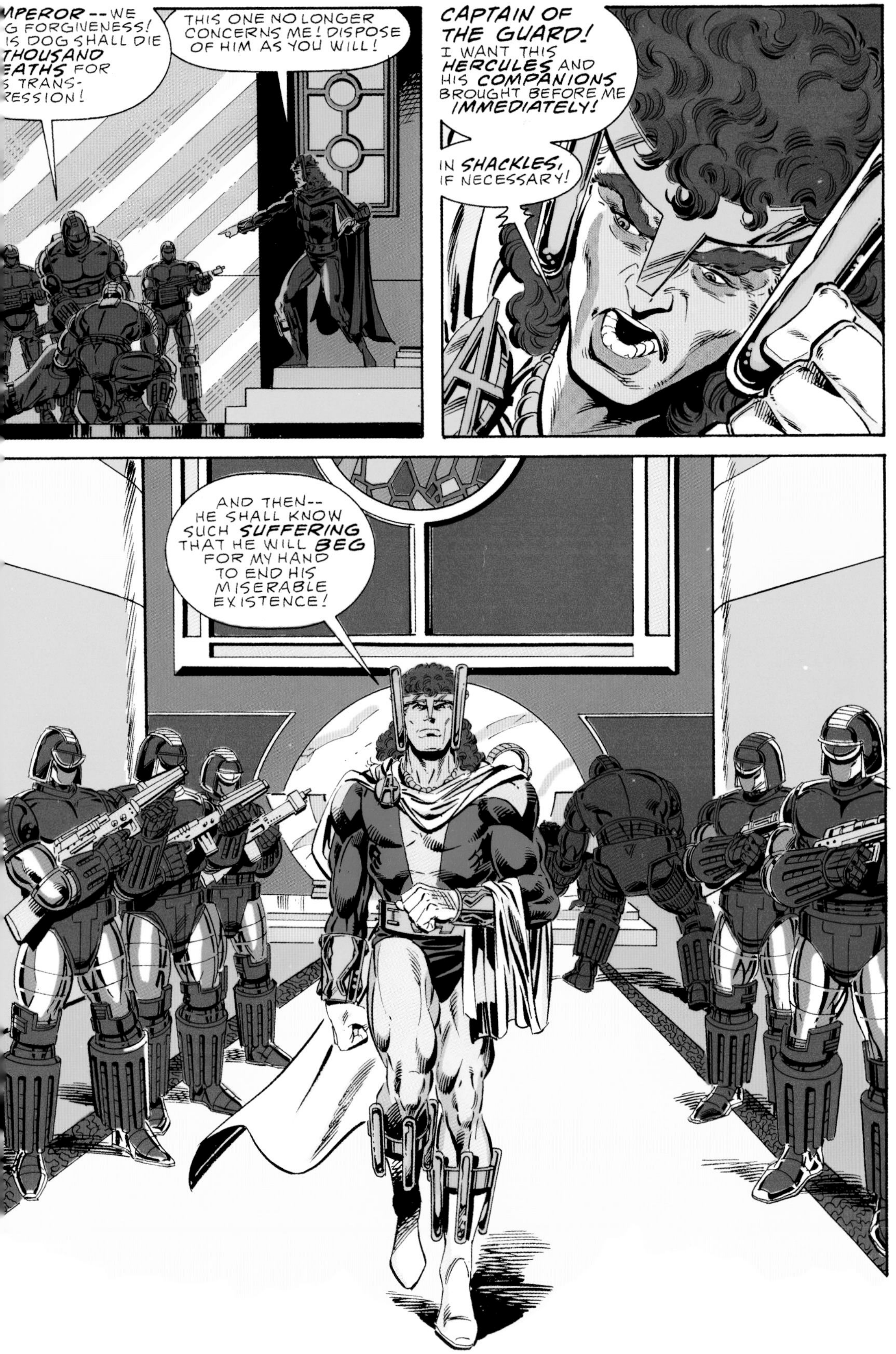
MPEROR -- WE
G FORGIVENESS!
IS DOG SHALL DIE
THOUSAND
EATHS FOR
S TRANS-
RESSION!
THIS ONE NO LONGER CONCERNS ME! DISPOSE OF HIM AS YOU WILL!
CAPTAIN OF THE GUARD! I WANT THIS HERCULES AND HIS COMPANIONS BROUGHT BEFORE ME IMMEDIATELY!
IN SHACKLES, IF NECESSARY!
AND THEN-- HE SHALL KNOW SUCH SUFFERING THAT HE WILL BEG FOR MY HAND TO END HIS MISERABLE EXISTENCE!

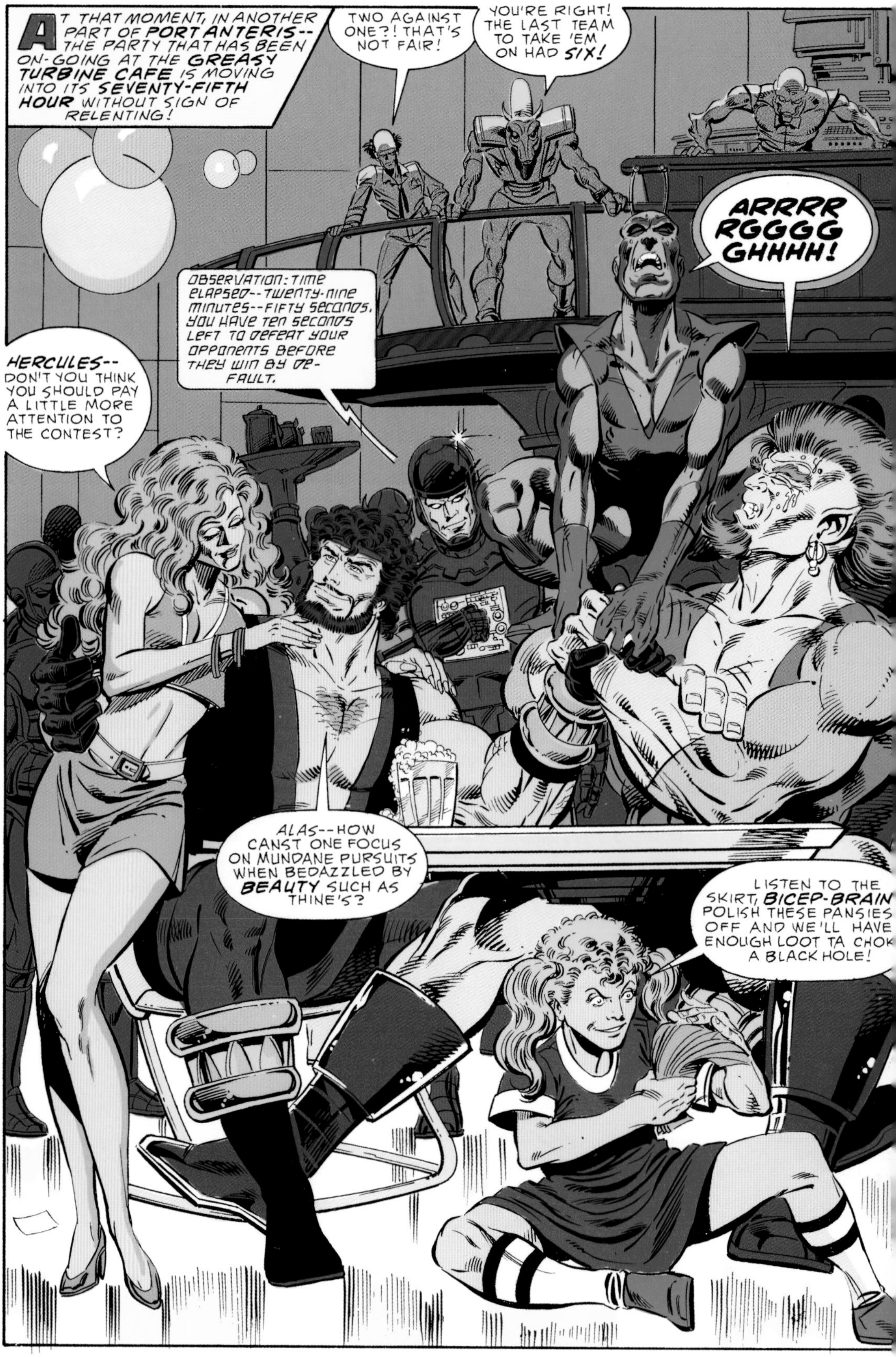
AT THAT MOMENT, IN ANOTHER PART OF PORT ANTERIS-- THE PARTY THAT HAS BEEN ON-GOING AT THE GREASY TURBINE CAFE IS MOVING INTO ITS SEVENTY-FIFTH HOUR WITHOUT SIGN OF RELENTING!
TWO AGAINST ONE?! THAT'S NOT FAIR!
YOU'RE RIGHT! THE LAST TEAM TO TAKE 'EM ON HAD SIX!
ARRRR RGGGG GHHHH!
OBSERVATION: TIME ELAPSED--TWENTY-NINE MINUTES--FIFTY SECONDS. YOU HAVE TEN SECONDS LEFT TO DEFEAT YOUR OPPONENTS BEFORE THEY WIN BY DE-FAULT.
HERCULES-- DON'T YOU THINK YOU SHOULD PAY A LITTLE MORE ATTENTION TO THE CONTEST?
ALAS--HOW CANST ONE FOCUS ON MUNDANE PURSUITS WHEN BEDAZZLED BY BEAUTY SUCH AS THINE'S?
LISTEN TO THE SKIRT, BICEP-BRAIN POLISH THESE PANSIES OFF AND WE'LL HAVE ENOUGH LOOT TA CHOK A BLACK HOLE!

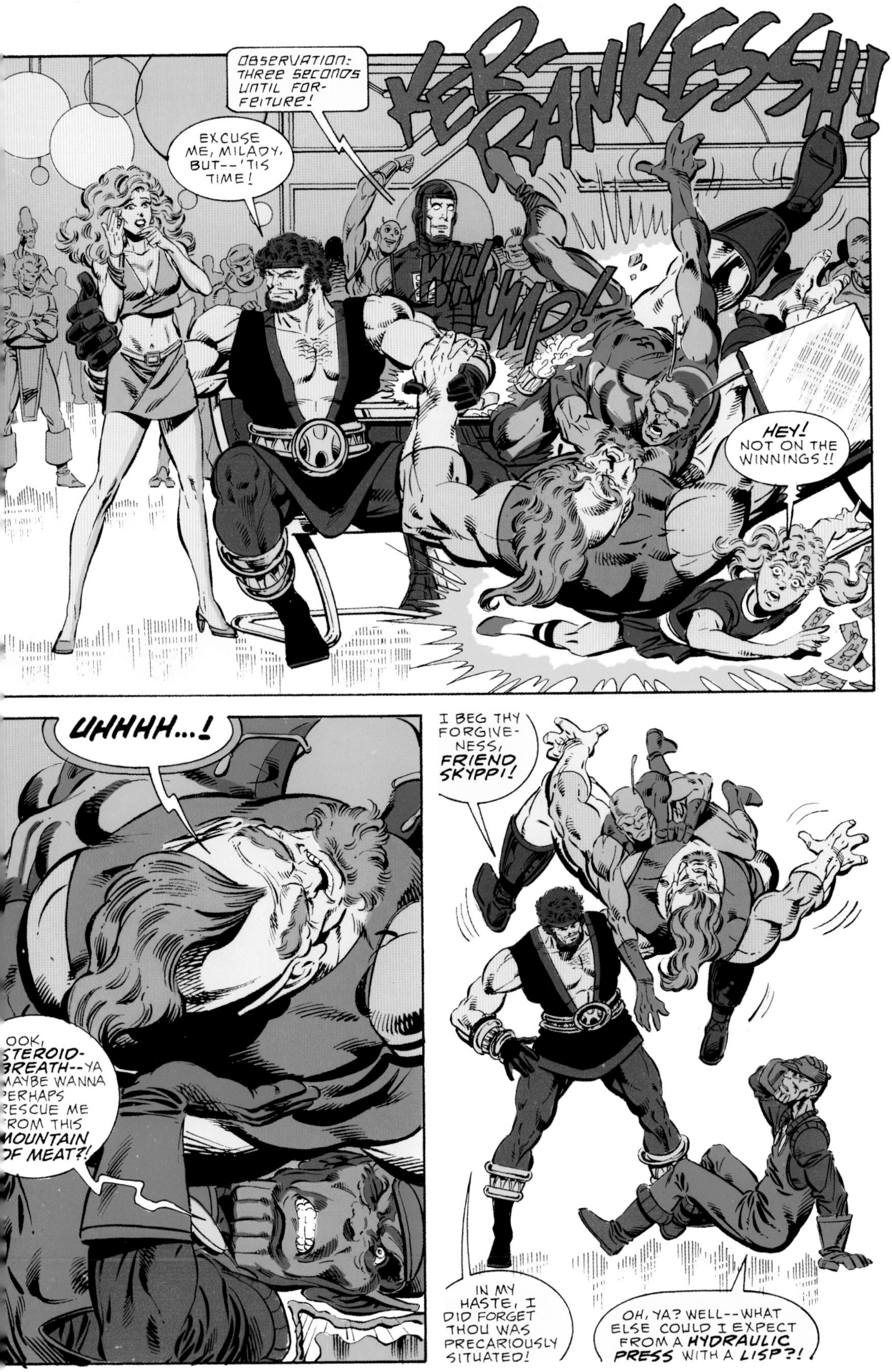
OBSERVATION: THREE SECONDS UNTIL FORFEITURE!
KER-RANKESSH!
EXCUSE ME, MILADY, BUT--'TIS TIME!
WHUMP!
HEY! NOT ON THE WINNINGS!!
UHHHH...!
LOOK, STEROID-BREATH--YA MAYBE WANNA PERHAPS RESCUE ME FROM THIS MOUNTAIN OF MEAT?!
I BEG THY FORGIVENESS, FRIEND SKYPP!!
IN MY HASTE, I DID FORGET THOU WAS PRECARIOUSLY SITUATED!
OH, YA? WELL--WHAT ELSE COULD I EXPECT FROM A HYDRAULIC PRESS WITH A LISP?!

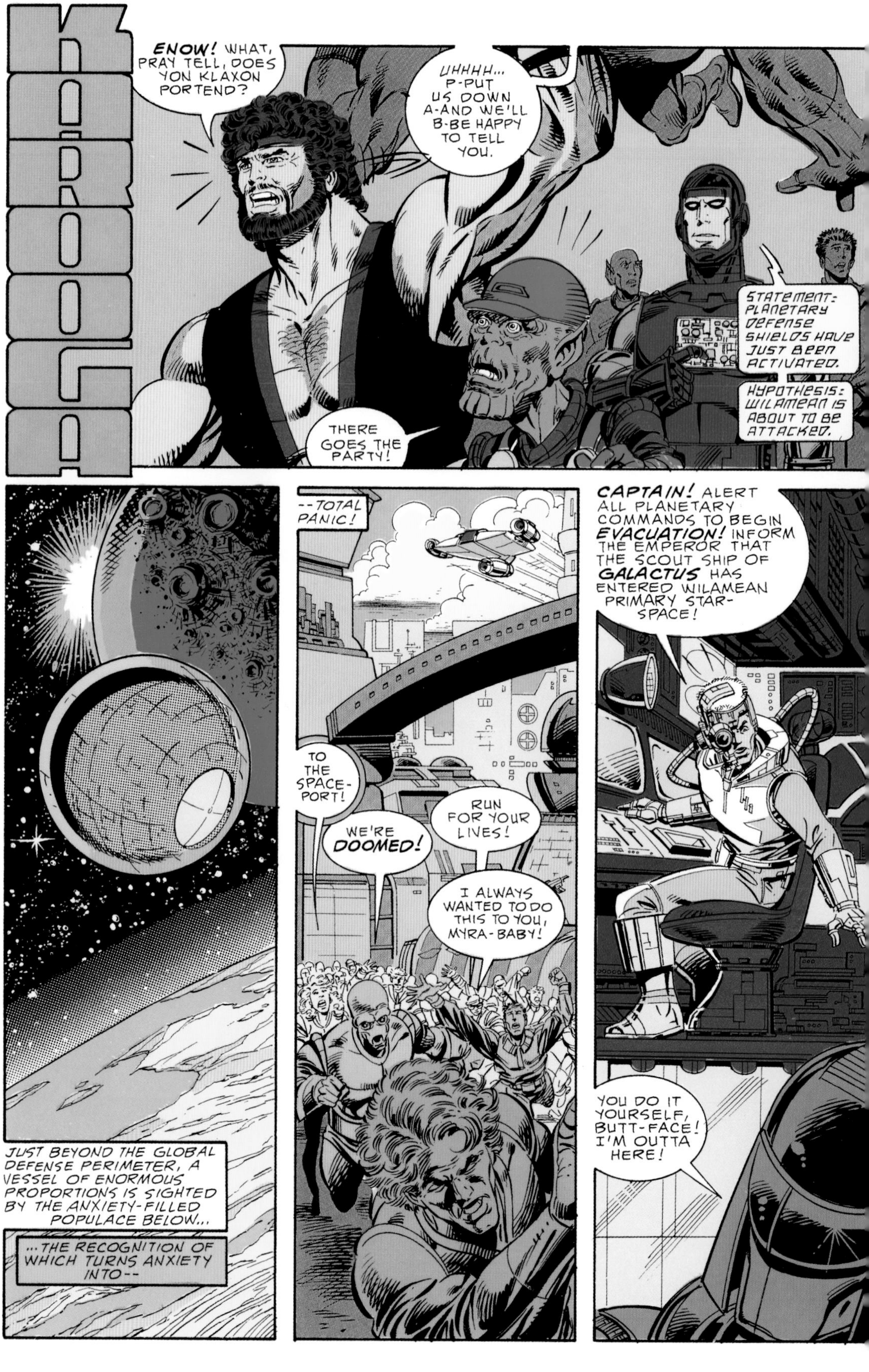
KOROGA
ENOW! WHAT, PRAY TELL, DOES YON KLAXON PORTEND?
UHHHH... P-PUT US DOWN A-AND WE'LL B-BE HAPPY TO TELL YOU.
THERE GOES THE PARTY!
STATEMENT: PLANETARY DEFENSE SHIELDS HAVE JUST BEEN ACTIVATED.
HYPOTHESIS: WILAMEAN IS ABOUT TO BE ATTACKED.
JUST BEYOND THE GLOBAL DEFENSE PERIMETER, A VESSEL OF ENORMOUS PROPORTIONS IS SIGHTED BY THE ANXIETY-FILLED POPULACE BELOW...
...THE RECOGNITION OF WHICH TURNS ANXIETY INTO--
--TOTAL PANIC!
TO THE SPACE-PORT!
WE'RE DOOMED!
RUN FOR YOUR LIVES!
I ALWAYS WANTED TO DO THIS TO YOU, MYRA-BABY!
CAPTAIN! ALERT ALL PLANETARY COMMANDS TO BEGIN EVACUATION! INFORM THE EMPEROR THAT THE SCOUT SHIP OF GALACTUS HAS ENTERED WILAMEAN PRIMARY STAR-SPACE!
YOU DO IT YOURSELF, BUTT-FACE! I'M OUTTA HERE!

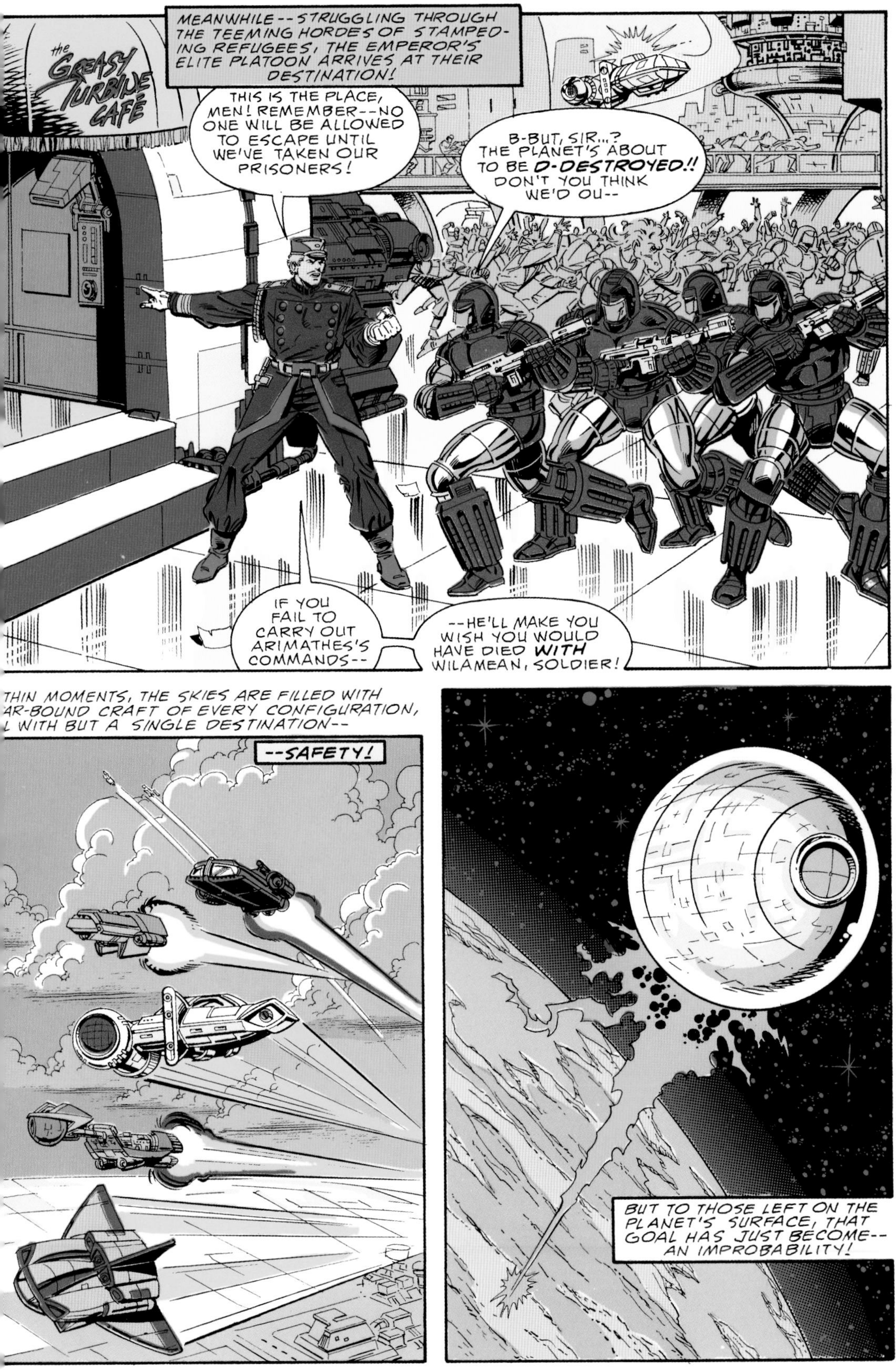

the GREASY TURBINE CAFÉ
MEANWHILE--STRUGGLING THROUGH THE TEEMING HORDES OF STAMPEDING REFUGEES, THE EMPEROR'S ELITE PLATOON ARRIVES AT THEIR DESTINATION!
THIS IS THE PLACE, MEN! REMEMBER--NO ONE WILL BE ALLOWED TO ESCAPE UNTIL WE'VE TAKEN OUR PRISONERS!
B-BUT, SIR...? THE PLANET'S ABOUT TO BE D-DESTROYED!! DON'T YOU THINK WE'D OU--
IF YOU FAIL TO CARRY OUT ARIMATHES'S COMMANDS--
--HE'LL MAKE YOU WISH YOU WOULD HAVE DIED WITH WILAMEAN, SOLDIER!
THIN MOMENTS, THE SKIES ARE FILLED WITH AR-BOUND CRAFT OF EVERY CONFIGURATION, L WITH BUT A SINGLE DESTINATION--
--SAFETY!
BUT TO THOSE LEFT ON THE PLANET'S SURFACE, THAT GOAL HAS JUST BECOME--AN IMPROBABILITY!

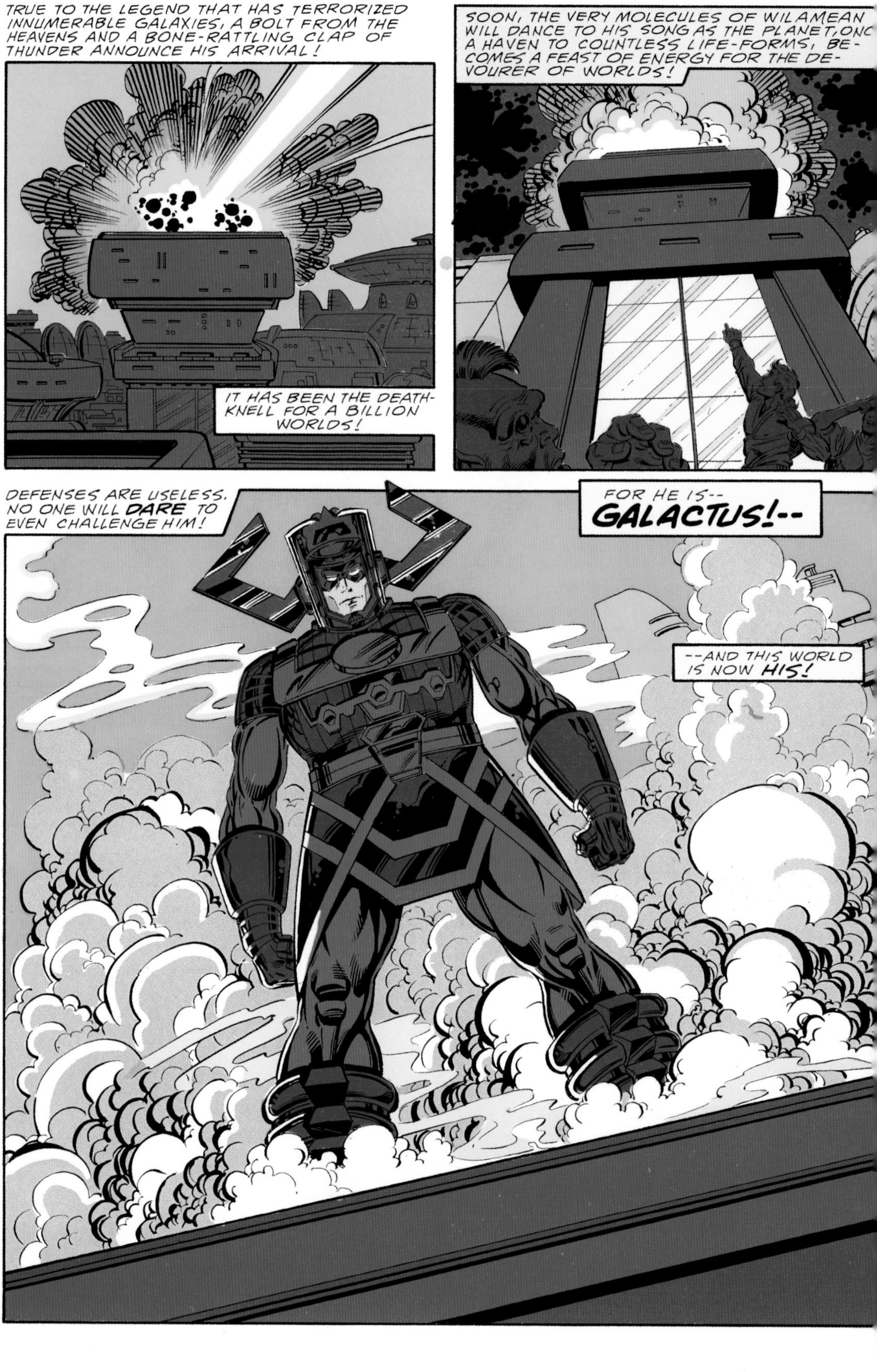
TRUE TO THE LEGEND THAT HAS TERRORIZED INNUMERABLE GALAXIES, A BOLT FROM THE HEAVENS AND A BONE-RATTLING CLAP OF THUNDER ANNOUNCE HIS ARRIVAL!
IT HAS BEEN THE DEATH-KNELL FOR A BILLION WORLDS!
SOON, THE VERY MOLECULES OF WILAMEAN WILL DANCE TO HIS SONG AS THE PLANET, ONC A HAVEN TO COUNTLESS LIFE-FORMS, BECOMES A FEAST OF ENERGY FOR THE DEVOURER OF WORLDS!
DEFENSES ARE USELESS. NO ONE WILL DARE TO EVEN CHALLENGE HIM!
FOR HE IS--
GALACTUS!--
--AND THIS WORLD IS NOW HIS!

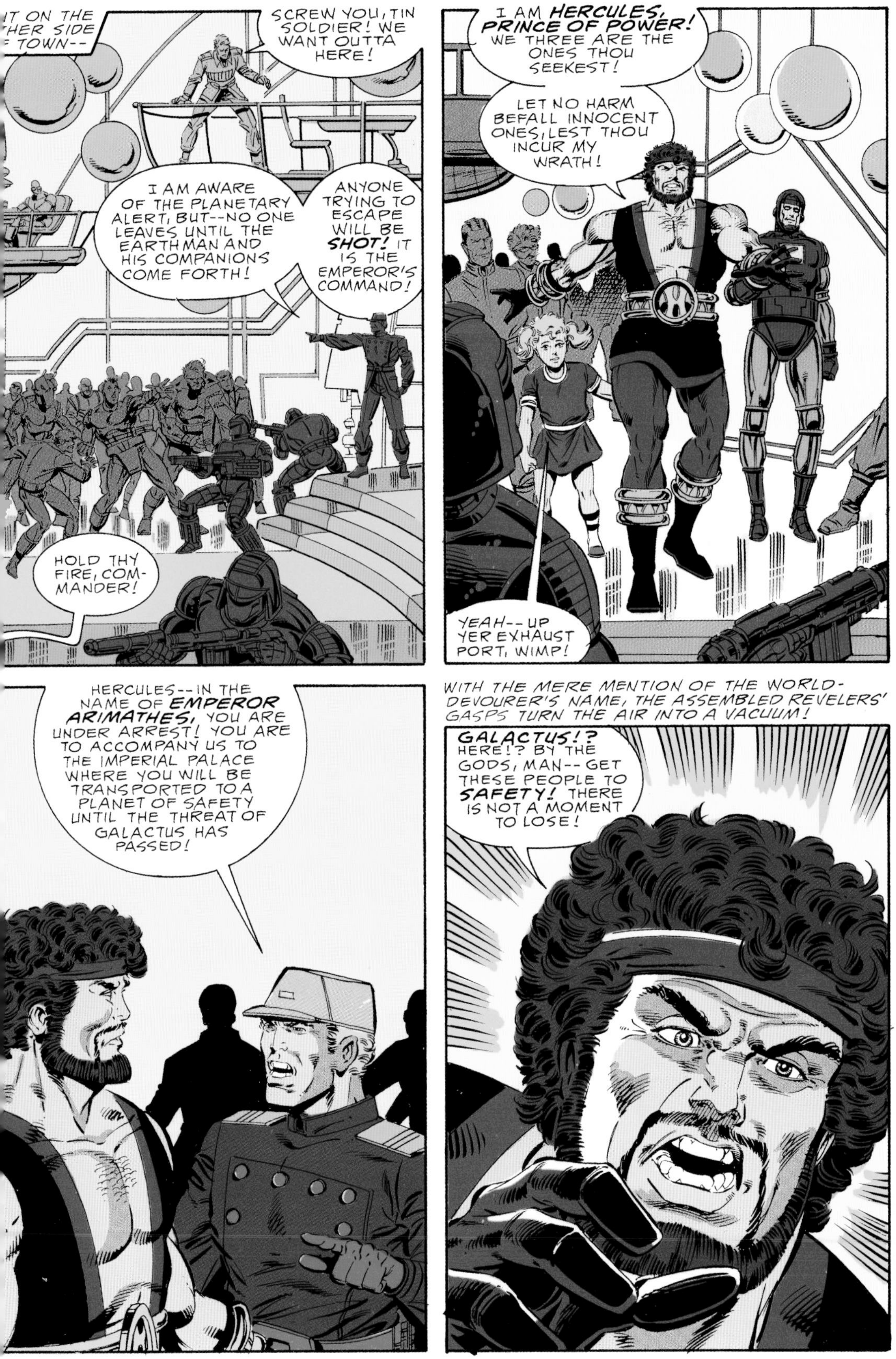
IT ON THE THER SIDE TOWN--
SCREW YOU, TIN SOLDIER! WE WANT OUTTA HERE!
I AM AWARE OF THE PLANETARY ALERT, BUT--NO ONE LEAVES UNTIL THE EARTHMAN AND HIS COMPANIONS COME FORTH!
ANYONE TRYING TO ESCAPE WILL BE SHOT! IT IS THE EMPEROR'S COMMAND!
HOLD THY FIRE, COM-MANDER!
I AM HERCULES, PRINCE OF POWER! WE THREE ARE THE ONES THOU SEEKEST!
LET NO HARM BEFALL INNOCENT ONES, LEST THOU INCUR MY WRATH!
YEAH--UP YER EXHAUST PORT, WIMP!
HERCULES--IN THE NAME OF EMPEROR ARIMATHES, YOU ARE UNDER ARREST! YOU ARE TO ACCOMPANY US TO THE IMPERIAL PALACE WHERE YOU WILL BE TRANSPORTED TO A PLANET OF SAFETY UNTIL THE THREAT OF GALACTUS HAS PASSED!
WITH THE MERE MENTION OF THE WORLD-DEVOURER'S NAME, THE ASSEMBLED REVELERS' GASPS TURN THE AIR INTO A VACUUM!
GALACTUS!? HERE!? BY THE GODS, MAN--GET THESE PEOPLE TO SAFETY! THERE IS NOT A MOMENT TO LOSE!

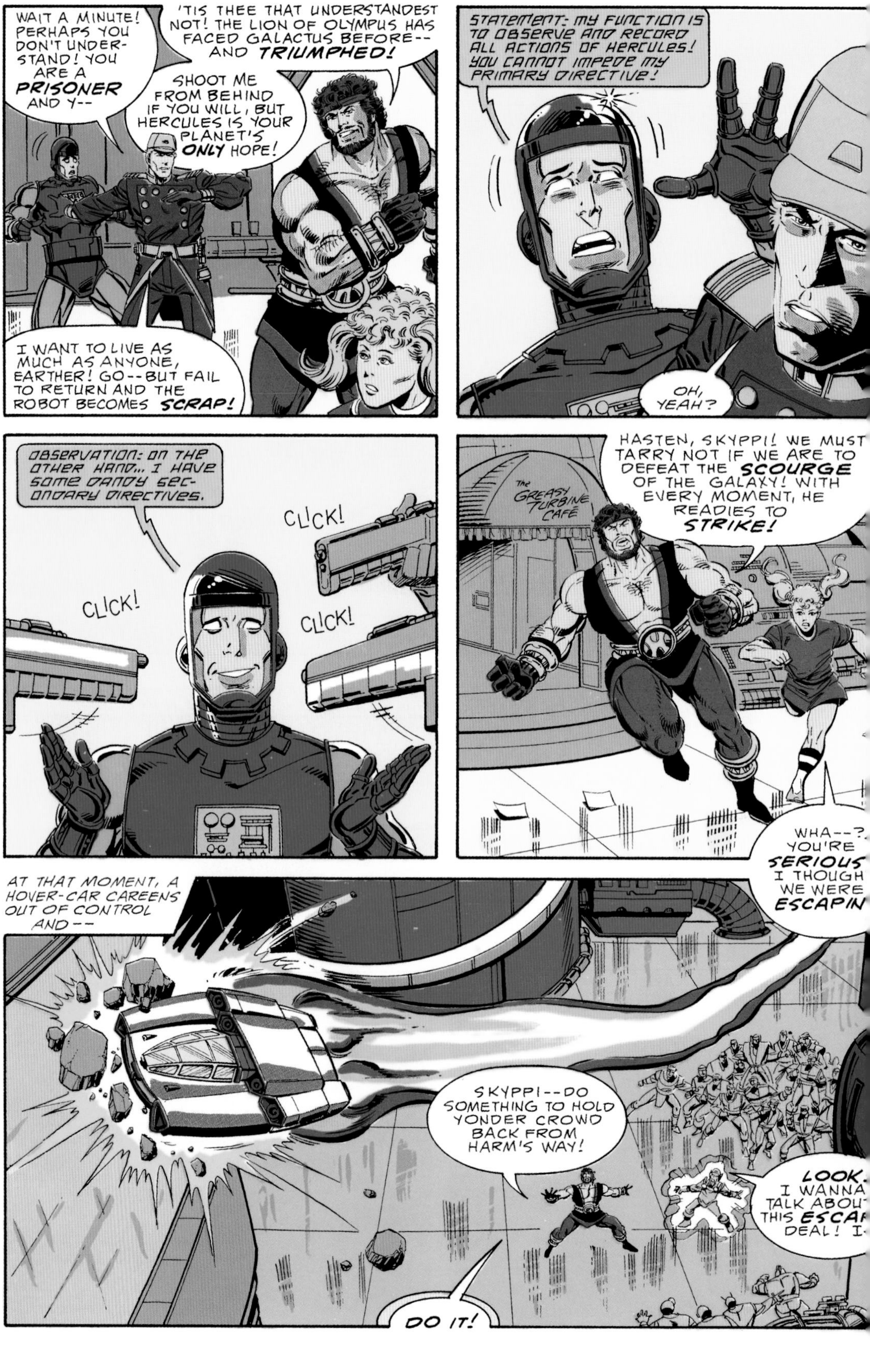
WAIT A MINUTE! PERHAPS YOU DON'T UNDERSTAND! YOU ARE A PRISONER AND Y--
'TIS THEE THAT UNDERSTANDEST NOT! THE LION OF OLYMPUS HAS FACED GALACTUS BEFORE-- AND TRIUMPHED!
SHOOT ME FROM BEHIND IF YOU WILL, BUT HERCULES IS YOUR PLANET'S ONLY HOPE!
I WANT TO LIVE AS MUCH AS ANYONE, EARTHER! GO--BUT FAIL TO RETURN AND THE ROBOT BECOMES SCRAP!
STATEMENT: MY FUNCTION IS TO OBSERVE AND RECORD ALL ACTIONS OF HERCULES! YOU CANNOT IMPEDE MY PRIMARY DIRECTIVE!
OH, YEAH?
OBSERVATION: ON THE OTHER HAND... I HAVE SOME DANDY SECONDARY DIRECTIVES.
CLICK!
CLICK!
CLICK!
HASTEN, SKYPPI! WE MUST TARRY NOT IF WE ARE TO DEFEAT THE SCOURGE OF THE GALAXY! WITH EVERY MOMENT, HE READIES TO STRIKE!
The GREASY TURBINE CAFÉ
WHA--? YOU'RE SERIOUS I THOUGH WE WERE ESCAPIN
AT THAT MOMENT, A HOVER-CAR CAREENS OUT OF CONTROL AND--
SKYPPI--DO SOMETHING TO HOLD YONDER CROWD BACK FROM HARM'S WAY!
LOOK. I WANNA TALK ABOUT THIS ESCAP DEAL! I-
DO IT!

BITCH, BITCH, BITCH! AND WHERE DOES IT GET ME?

ROARR RGHH!

FULL TANK RUPTURED!

IT'LL *BLOW* WHEN IT HITS!

WHUMP!

AFTER GENTLY LOWERING THE DAMAGED CRAFT--

WELL DONE, *SKRULL!* AND NOW-- *GALACTUS* AWAITS!

THAT ORION *SLIME-SERPENT* GETS THEM EVERY TIME! THEY'RE ALL GONNA NEED TO CHANGE THEIR DIAPERS!

YOU LISTEN TO ME, LAME-O OF OLYMPUS!

RECORDER--IS *HISTORY!*

THIS *PLANET* --IS HISTORY!

AND IF YOU THINK YOU'RE GONNA GET ME TO THROW MY LIFE AWAY FOR ONE OF YOUR *STUPID, NOBLE* GESTURES--

NO WAY!

END OF SUBJECT!

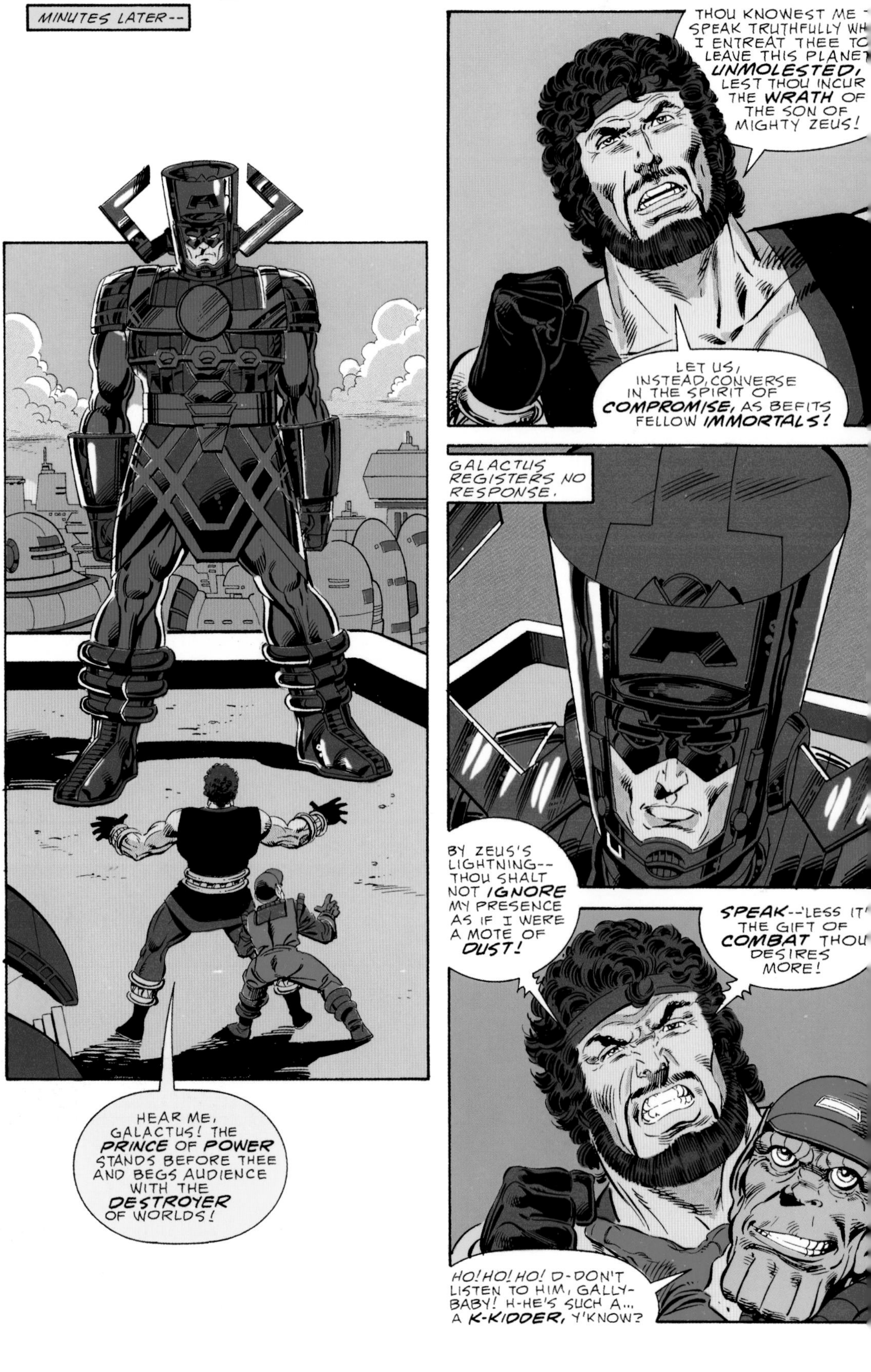
MINUTES LATER--
HEAR ME, GALACTUS! THE PRINCE OF POWER STANDS BEFORE THEE AND BEGS AUDIENCE WITH THE DESTROYER OF WORLDS!
THOU KNOWEST ME - SPEAK TRUTHFULLY WH I ENTREAT THEE TO LEAVE THIS PLANET UNMOLESTED, LEST THOU INCUR THE WRATH OF THE SON OF MIGHTY ZEUS!
LET US, INSTEAD, CONVERSE IN THE SPIRIT OF COMPROMISE, AS BEFITS FELLOW IMMORTALS!
GALACTUS REGISTERS NO RESPONSE.
BY ZEUS'S LIGHTNING-- THOU SHALT NOT IGNORE MY PRESENCE AS IF I WERE A MOTE OF DUST!
SPEAK--'LESS IT THE GIFT OF COMBAT THOU DESIRES MORE!
HO! HO! HO! D-DON'T LISTEN TO HIM, GALLY-BABY! H-HE'S SUCH A... A K-KIDDER, Y'KNOW?

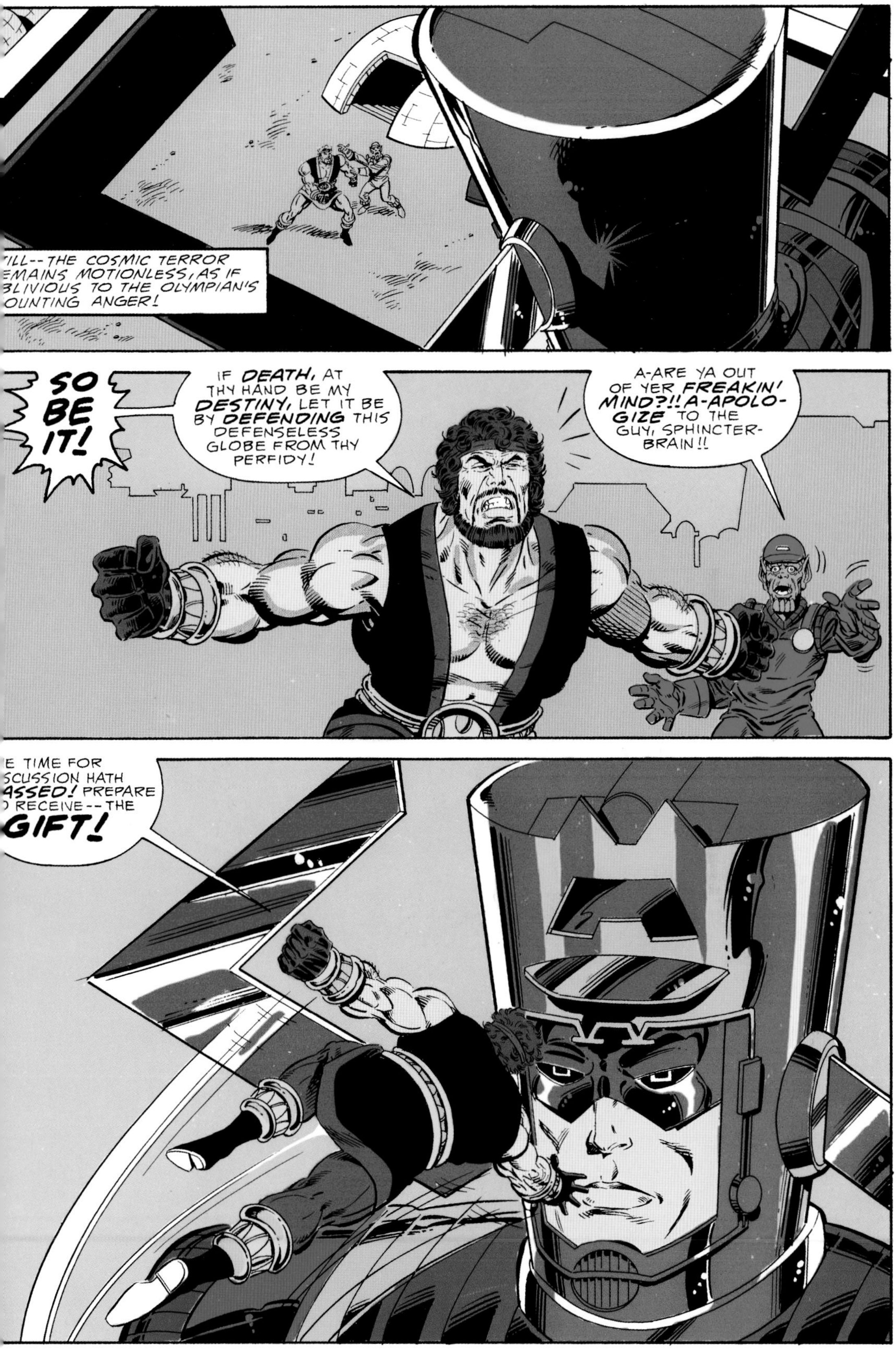
ILL--THE COSMIC TERROR
EMAINS MOTIONLESS, AS IF
BLIVIOUS TO THE OLYMPIAN'S
OUNTING ANGER!
SO BE IT!
IF DEATH, AT THY HAND BE MY DESTINY, LET IT BE BY DEFENDING THIS DEFENSELESS GLOBE FROM THY PERFIDY!
A-ARE YA OUT OF YER FREAKIN' MIND?!! A-APOLOGIZE TO THE GUY, SPHINCTER-BRAIN!!
E TIME FOR
SCUSSION HATH
ASSED! PREPARE
RECEIVE--THE
GIFT!

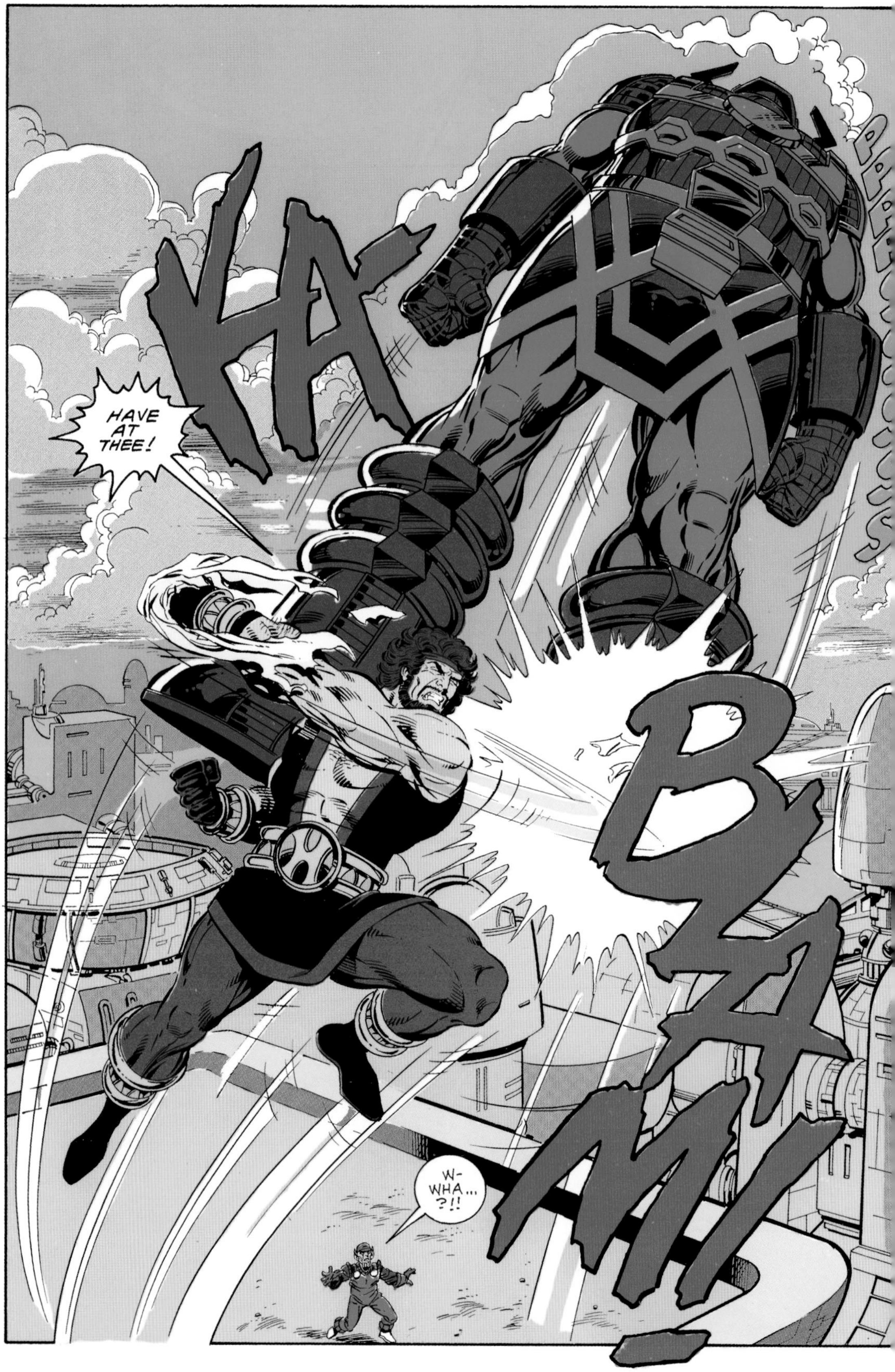
KA-
HAVE AT THEE!
BLAM!
W-WHA...?!!

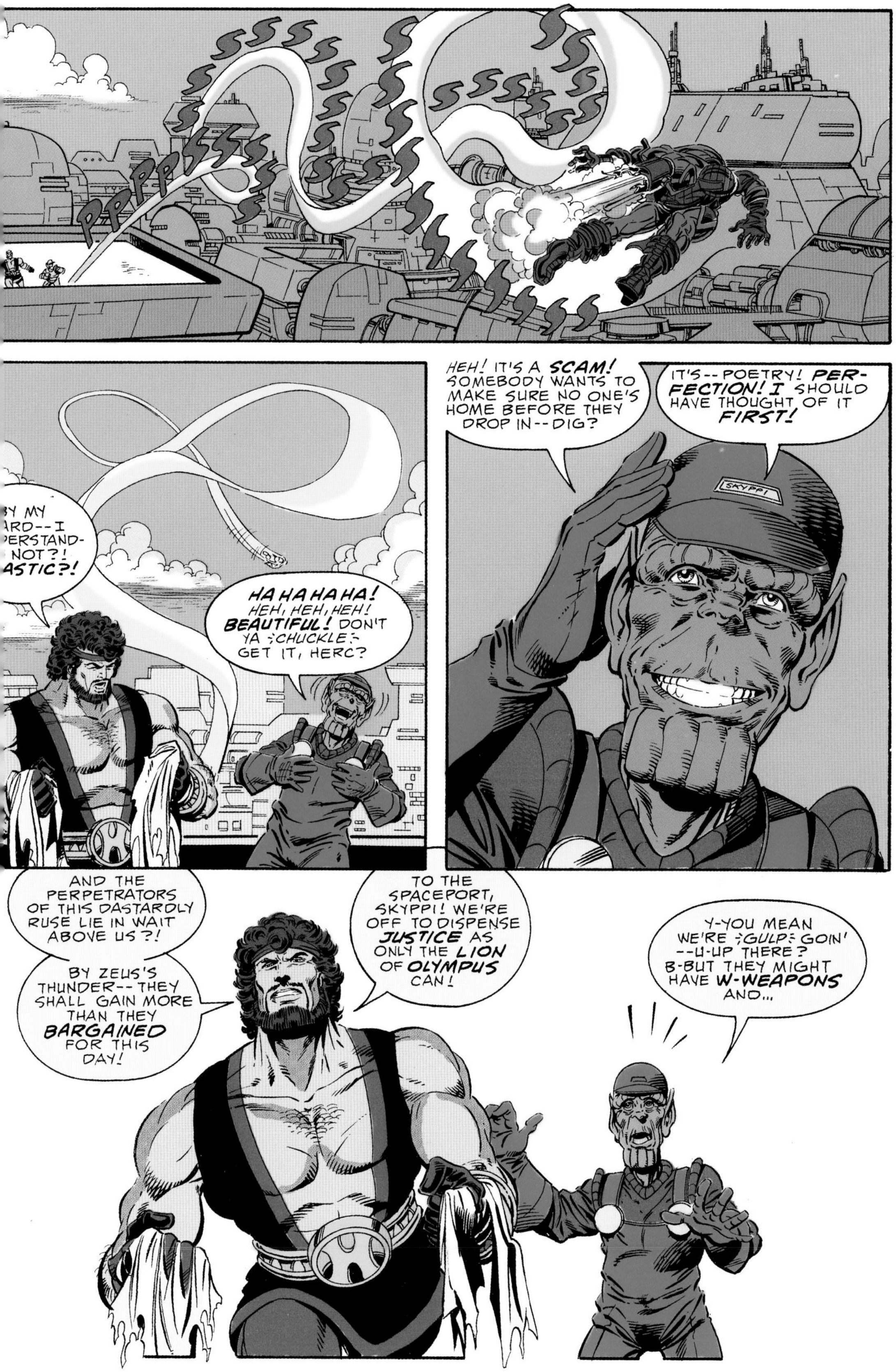

ARD--I
ERSTAND-
NOT?!
ASTIC?!
HAHAHAHA! HEH, HEH, HEH! BEAUTIFUL! DON'T YA -CHUCKLE- GET IT, HERC?
HEH! IT'S A SCAM! SOMEBODY WANTS TO MAKE SURE NO ONE'S HOME BEFORE THEY DROP IN--DIG?
IT'S--POETRY! PERFECTION! I SHOULD HAVE THOUGHT OF IT FIRST!
SKYPPI
AND THE PERPETRATORS OF THIS DASTARDLY RUSE LIE IN WAIT ABOVE US?!
BY ZEUS'S THUNDER--THEY SHALL GAIN MORE THAN THEY BARGAINED FOR THIS DAY!
TO THE SPACEPORT, SKYPPI! WE'RE OFF TO DISPENSE JUSTICE AS ONLY THE LION OF OLYMPUS CAN!
Y-YOU MEAN WE'RE -GULP- GOIN' --U-UP THERE? B-BUT THEY MIGHT HAVE W-WEAPONS AND...

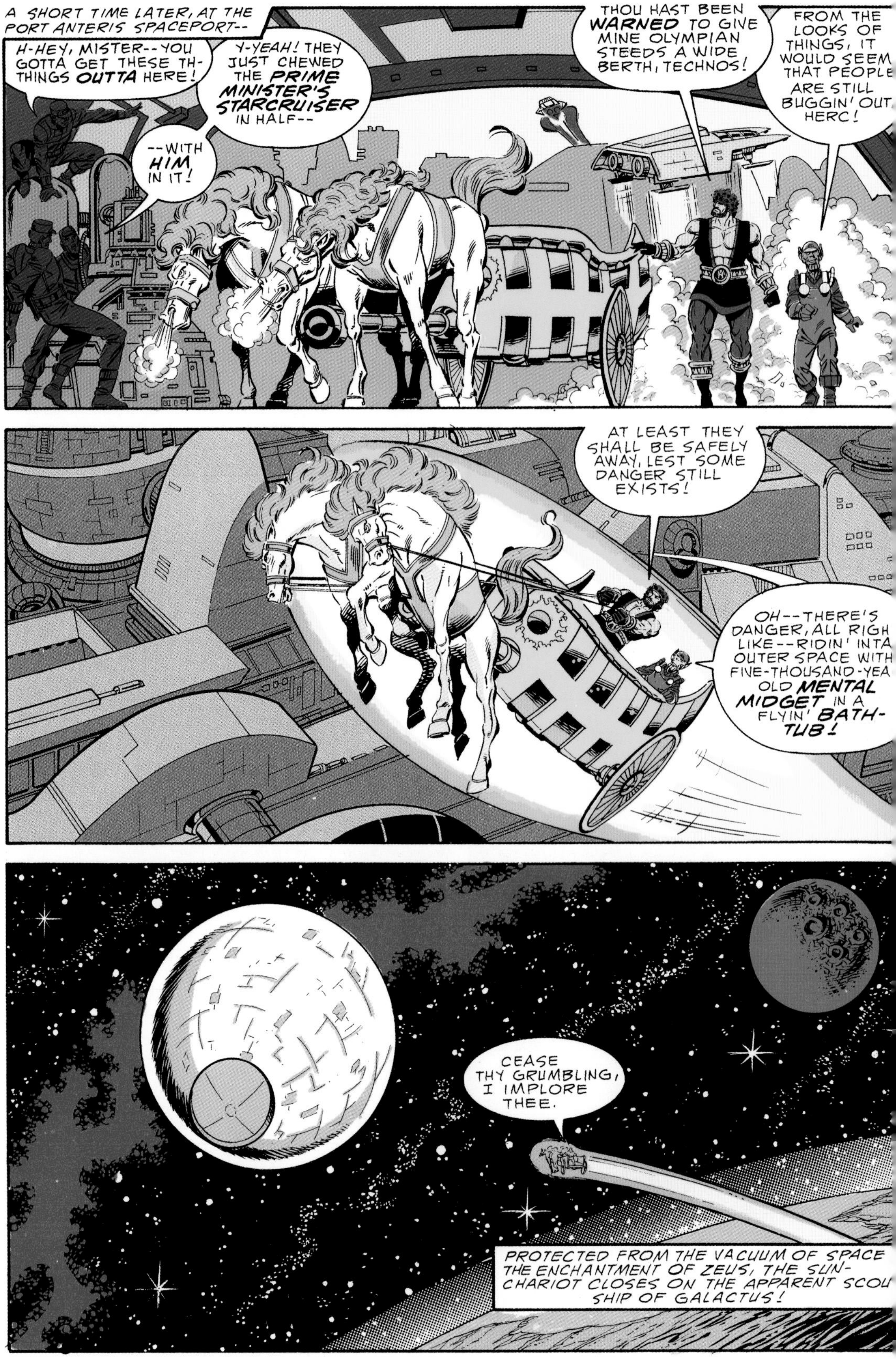
A SHORT TIME LATER, AT THE PORT ANTERIS SPACEPORT--
H-HEY, MISTER--YOU GOTTA GET THESE TH-THINGS OUTTA HERE!
Y-YEAH! THEY JUST CHEWED THE PRIME MINISTER'S STARCRUISER IN HALF--
--WITH HIM IN IT!
THOU HAST BEEN WARNED TO GIVE MINE OLYMPIAN STEEDS A WIDE BERTH, TECHNOS!
FROM THE LOOKS OF THINGS, IT WOULD SEEM THAT PEOPLE ARE STILL BUGGIN' OUT, HERC!
AT LEAST THEY SHALL BE SAFELY AWAY, LEST SOME DANGER STILL EXISTS!
OH--THERE'S DANGER, ALL RIGH LIKE--RIDIN' INTA OUTER SPACE WITH FIVE-THOUSAND-YEA OLD MENTAL MIDGET IN A FLYIN' BATH-TUB!
CEASE THY GRUMBLING, I IMPLORE THEE.
PROTECTED FROM THE VACUUM OF SPACE THE ENCHANTMENT OF ZEUS, THE SUN-CHARIOT CLOSES ON THE APPARENT SCOU SHIP OF GALACTUS!

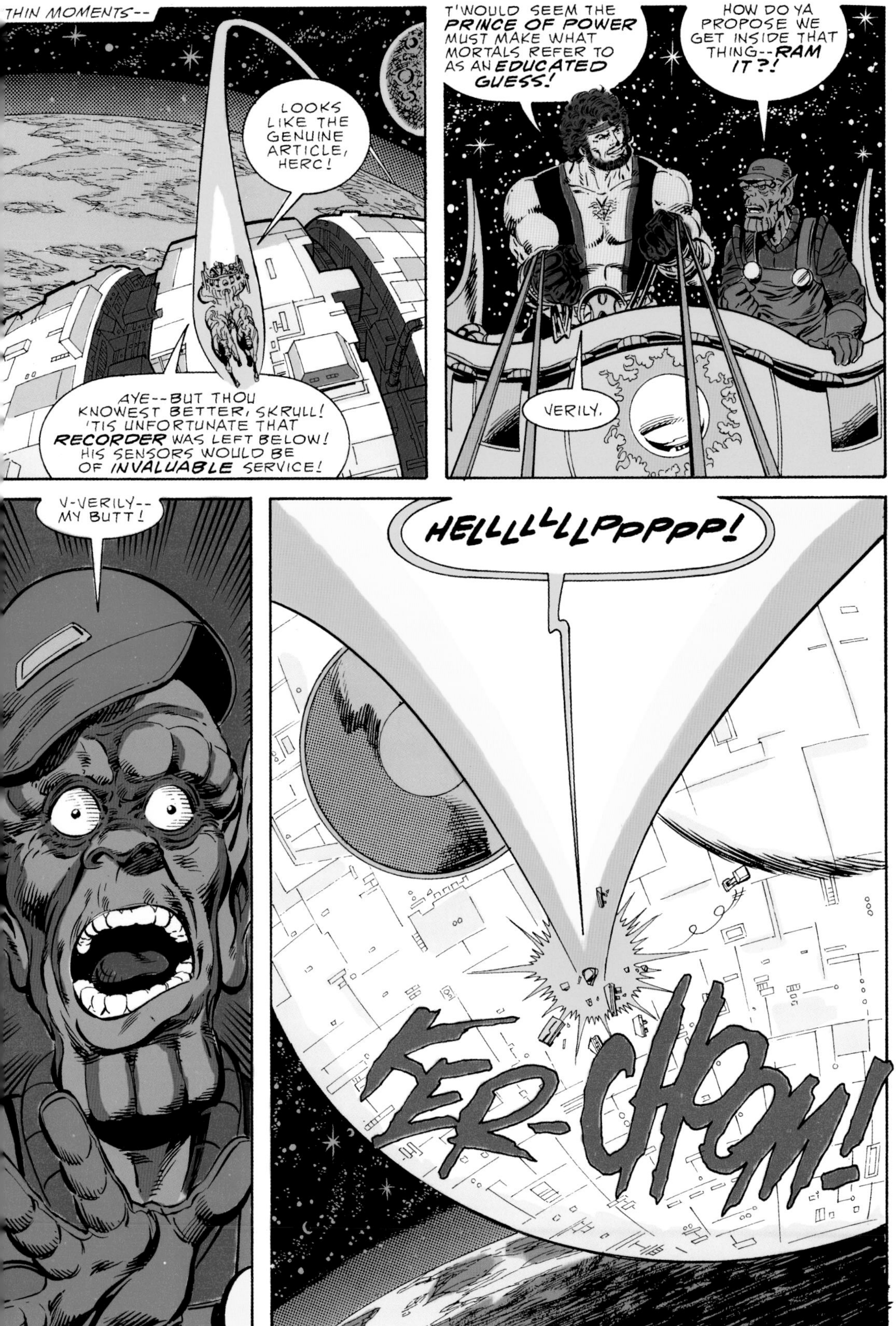

THIN MOMENTS--
LOOKS LIKE THE GENUINE ARTICLE, HERC!
AYE--BUT THOU KNOWEST BETTER, SKRULL! 'TIS UNFORTUNATE THAT RECORDER WAS LEFT BELOW! HIS SENSORS WOULD BE OF INVALUABLE SERVICE!
T'WOULD SEEM THE PRINCE OF POWER MUST MAKE WHAT MORTALS REFER TO AS AN EDUCATED GUESS!
HOW DO YA PROPOSE WE GET INSIDE THAT THING--RAM IT?!
VERILY.
V-VERILY--MY BUTT!
HELLLLLLPPPPP!
KER-CHOOM!

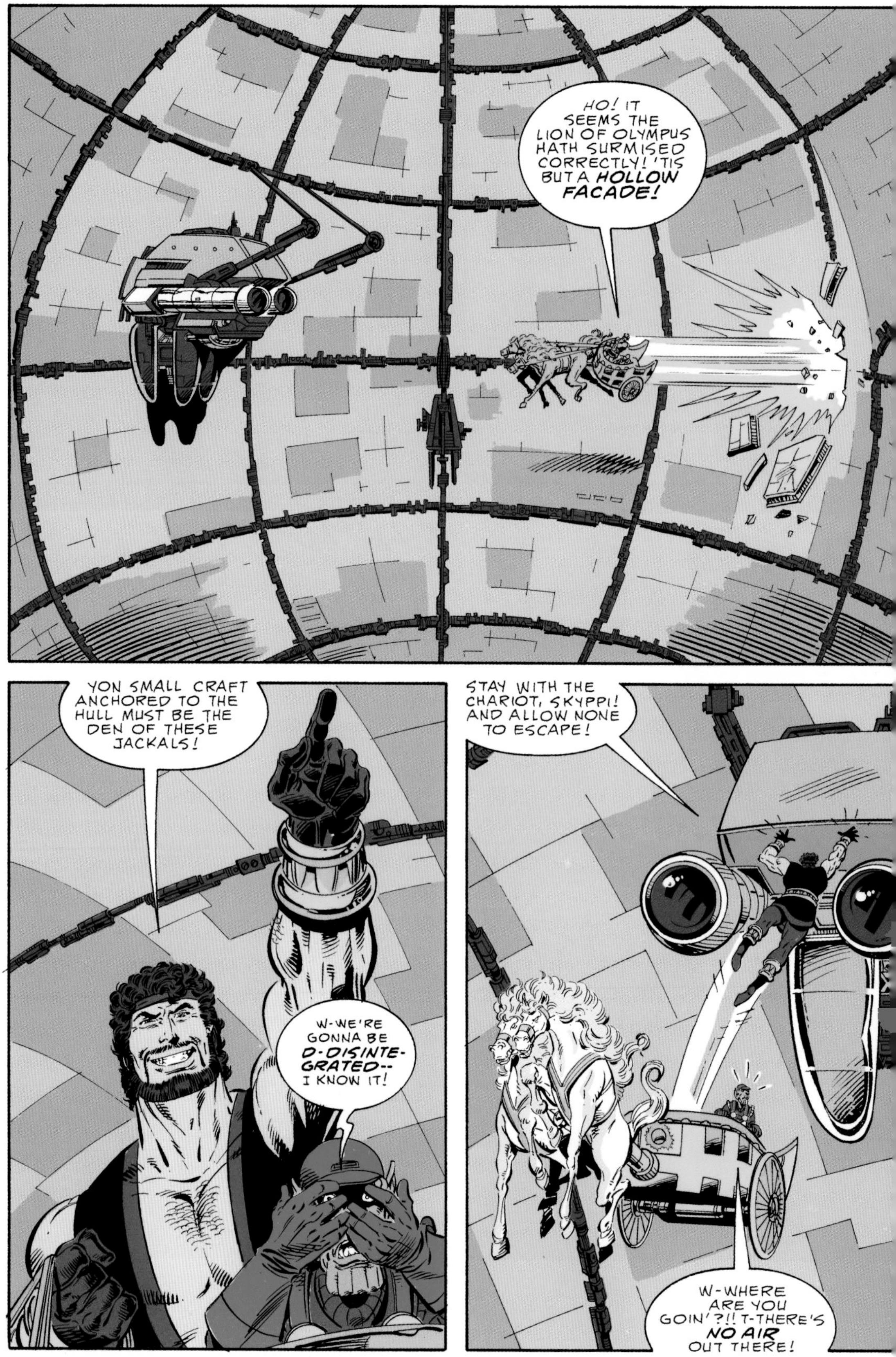
HO! IT SEEMS THE LION OF OLYMPUS HATH SURMISED CORRECTLY! 'TIS BUT A HOLLOW FACADE!
YON SMALL CRAFT ANCHORED TO THE HULL MUST BE THE DEN OF THESE JACKALS!
W-WE'RE GONNA BE D-DISINTE-GRATED-- I KNOW IT!
STAY WITH THE CHARIOT, SKYPPI! AND ALLOW NONE TO ESCAPE!
W-WHERE ARE YOU GOIN'?!! T-THERE'S NO AIR OUT THERE!

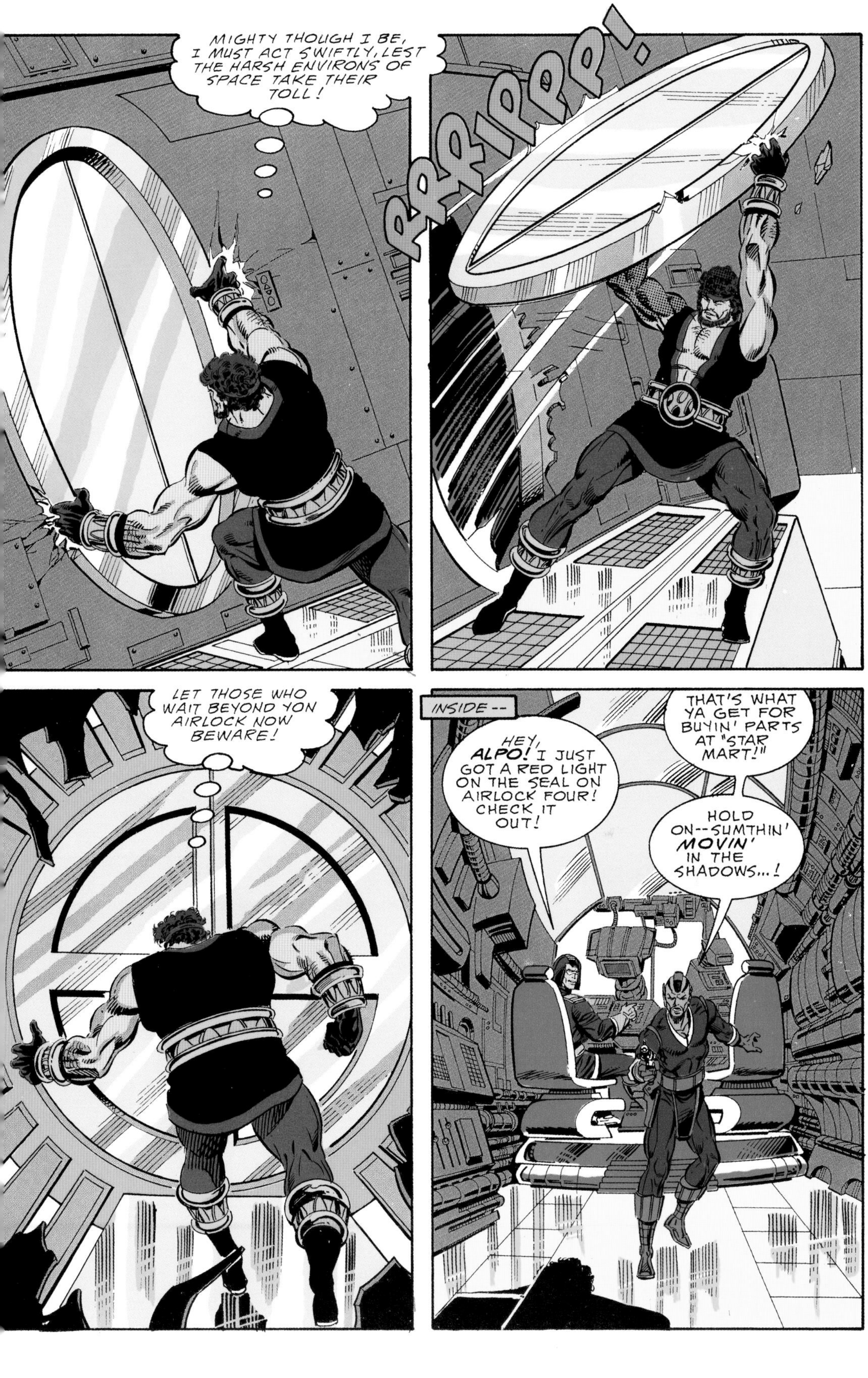
MIGHTY THOUGH I BE, I MUST ACT SWIFTLY, LEST THE HARSH ENVIRONS OF SPACE TAKE THEIR TOLL!
RRRIPPP!
LET THOSE WHO WAIT BEYOND YON AIRLOCK NOW BEWARE!
INSIDE--
HEY, ALPO! I JUST GOT A RED LIGHT ON THE SEAL ON AIRLOCK FOUR! CHECK IT OUT!
THAT'S WHAT YA GET FOR BUYIN' PARTS AT "STAR MART!"
HOLD ON--SUMTHIN' MOVIN' IN THE SHADOWS...!

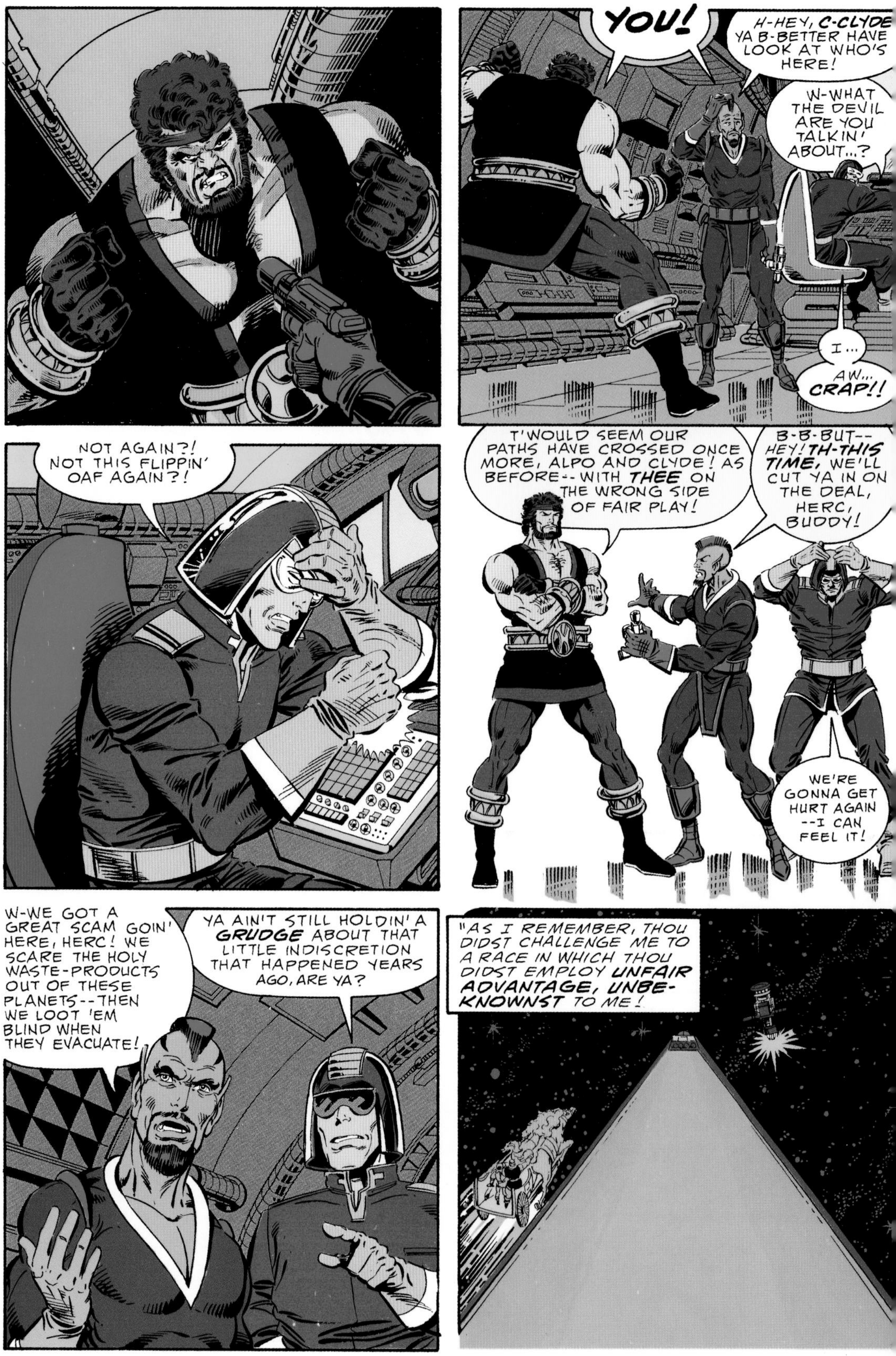
YOU!
H-HEY, C-CLYDE YA B-BETTER HAVE LOOK AT WHO'S HERE!
W-WHAT THE DEVIL ARE YOU TALKIN' ABOUT...?
I...
AW... CRAP!!
NOT AGAIN?! NOT THIS FLIPPIN' OAF AGAIN?!
T'WOULD SEEM OUR PATHS HAVE CROSSED ONCE MORE, ALPO AND CLYDE! AS BEFORE--WITH THEE ON THE WRONG SIDE OF FAIR PLAY!
B-B-BUT--HEY! TH-THIS TIME, WE'LL CUT YA IN ON THE DEAL, HERC, BUDDY!
WE'RE GONNA GET HURT AGAIN --I CAN FEEL IT!
W-WE GOT A GREAT SCAM GOIN' HERE, HERC! WE SCARE THE HOLY WASTE-PRODUCTS OUT OF THESE PLANETS--THEN WE LOOT 'EM BLIND WHEN THEY EVACUATE!
YA AIN'T STILL HOLDIN' A GRUDGE ABOUT THAT LITTLE INDISCRETION THAT HAPPENED YEARS AGO, ARE YA?
"AS I REMEMBER, THOU DIDST CHALLENGE ME TO A RACE IN WHICH THOU DIDST EMPLOY UNFAIR ADVANTAGE, UNBE-KNOWNST TO ME!

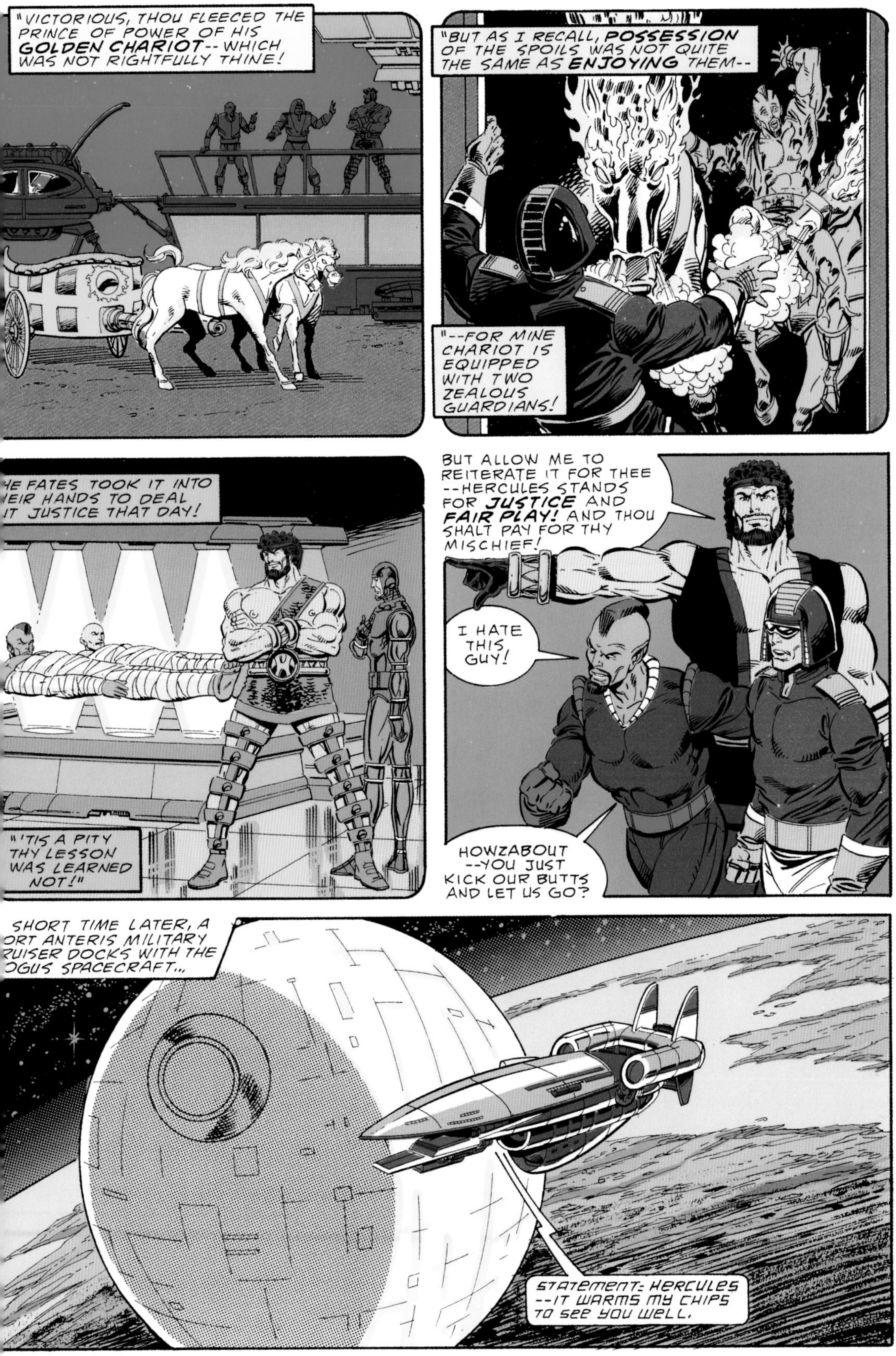
"VICTORIOUS, THOU FLEECED THE PRINCE OF POWER OF HIS GOLDEN CHARIOT--WHICH WAS NOT RIGHTFULLY THINE!
"BUT AS I RECALL, POSSESSION OF THE SPOILS WAS NOT QUITE THE SAME AS ENJOYING THEM--
"--FOR MINE CHARIOT IS EQUIPPED WITH TWO ZEALOUS GUARDIANS!
HE FATES TOOK IT INTO EIR HANDS TO DEAL IT JUSTICE THAT DAY!
"'TIS A PITY THY LESSON WAS LEARNED NOT!"
BUT ALLOW ME TO REITERATE IT FOR THEE --HERCULES STANDS FOR JUSTICE AND FAIR PLAY! AND THOU SHALT PAY FOR THY MISCHIEF!
I HATE THIS GUY!
HOWZABOUT --YOU JUST KICK OUR BUTTS AND LET US GO?
SHORT TIME LATER, A ORT ANTERIS MILITARY RUISER DOCKS WITH THE OGUS SPACECRAFT...
STATEMENT: HERCULES --IT WARMS MY CHIPS TO SEE YOU WELL.

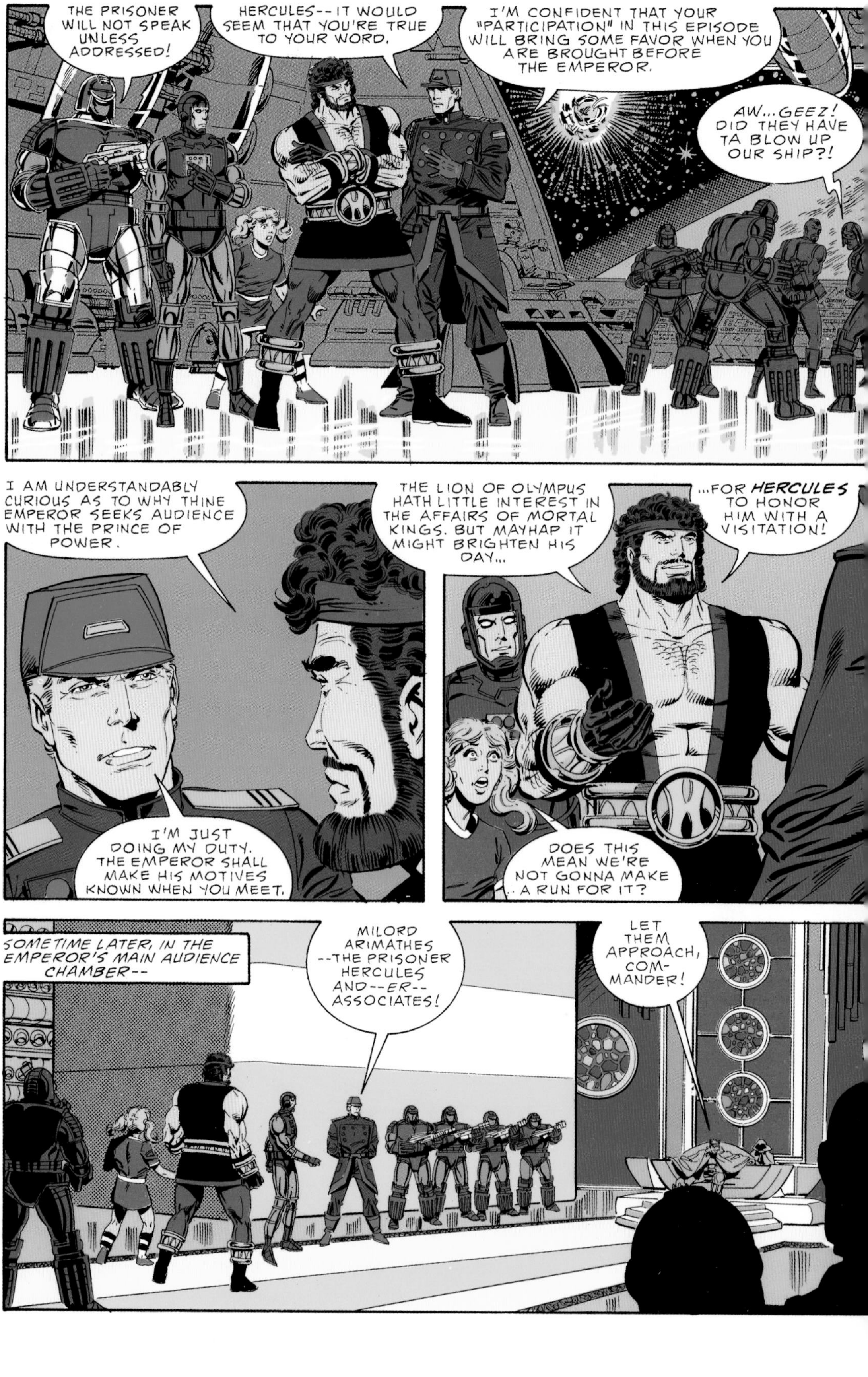
THE PRISONER WILL NOT SPEAK UNLESS ADDRESSED!
HERCULES--IT WOULD SEEM THAT YOU'RE TRUE TO YOUR WORD.
I'M CONFIDENT THAT YOUR "PARTICIPATION" IN THIS EPISODE WILL BRING SOME FAVOR WHEN YOU ARE BROUGHT BEFORE THE EMPEROR.
AW...GEEZ! DID THEY HAVE TA BLOW UP OUR SHIP?!
I AM UNDERSTANDABLY CURIOUS AS TO WHY THINE EMPEROR SEEKS AUDIENCE WITH THE PRINCE OF POWER.
I'M JUST DOING MY DUTY. THE EMPEROR SHALL MAKE HIS MOTIVES KNOWN WHEN YOU MEET.
THE LION OF OLYMPUS HATH LITTLE INTEREST IN THE AFFAIRS OF MORTAL KINGS. BUT MAYHAP IT MIGHT BRIGHTEN HIS DAY...
...FOR HERCULES TO HONOR HIM WITH A VISITATION!
DOES THIS MEAN WE'RE NOT GONNA MAKE A RUN FOR IT?
SOMETIME LATER, IN THE EMPEROR'S MAIN AUDIENCE CHAMBER--
MILORD ARIMATHES--THE PRISONER HERCULES AND--ER--ASSOCIATES!
LET THEM APPROACH, COM-MANDER!

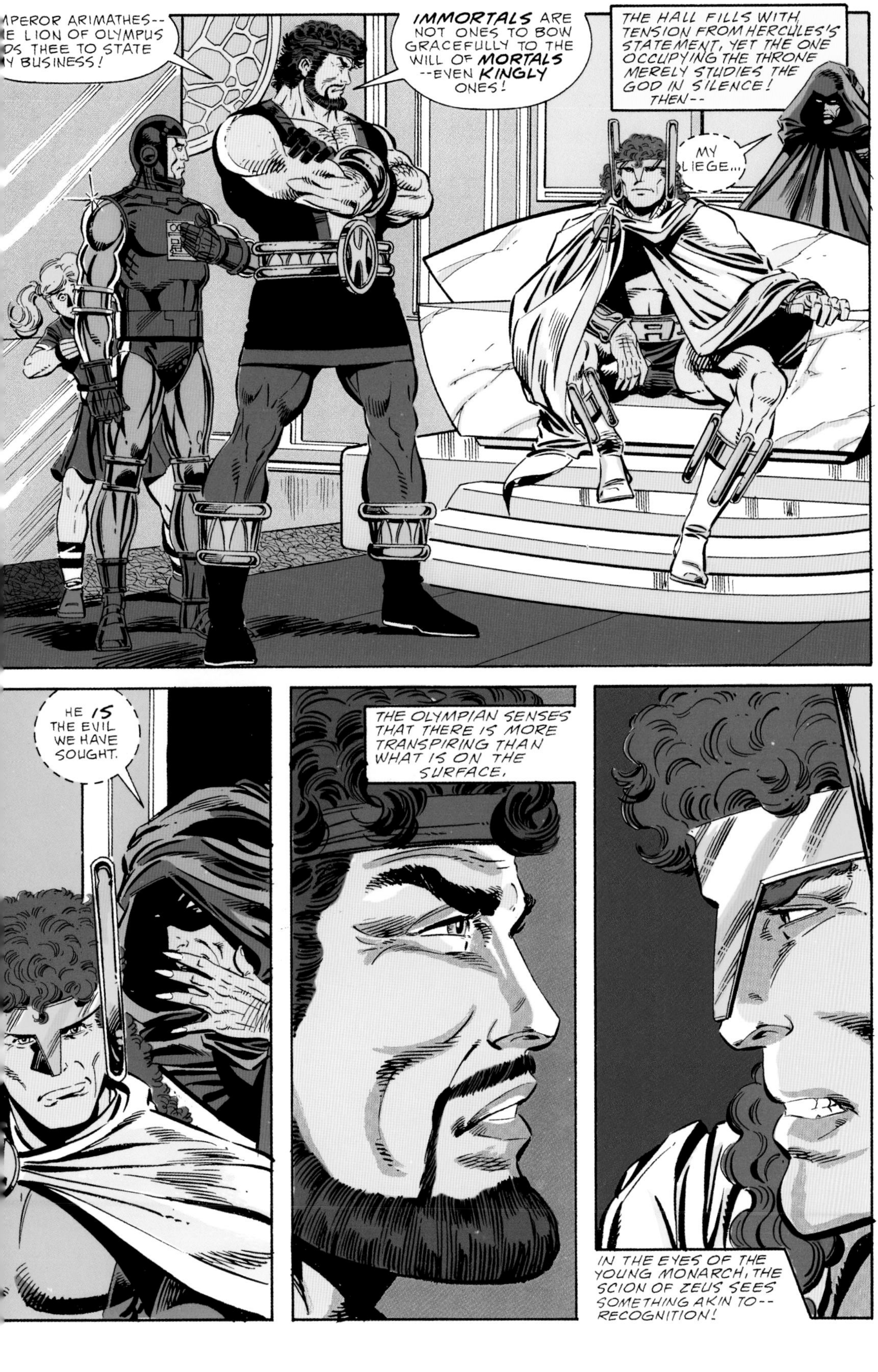
MPEROR ARIMATHES--
E LION OF OLYMPUS
DS THEE TO STATE
Y BUSINESS!
IMMORTALS ARE NOT ONES TO BOW GRACEFULLY TO THE WILL OF MORTALS --EVEN KINGLY ONES!
THE HALL FILLS WITH TENSION FROM HERCULES'S STATEMENT, YET THE ONE OCCUPYING THE THRONE MERELY STUDIES THE GOD IN SILENCE! THEN--
MY LIEGE...
HE IS THE EVIL WE HAVE SOUGHT.
THE OLYMPIAN SENSES THAT THERE IS MORE TRANSPIRING THAN WHAT IS ON THE SURFACE.
IN THE EYES OF THE YOUNG MONARCH, THE SCION OF ZEUS SEES SOMETHING AKIN TO-- RECOGNITION!

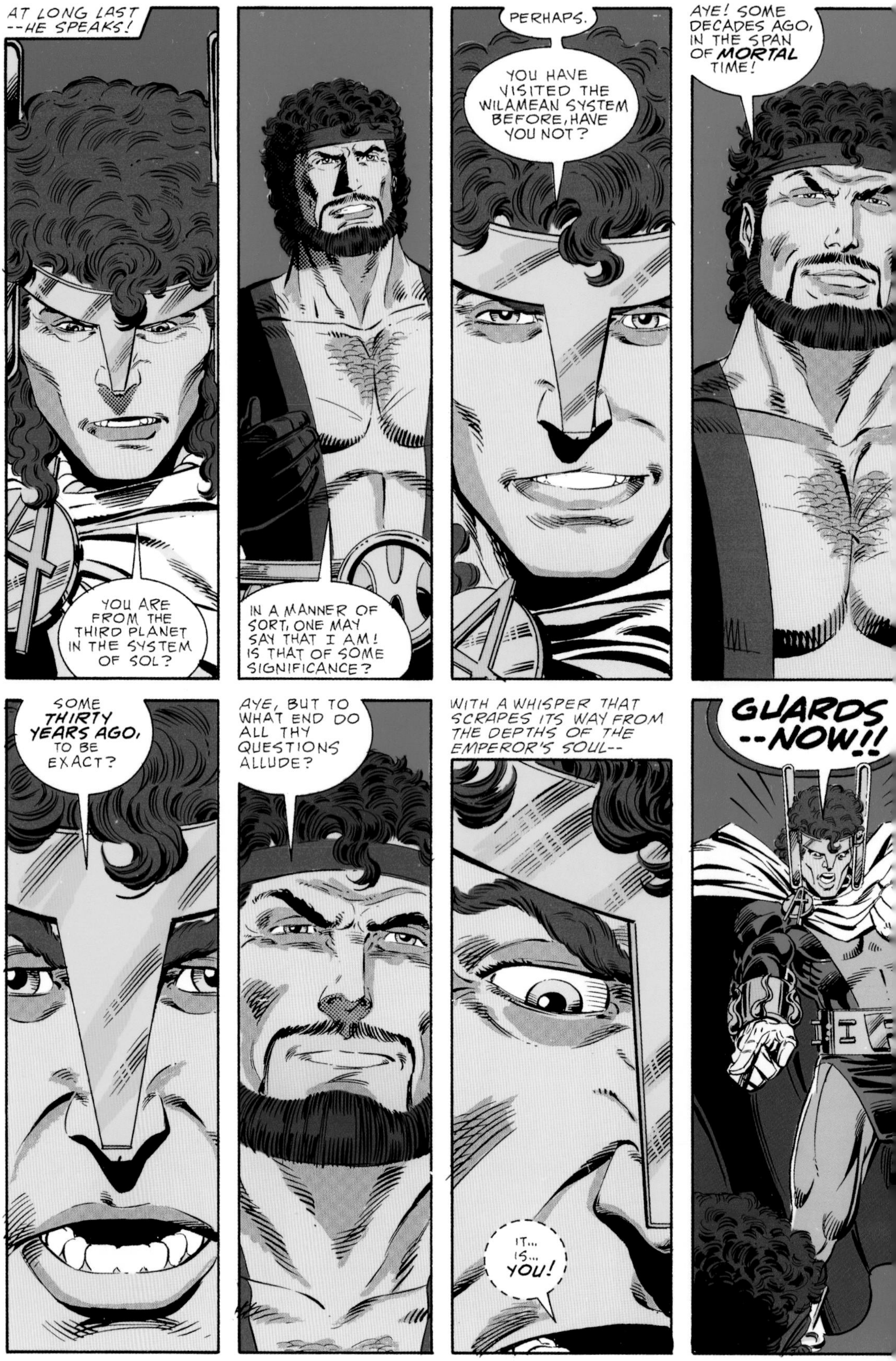
AT LONG LAST --HE SPEAKS!
YOU ARE FROM THE THIRD PLANET IN THE SYSTEM OF SOL?
IN A MANNER OF SORT, ONE MAY SAY THAT I AM! IS THAT OF SOME SIGNIFICANCE?
PERHAPS.
YOU HAVE VISITED THE WILAMEAN SYSTEM BEFORE, HAVE YOU NOT?
AYE! SOME DECADES AGO, IN THE SPAN OF MORTAL TIME!
SOME THIRTY YEARS AGO, TO BE EXACT?
AYE, BUT TO WHAT END DO ALL THY QUESTIONS ALLUDE?
WITH A WHISPER THAT SCRAPES ITS WAY FROM THE DEPTHS OF THE EMPEROR'S SOUL--
IT... IS... YOU!
GUARDS --NOW!!

EXCLAMATION: LORD HERCULES...!

B-DDOOWNN

B-DDOOWNN

B-DDOOWNN

B-DDOOWNN

...UARDS! ...ARE ...HEY...?

UNCONSCIOUS, MY LIEGE! AS YOU WISHED!

EMPEROR-- WHAT OF THE CYBERNETIC?

TAKE HIM TO THE STASIS CHAMBER WITH THE OTHERS! I WANT NO HARM TO COME TO ANY OF THEM UNTIL *I* COMMAND OTHERWISE!

AND--I DO PLAN OTHER-WISE!

WELCOME BACK-- *FATHER!!*

AS ABRUPTLY AS CONSCIOUSNESS FLED THE OLYMPIAN, IT AS QUICKLY RETURNS --BUT IN A SITUATION FAR LESS DESIRABLE!

B-BY MY BEARD! WHAT SORCERY DOES THIS BE? I-- I CANNOT MOVE!

IT'S THESE STASIS BEDS, MUSCLE-MOUTH! THEY KEEP US PARALYZED FROM THE NECK DOWN! KINDA LIKE THE **OPPOSITE** OF YOUR NORMAL CONDITION!

THE SKRULL IS CORRECT! EVEN HIS SHAPE-CHANGING ABILITIES ARE NEUTRALIZED BY THE RESTRAINING FIELD THESE TABLES GENERATE.

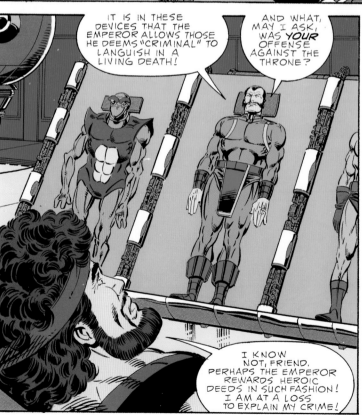

IT IS IN THESE DEVICES THAT THE EMPEROR ALLOWS THOSE HE DEEMS "CRIMINAL" TO LANGUISH IN A LIVING DEATH!

AND WHAT, MAY I ASK, WAS **YOUR** OFFENSE AGAINST THE THRONE?

I KNOW NOT, FRIEND. PERHAPS THE EMPEROR REWARDS HEROIC DEEDS IN SUCH FASHION! I AM AT A LOSS TO EXPLAIN MY CRIME!

AH-- THEN YOU ARE NOT ALONE. MOST OF THE HAPLESS VICTIMS YOU SEE BEFORE YOU ARE, AS WELL, UNAWARE OF WHY THEY ARE HERE. A GREAT INJUSTICE EXISTS IN THIS GALAXY, MY FRIEND!

I'M **MALLAX FORTNITE** AND I'M HERE BECAUSE I STOOD FAST TO **OPPOSE** SUCH TYRANNY!

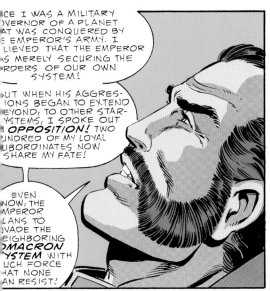

...CE I WAS A MILITARY ...OVERNOR OF A PLANET ...AT WAS CONQUERED BY ...E EMPEROR'S ARMY. I ...LIEVED THAT THE EMPEROR ...AS MERELY SECURING THE ...RDERS OF OUR OWN SYSTEM!

...UT WHEN HIS AGGRES-...IONS BEGAN TO EXTEND ...EYOND, TO OTHER STAR-...YSTEMS, I SPOKE OUT ...OPPOSITION! TWO ...UNDRED OF MY LOYAL ...UBORDINATES NOW ...HARE MY FATE!

EVEN ...NOW, THE EMPEROR ...LANS TO ...VADE THE ...EIGHBORING ...OMACRON ...YSTEM WITH ...UCH FORCE ...HAT NONE ...AN RESIST!

BY THE GODS! THIS IS AN OUTRAGE! YONDER SYSTEM IS ONE OF THE MOST PEACE-LOVING IN ALL THE GALAXY! FOR A TIME, I DID CALL IT--HOME!*

*HERC, VOL. 1, ISH. NUMBER 4.

...EY SHALL BE ...LAMBS BEFORE ...HE WOLF PACK! I--

NAY! THEY SHALL NOT ENTER THE OMACRON SYSTEM AS LONG AS BREATH REMAINS IN ME! SO SWEARS HERCULES!

...HAVE NEWS ...R YOU, MISTER-- ...--HERCULES! ...'RE GOING TO ...HERE FOR A ...ERY LONG... ...EH?

QUIET-- SOMEONE'S COMING!

OH, MY L-LORD--IT'S--

"--THE EMPEROR MOTHER!

"DOWN HERE--IN THE STASIS CHAMBER?! IT'S UNTHINKABLE!"

47

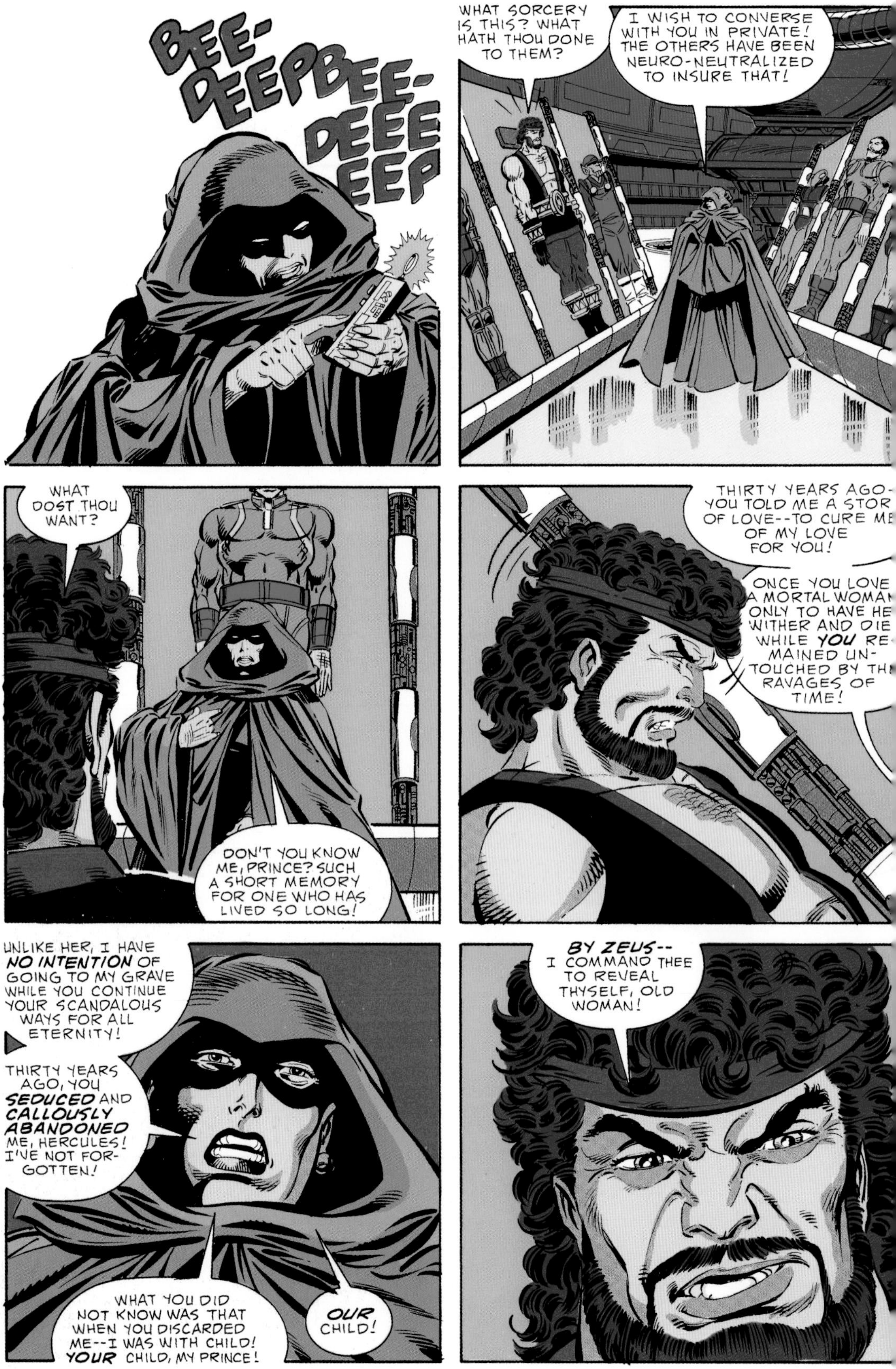
BEE-DEEP BEE-DEEE EEP
WHAT SORCERY IS THIS? WHAT HATH THOU DONE TO THEM?
I WISH TO CONVERSE WITH YOU IN PRIVATE! THE OTHERS HAVE BEEN NEURO-NEUTRALIZED TO INSURE THAT!
WHAT DOST THOU WANT?
DON'T YOU KNOW ME, PRINCE? SUCH A SHORT MEMORY FOR ONE WHO HAS LIVED SO LONG!
THIRTY YEARS AGO- YOU TOLD ME A STOR OF LOVE--TO CURE ME OF MY LOVE FOR YOU!
ONCE YOU LOVE A MORTAL WOMAN ONLY TO HAVE HE WITHER AND DIE WHILE YOU RE- MAINED UN- TOUCHED BY TH RAVAGES OF TIME!
UNLIKE HER, I HAVE NO INTENTION OF GOING TO MY GRAVE WHILE YOU CONTINUE YOUR SCANDALOUS WAYS FOR ALL ETERNITY!
THIRTY YEARS AGO, YOU SEDUCED AND CALLOUSLY ABANDONED ME, HERCULES! I'VE NOT FOR- GOTTEN!
WHAT YOU DID NOT KNOW WAS THAT WHEN YOU DISCARDED ME--I WAS WITH CHILD! YOUR CHILD, MY PRINCE!
OUR CHILD!
BY ZEUS-- I COMMAND THEE TO REVEAL THYSELF, OLD WOMAN!

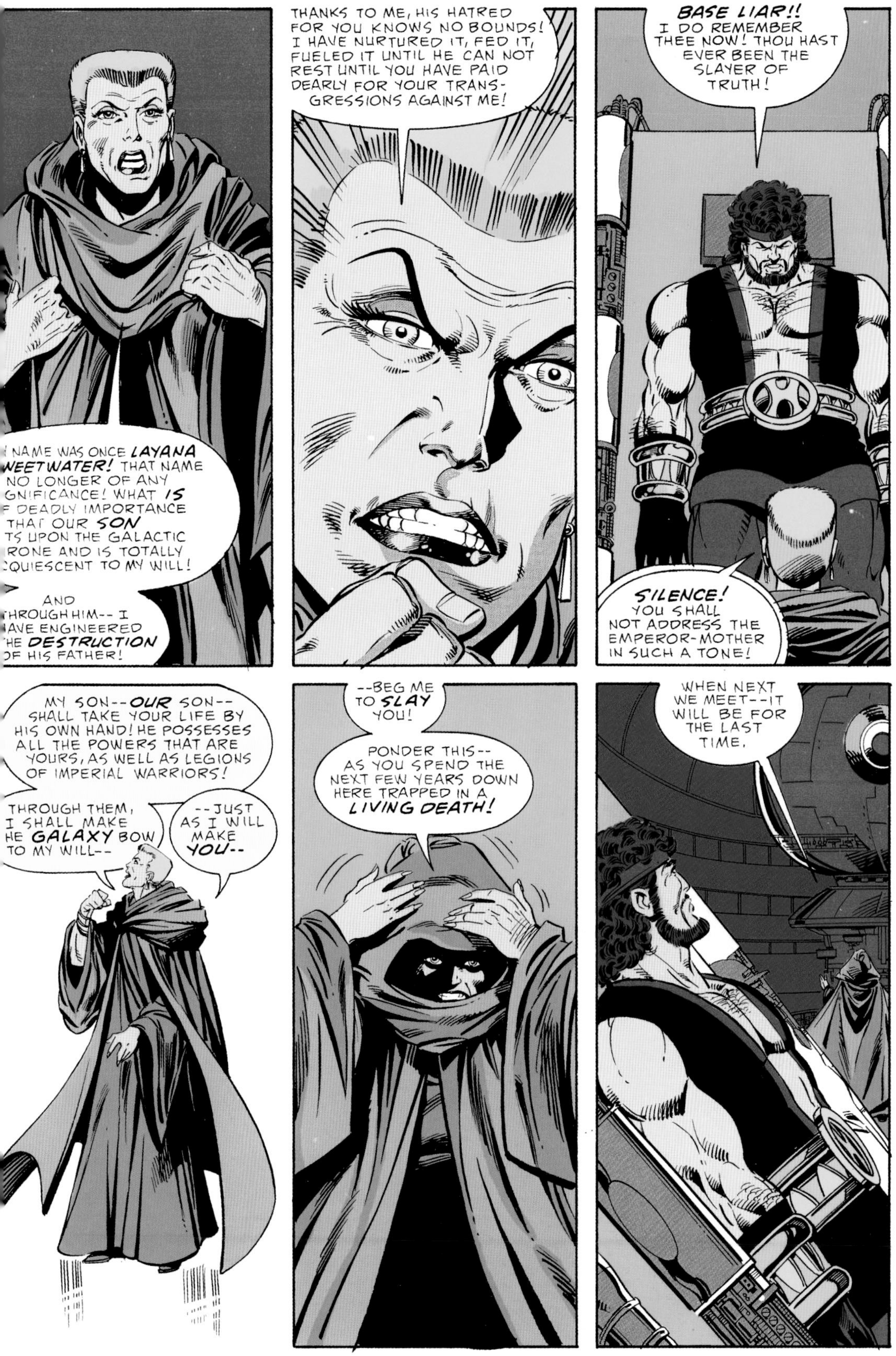
NAME WAS ONCE LAYANA WEETWATER! THAT NAME NO LONGER OF ANY GNIFICANCE! WHAT IS F DEADLY IMPORTANCE THAT OUR SON TS UPON THE GALACTIC RONE AND IS TOTALLY CQUIESCENT TO MY WILL!
AND HROUGH HIM-- I AVE ENGINEERED HE DESTRUCTION OF HIS FATHER!
THANKS TO ME, HIS HATRED FOR YOU KNOWS NO BOUNDS! I HAVE NURTURED IT, FED IT, FUELED IT UNTIL HE CAN NOT REST UNTIL YOU HAVE PAID DEARLY FOR YOUR TRANS-GRESSIONS AGAINST ME!
BASE LIAR!! I DO REMEMBER THEE NOW! THOU HAST EVER BEEN THE SLAYER OF TRUTH!
SILENCE! YOU SHALL NOT ADDRESS THE EMPEROR-MOTHER IN SUCH A TONE!
MY SON--OUR SON--SHALL TAKE YOUR LIFE BY HIS OWN HAND! HE POSSESSES ALL THE POWERS THAT ARE YOURS, AS WELL AS LEGIONS OF IMPERIAL WARRIORS!
THROUGH THEM, I SHALL MAKE HE GALAXY BOW TO MY WILL--
--JUST AS I WILL MAKE YOU--
--BEG ME TO SLAY YOU!
PONDER THIS--AS YOU SPEND THE NEXT FEW YEARS DOWN HERE TRAPPED IN A LIVING DEATH!
WHEN NEXT WE MEET--IT WILL BE FOR THE LAST TIME.

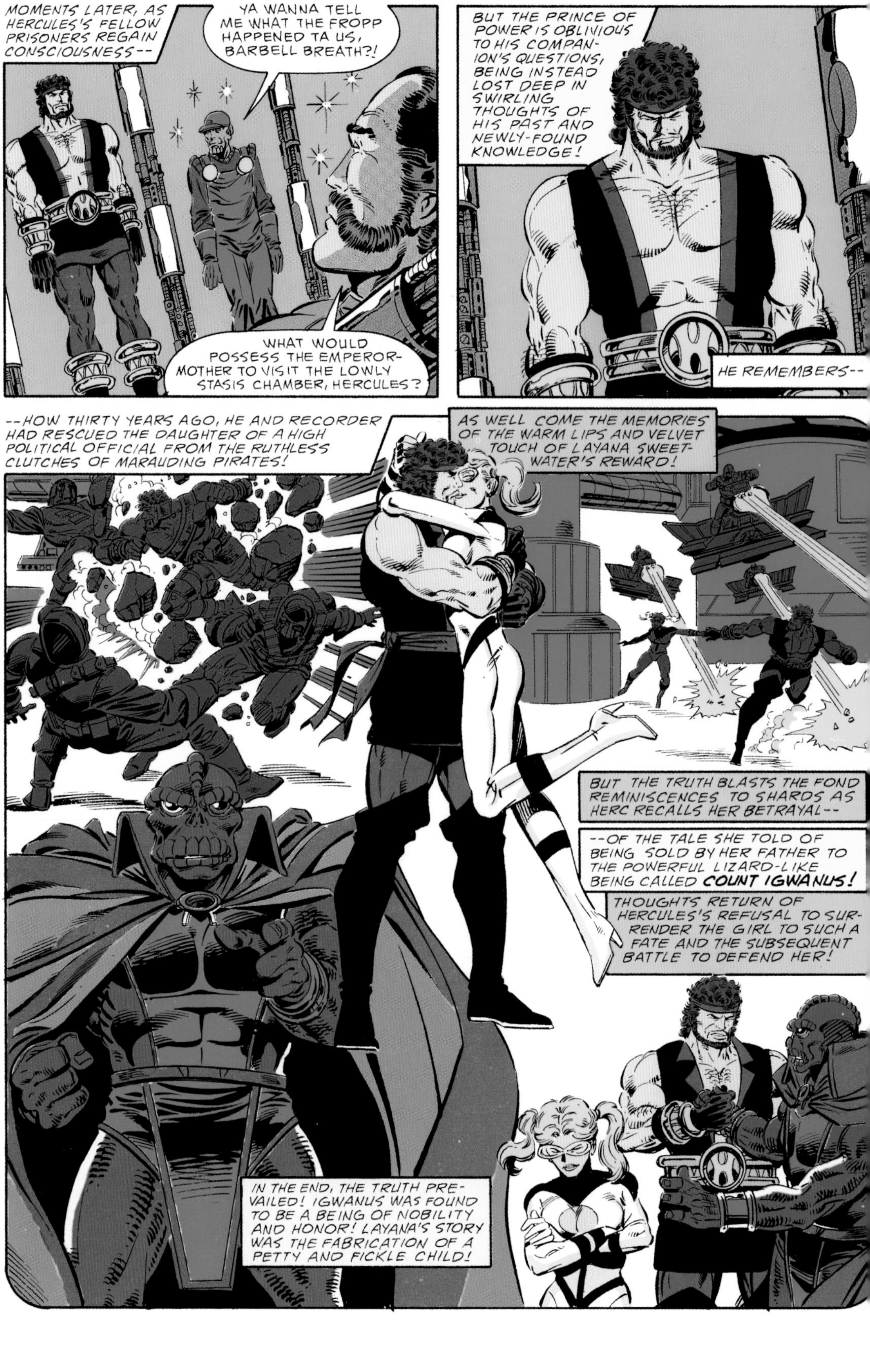
MOMENTS LATER, AS HERCULES'S FELLOW PRISONERS REGAIN CONSCIOUSNESS--
YA WANNA TELL ME WHAT THE FROPP HAPPENED TA US, BARBELL BREATH?!
WHAT WOULD POSSESS THE EMPEROR-MOTHER TO VISIT THE LOWLY STASIS CHAMBER, HERCULES?
BUT THE PRINCE OF POWER IS OBLIVIOUS TO HIS COMPANION'S QUESTIONS, BEING INSTEAD LOST DEEP IN SWIRLING THOUGHTS OF HIS PAST AND NEWLY-FOUND KNOWLEDGE!
HE REMEMBERS--
--HOW THIRTY YEARS AGO, HE AND RECORDER HAD RESCUED THE DAUGHTER OF A HIGH POLITICAL OFFICIAL FROM THE RUTHLESS CLUTCHES OF MARAUDING PIRATES!
AS WELL COME THE MEMORIES OF THE WARM LIPS AND VELVET TOUCH OF LAYANA SWEETWATER'S REWARD!
BUT THE TRUTH BLASTS THE FOND REMINISCENCES TO SHARDS AS HERC RECALLS HER BETRAYAL--
--OF THE TALE SHE TOLD OF BEING SOLD BY HER FATHER TO THE POWERFUL LIZARD-LIKE BEING CALLED COUNT IGWANUS!
THOUGHTS RETURN OF HERCULES'S REFUSAL TO SURRENDER THE GIRL TO SUCH A FATE AND THE SUBSEQUENT BATTLE TO DEFEND HER!
IN THE END, THE TRUTH PREVAILED! IGWANUS WAS FOUND TO BE A BEING OF NOBILITY AND HONOR! LAYANA'S STORY WAS THE FABRICATION OF A PETTY AND FICKLE CHILD!

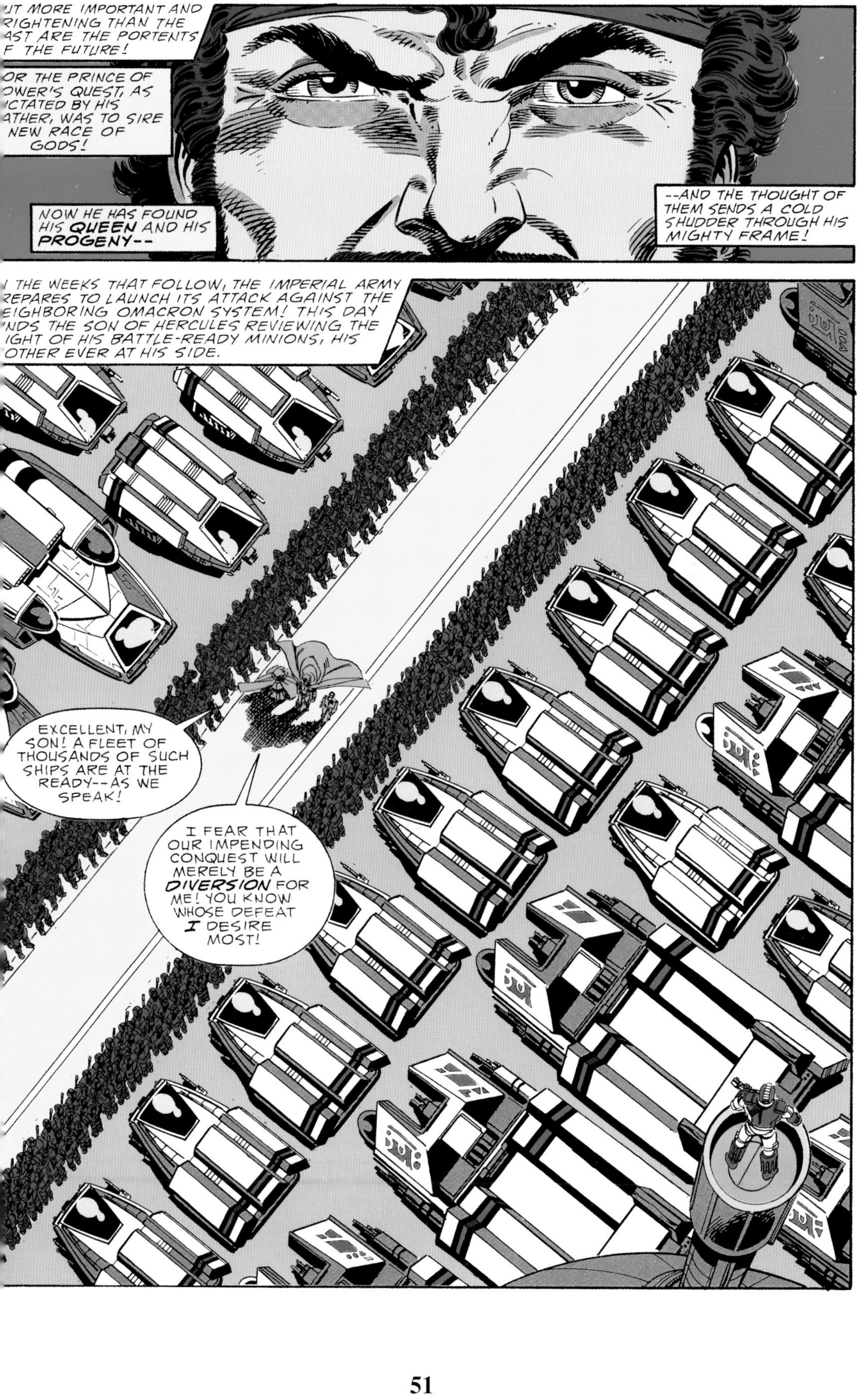
UT MORE IMPORTANT AND RIGHTENING THAN THE AST ARE THE PORTENTS F THE FUTURE!
OR THE PRINCE OF OWER'S QUEST, AS CTATED BY HIS ATHER, WAS TO SIRE NEW RACE OF GODS!
NOW HE HAS FOUND HIS QUEEN AND HIS PROGENY--
--AND THE THOUGHT OF THEM SENDS A COLD SHUDDER THROUGH HIS MIGHTY FRAME!
THE WEEKS THAT FOLLOW, THE IMPERIAL ARMY REPARES TO LAUNCH ITS ATTACK AGAINST THE EIGHBORING OMACRON SYSTEM! THIS DAY NDS THE SON OF HERCULES REVIEWING THE IGHT OF HIS BATTLE-READY MINIONS, HIS OTHER EVER AT HIS SIDE.
EXCELLENT, MY SON! A FLEET OF THOUSANDS OF SUCH SHIPS ARE AT THE READY--AS WE SPEAK!
I FEAR THAT OUR IMPENDING CONQUEST WILL MERELY BE A DIVERSION FOR ME! YOU KNOW WHOSE DEFEAT I DESIRE MOST!

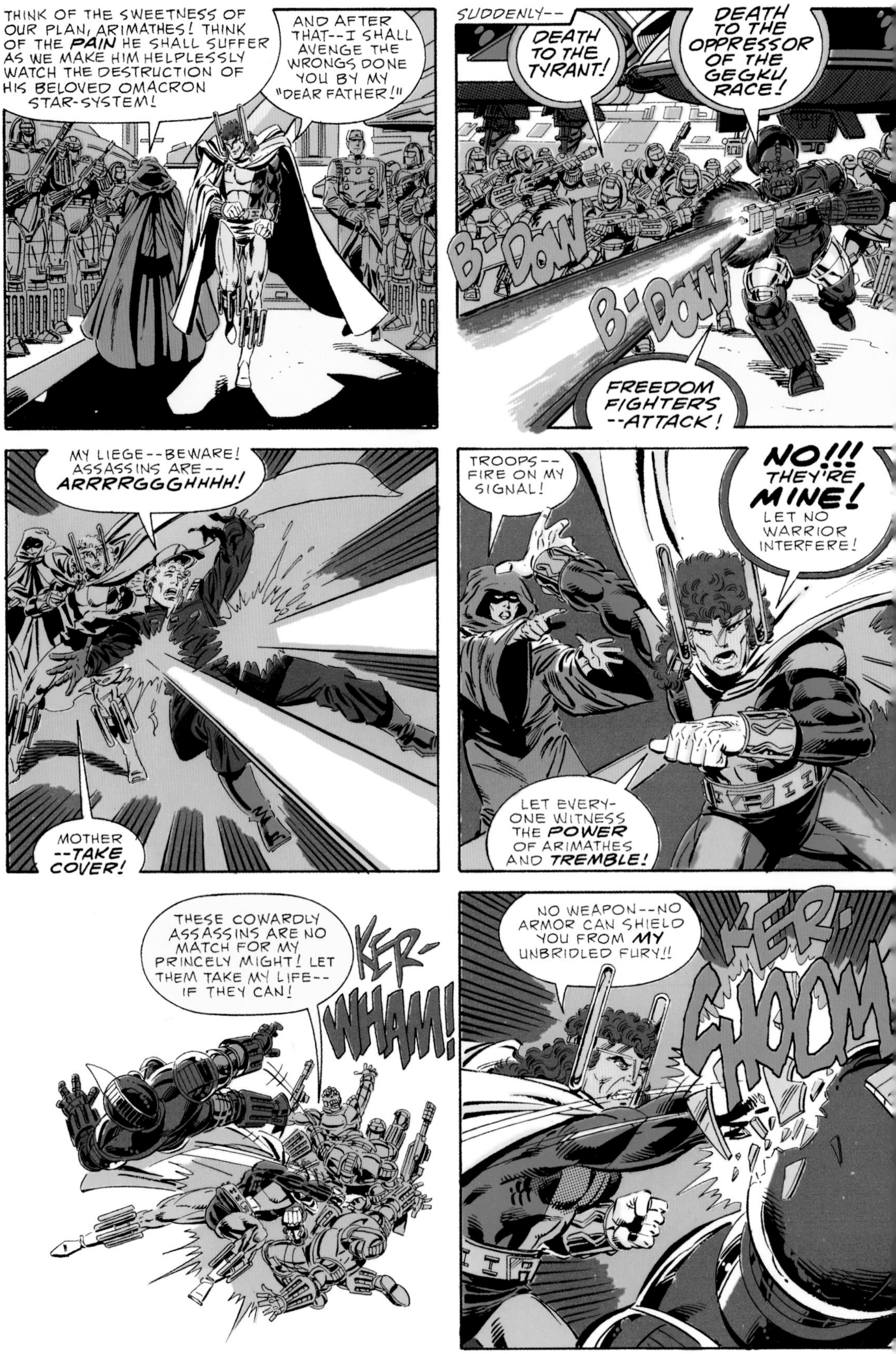
THINK OF THE SWEETNESS OF OUR PLAN, ARIMATHES! THINK OF THE PAIN HE SHALL SUFFER AS WE MAKE HIM HELPLESSLY WATCH THE DESTRUCTION OF HIS BELOVED OMACRON STAR-SYSTEM!
AND AFTER THAT--I SHALL AVENGE THE WRONGS DONE YOU BY MY "DEAR FATHER!"
SUDDENLY--
DEATH TO THE TYRANT!
DEATH TO THE OPPRESSOR OF THE GEGKU RACE!
B-DOW
B-DOW
FREEDOM FIGHTERS --ATTACK!
MY LIEGE--BEWARE! ASSASSINS ARE-- ARRRRGGGHHHH!
MOTHER --TAKE COVER!
TROOPS-- FIRE ON MY SIGNAL!
NO!!! THEY'RE MINE! LET NO WARRIOR INTERFERE!
LET EVERY-ONE WITNESS THE POWER OF ARIMATHES AND TREMBLE!
THESE COWARDLY ASSASSINS ARE NO MATCH FOR MY PRINCELY MIGHT! LET THEM TAKE MY LIFE-- IF THEY CAN!
KER-WHAM!
NO WEAPON--NO ARMOR CAN SHIELD YOU FROM MY UNBRIDLED FURY!!
KER-CHOOM

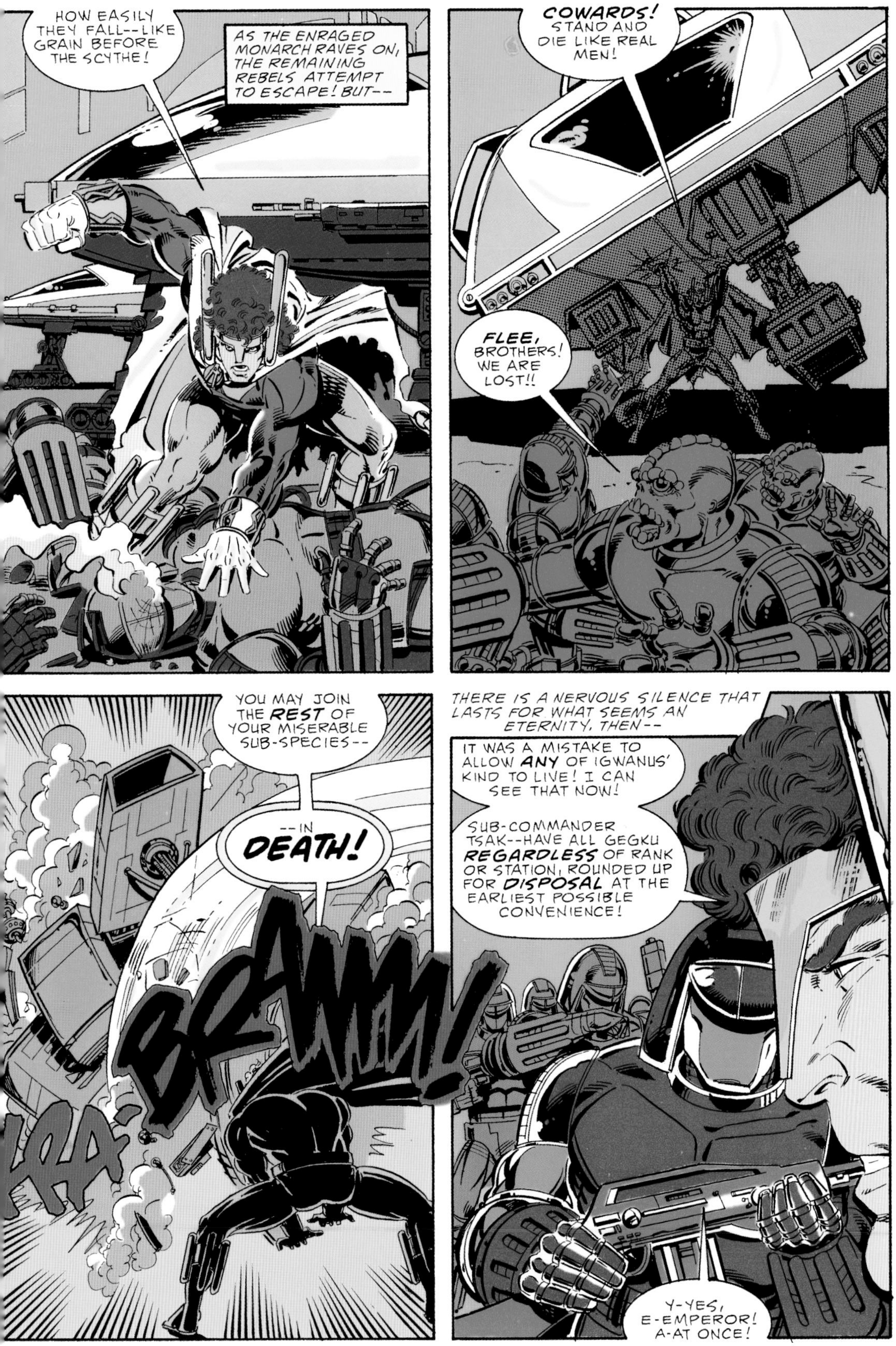
HOW EASILY THEY FALL--LIKE GRAIN BEFORE THE SCYTHE!
AS THE ENRAGED MONARCH RAVES ON, THE REMAINING REBELS ATTEMPT TO ESCAPE! BUT--
COWARDS! STAND AND DIE LIKE REAL MEN!
FLEE, BROTHERS! WE ARE LOST!!
YOU MAY JOIN THE REST OF YOUR MISERABLE SUB-SPECIES--
--IN DEATH!
THERE IS A NERVOUS SILENCE THAT LASTS FOR WHAT SEEMS AN ETERNITY. THEN--
IT WAS A MISTAKE TO ALLOW ANY OF IGWANUS' KIND TO LIVE! I CAN SEE THAT NOW!
SUB-COMMANDER TSAK--HAVE ALL GEGKU REGARDLESS OF RANK OR STATION, ROUNDED UP FOR DISPOSAL AT THE EARLIEST POSSIBLE CONVENIENCE!
Y-YES, E-EMPEROR! A-AT ONCE!

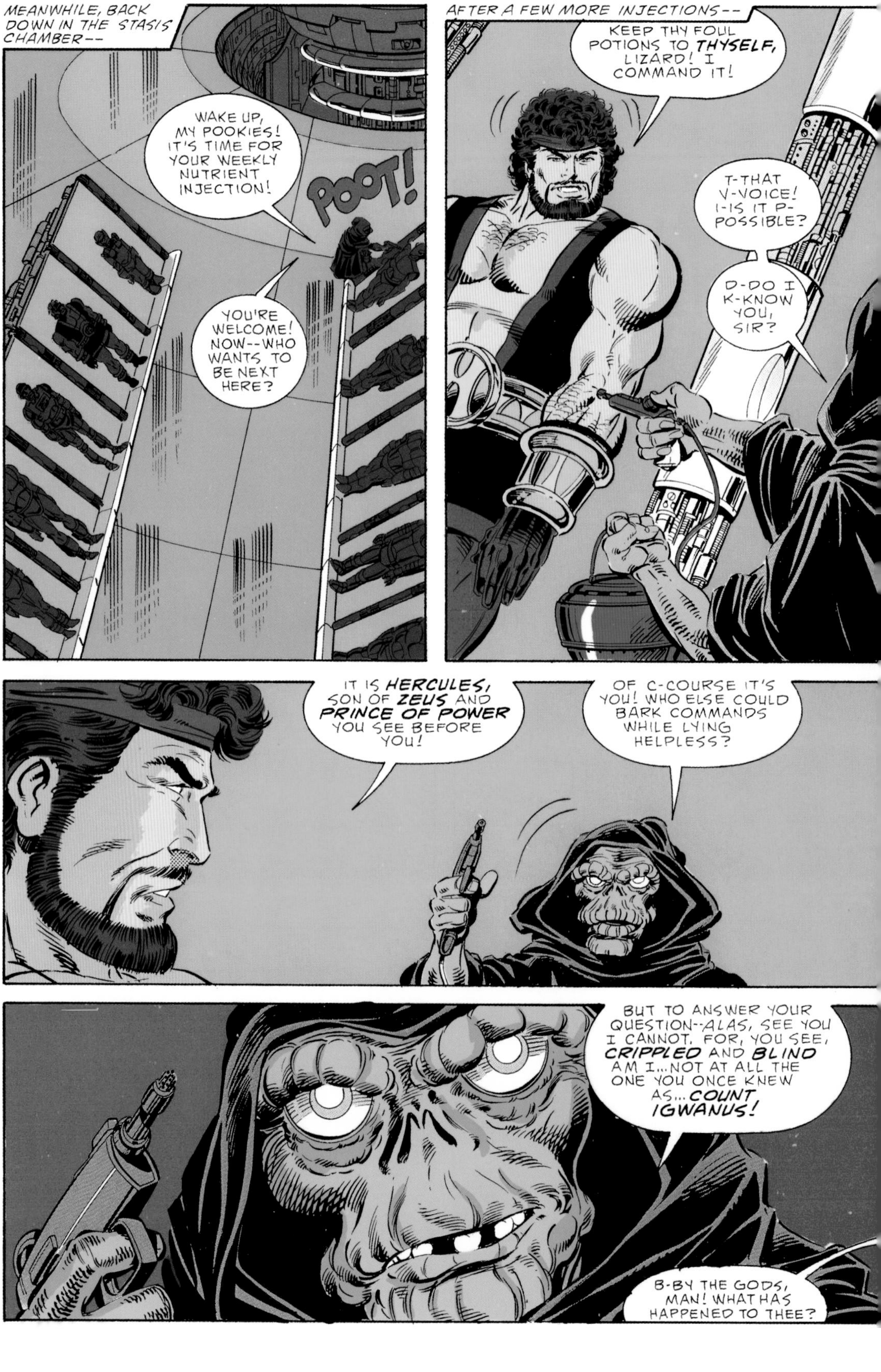
MEANWHILE, BACK DOWN IN THE STASIS CHAMBER--
WAKE UP, MY POOKIES! IT'S TIME FOR YOUR WEEKLY NUTRIENT INJECTION!
POOT!
YOU'RE WELCOME! NOW--WHO WANTS TO BE NEXT HERE?
AFTER A FEW MORE INJECTIONS--
KEEP THY FOUL POTIONS TO THYSELF, LIZARD! I COMMAND IT!
T-THAT V-VOICE! I-IS IT P-POSSIBLE?
D-DO I K-KNOW YOU, SIR?
IT IS HERCULES, SON OF ZEUS AND PRINCE OF POWER YOU SEE BEFORE YOU!
OF C-COURSE IT'S YOU! WHO ELSE COULD BARK COMMANDS WHILE LYING HELPLESS?
BUT TO ANSWER YOUR QUESTION--ALAS, SEE YOU I CANNOT. FOR, YOU SEE, CRIPPLED AND BLIND AM I...NOT AT ALL THE ONE YOU ONCE KNEW AS...COUNT IGWANUS!
B-BY THE GODS, MAN! WHAT HAS HAPPENED TO THEE?

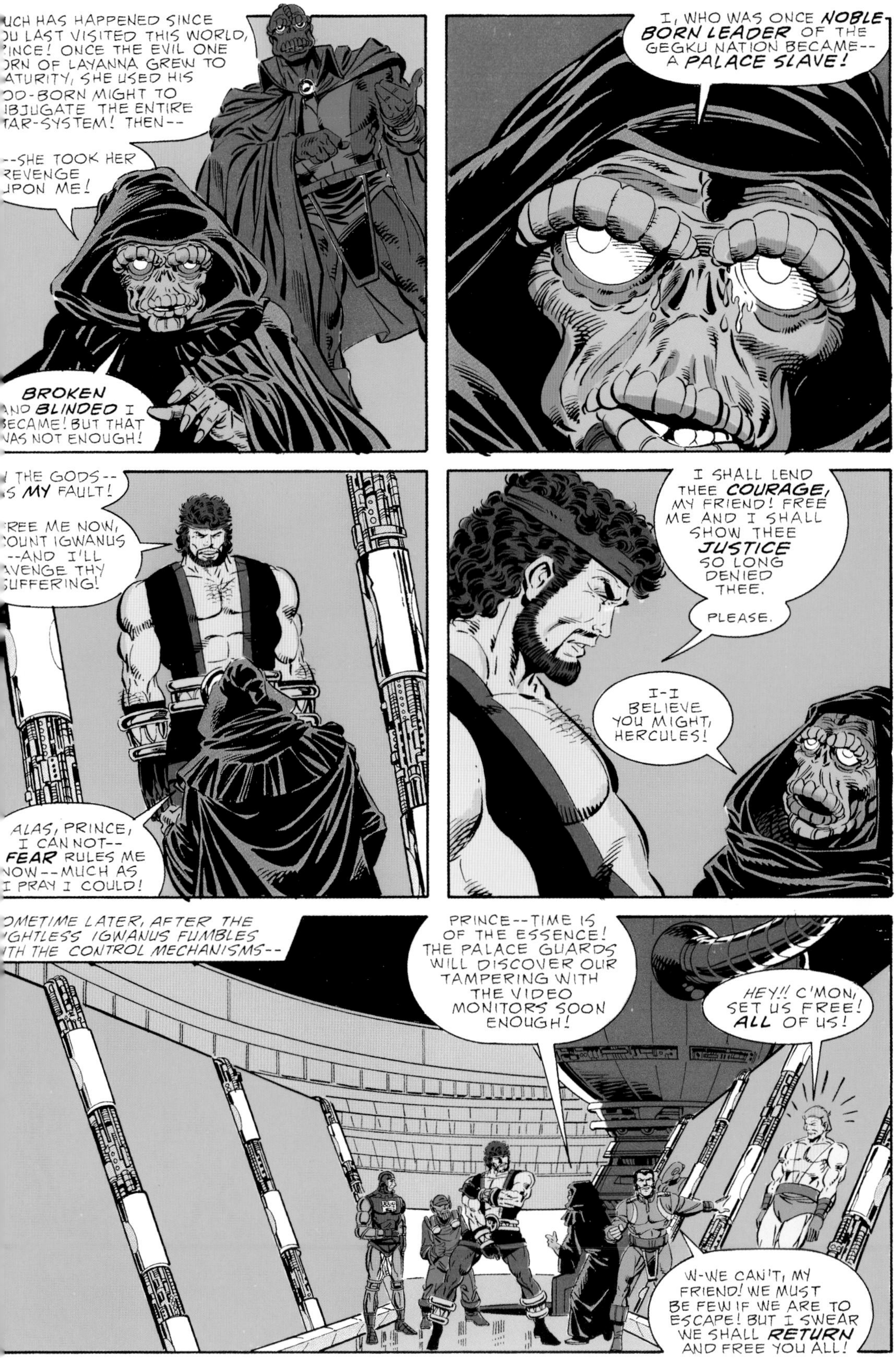
UCH HAS HAPPENED SINCE OU LAST VISITED THIS WORLD, RINCE! ONCE THE EVIL ONE ORN OF LAYANNA GREW TO ATURITY, SHE USED HIS OD-BORN MIGHT TO IBJUGATE THE ENTIRE TAR-SYSTEM! THEN--
--SHE TOOK HER REVENGE UPON ME!
BROKEN AND BLINDED I BECAME! BUT THAT WAS NOT ENOUGH!
I, WHO WAS ONCE NOBLE-BORN LEADER OF THE GEGKU NATION BECAME-- A PALACE SLAVE!
THE GODS-- S MY FAULT!
REE ME NOW, COUNT IGWANUS --AND I'LL AVENGE THY SUFFERING!
ALAS, PRINCE, I CAN NOT-- FEAR RULES ME NOW--MUCH AS I PRAY I COULD!
I SHALL LEND THEE COURAGE, MY FRIEND! FREE ME AND I SHALL SHOW THEE JUSTICE SO LONG DENIED THEE.
PLEASE.
I-I BELIEVE YOU MIGHT, HERCULES!
OMETIME LATER, AFTER THE IGHTLESS IGWANUS FUMBLES ITH THE CONTROL MECHANISMS--
PRINCE--TIME IS OF THE ESSENCE! THE PALACE GUARDS WILL DISCOVER OUR TAMPERING WITH THE VIDEO MONITORS SOON ENOUGH!
HEY!! C'MON, SET US FREE! ALL OF US!
W-WE CAN'T, MY FRIEND! WE MUST BE FEW IF WE ARE TO ESCAPE! BUT I SWEAR WE SHALL RETURN AND FREE YOU ALL!

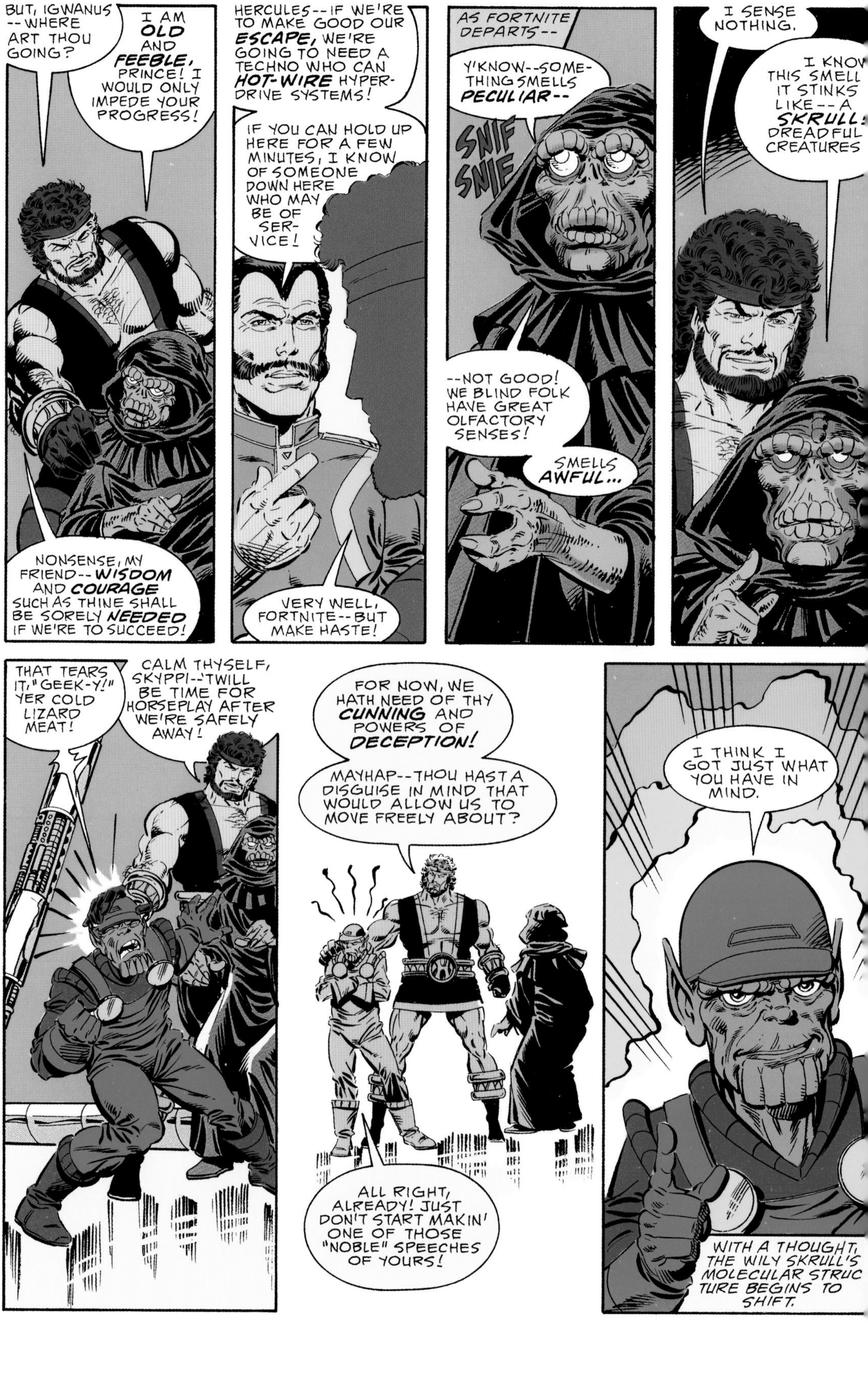

BUT, IGWANUS --WHERE ART THOU GOING?
I AM OLD AND FEEBLE, PRINCE! I WOULD ONLY IMPEDE YOUR PROGRESS!
NONSENSE, MY FRIEND--WISDOM AND COURAGE SUCH AS THINE SHALL BE SORELY NEEDED IF WE'RE TO SUCCEED!
HERCULES--IF WE'RE TO MAKE GOOD OUR ESCAPE, WE'RE GOING TO NEED A TECHNO WHO CAN HOT-WIRE HYPER-DRIVE SYSTEMS!
IF YOU CAN HOLD UP HERE FOR A FEW MINUTES, I KNOW OF SOMEONE DOWN HERE WHO MAY BE OF SER-VICE!
VERY WELL, FORTNITE--BUT MAKE HASTE!
AS FORTNITE DEPARTS--
Y'KNOW--SOME-THING SMELLS PECULIAR--
SNIF SNIF
--NOT GOOD! WE BLIND FOLK HAVE GREAT OLFACTORY SENSES!
SMELLS AWFUL...
I SENSE NOTHING.
I KNOW THIS SMELL IT STINKS LIKE--A SKRULL! DREADFUL CREATURES
THAT TEARS IT, "GEEK-Y!" YER COLD LIZARD MEAT!
CALM THYSELF, SKYPPI--'TWILL BE TIME FOR HORSEPLAY AFTER WE'RE SAFELY AWAY!
FOR NOW, WE HATH NEED OF THY CUNNING AND POWERS OF DECEPTION!
MAYHAP--THOU HAST A DISGUISE IN MIND THAT WOULD ALLOW US TO MOVE FREELY ABOUT?
ALL RIGHT, ALREADY! JUST DON'T START MAKIN' ONE OF THOSE "NOBLE" SPEECHES OF YOURS!
I THINK I GOT JUST WHAT YOU HAVE IN MIND.
WITH A THOUGHT, THE WILY SKRULL'S MOLECULAR STRUC TURE BEGINS TO SHIFT.

MOMENTS LATER, AS FORTNITE RETURNS...

HERCULES--I'D LIKE TO INTRODUCE YOU TO AN OLD PIRATE FRIEND, AND THE BEST *STARSHIP THIEF* IN THE GALAXY--

--LUCYNDA THRUST!

HI, GANG! MALLAX SAYS YOU'VE GOT A--

--P-PLAN ...OH, MY!

B-BY MY STARS! WE'VE BEEN DISCOVERED! IT'S--

--THE EMPEROR MOTHER!

THAT'S RIGHT, LACKEY! *KNEEL* BEFORE ME-- IF YOU WISH TO LIVE! AND AS FOR THE GIRL--

--HOWZABOUT A KISS, HOT-PANTS?!

SMEK!

W-WAIT A MINUTE! -HEH HEH- THIS BROAD'S NOT THE ROYAL MOTHER! WHAT'S GOIN' ON HERE?

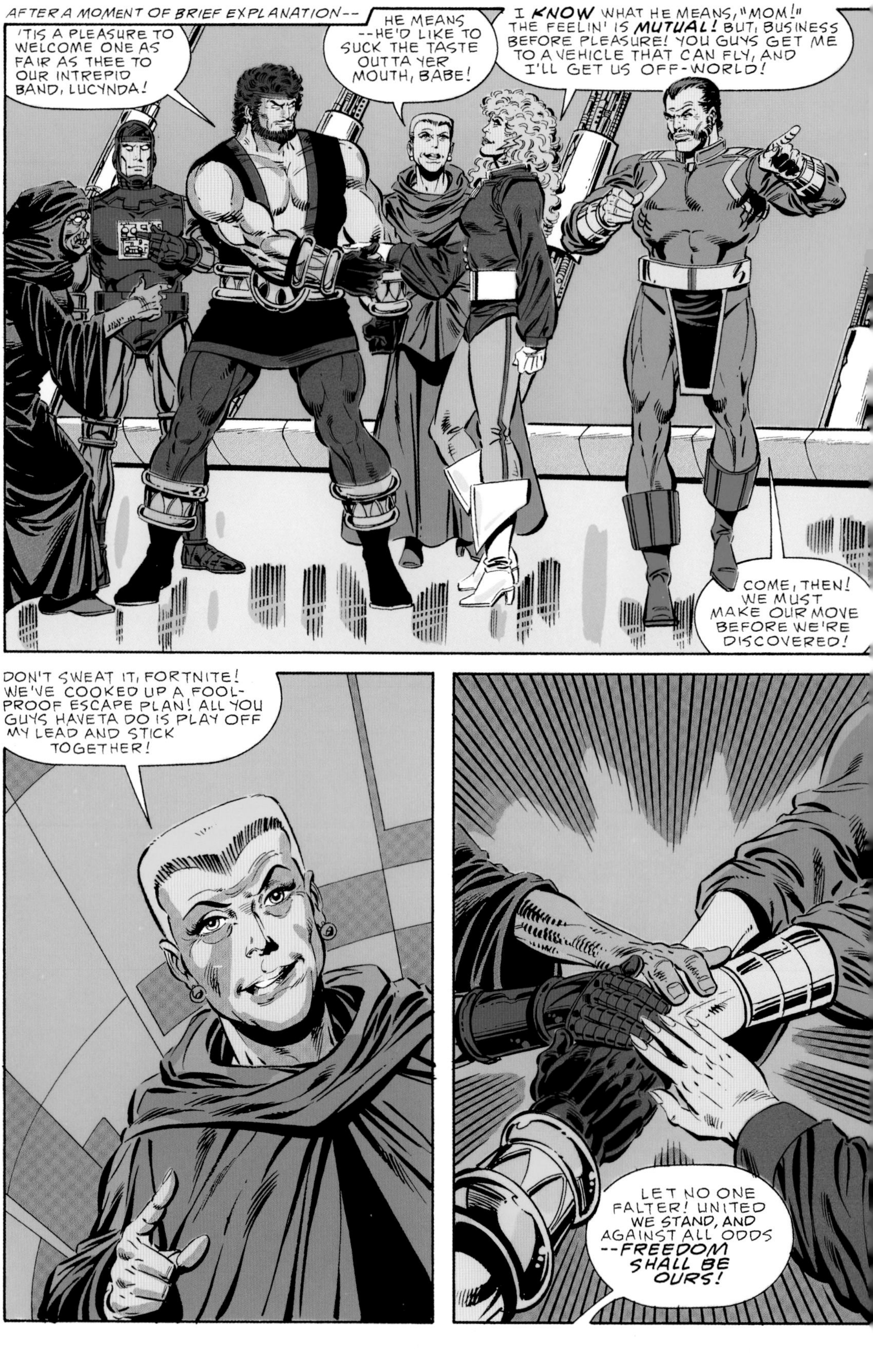

AFTER A MOMENT OF BRIEF EXPLANATION--
'TIS A PLEASURE TO WELCOME ONE AS FAIR AS THEE TO OUR INTREPID BAND, LUCYNDA!
HE MEANS --HE'D LIKE TO SUCK THE TASTE OUTTA YER MOUTH, BABE!
I KNOW WHAT HE MEANS, "MOM!" THE FEELIN' IS MUTUAL! BUT, BUSINESS BEFORE PLEASURE! YOU GUYS GET ME TO A VEHICLE THAT CAN FLY, AND I'LL GET US OFF-WORLD!
COME, THEN! WE MUST MAKE OUR MOVE BEFORE WE'RE DISCOVERED!
DON'T SWEAT IT, FORTNITE! WE'VE COOKED UP A FOOL-PROOF ESCAPE PLAN! ALL YOU GUYS HAVETA DO IS PLAY OFF MY LEAD AND STICK TOGETHER!
LET NO ONE FALTER! UNITED WE STAND, AND AGAINST ALL ODDS --FREEDOM SHALL BE OURS!

MINUTES LATER, AT THE EXIT OF THE MASSIVE STASIS CHAMBER--

HALT! WHAT ARE YOU PRISONERS DOING?! WHY AREN'T YOU IN YOUR STASIS BEDS?

WE'VE BEEN PARDONED BY THE EMPEROR-MOTHER HERSELF, AND WE'RE ON OUR WAY TO MEET WITH EMPEROR ARIMATHES.

BULL FROPP! BACK OFF, OR WE'LL FRY THE LOT OF YA! WE DON'T--

SILENCE! YOU WILL LET THEM PASS!

SON... OF...A...!?

THESE PRISONERS ARE IN MY CHARGE! ALLOW THEM THROUGH --AT ONCE!

WAIT A MINUTE -- HOW DO WE KNOW IT'S REALLY YOU?!

SUDDENLY, BURSTING THROUGH THE CROWD--

GANGWAY, PEOPLE! I GOTTA GET MY SLOP PAIL REFILLED--AND QUICK! I'M RUNNIN' BEHIND WITH MY GRUEL-X INJECTIONS!

OOPS... SORRY, BUDDY!

BUMP!

VILE CREATURE! YOU DARE TO TOUCH THE PERSON OF THE EMPEROR-MOTHER?!!

TWATT!

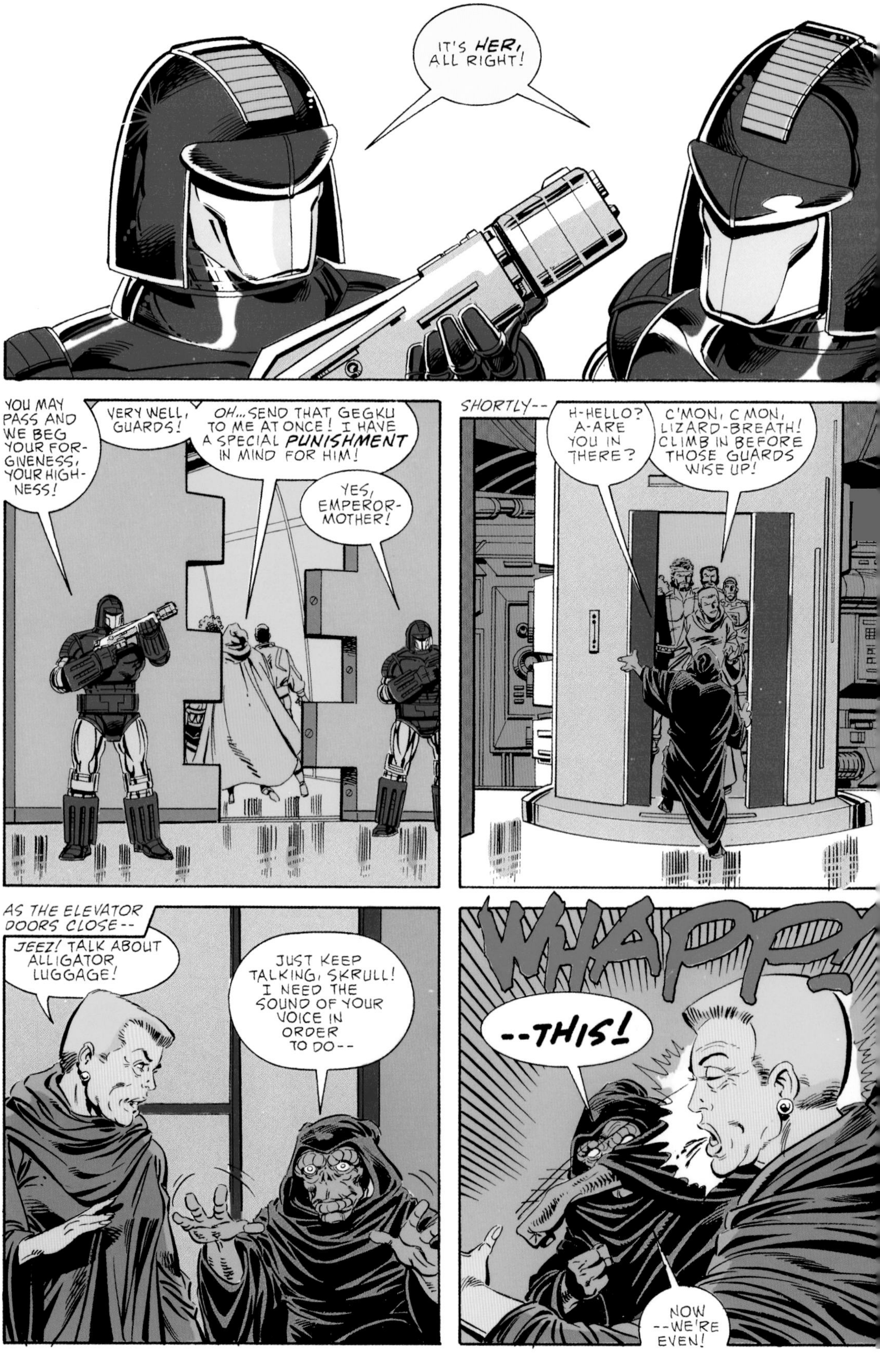

IT'S HER, ALL RIGHT!
YOU MAY PASS AND WE BEG YOUR FORGIVENESS, YOUR HIGHNESS!
VERY WELL, GUARDS!
OH... SEND THAT GEGKU TO ME AT ONCE! I HAVE A SPECIAL PUNISHMENT IN MIND FOR HIM!
YES, EMPEROR-MOTHER!
SHORTLY--
H-HELLO? A-ARE YOU IN THERE?
C'MON, C'MON, LIZARD-BREATH! CLIMB IN BEFORE THOSE GUARDS WISE UP!
AS THE ELEVATOR DOORS CLOSE--
JEEZ! TALK ABOUT ALLIGATOR LUGGAGE!
JUST KEEP TALKING, SKRULL! I NEED THE SOUND OF YOUR VOICE IN ORDER TO DO--
WHAPP!
--THIS!
NOW --WE'RE EVEN!

INTERROGATIVE: CAN YOU RESIST LONG ENOUGH TO CONTINUE THE RUSE, KYPPI? I'M ACTIVATING THE COMPUTER.

DECLARATION: GOOD DAY, COMPUTER.

INTERROGATIVE: WOULD YOU PLEASE TRANSPORT MY COMPANIONS AND ME TO THE MAIN PLAZA LEVEL?

PING!

HEY, MON...YOU GOTTA DEM ACCESS CODES?

NO CODE... YOU NO GONNA MOVE, MON!

I'M THE ROYAL MOTHER, BLAST YOU! YOU'LL TAKE US WHERE I SAY!

KISS MY PULLIES, THUNDER BUNS! IF YA NO GOTTA CODE--BAIL YO' BIG BUTT OUTTA HERE!

SPECULATION: I BELIEVE I MIGHT HAVE A SOLUTION, "YOUR HIGHNESS!"

STATEMENT: COMPUTER--AS EGOCENTRIC AS YOUR BEHAVIOR IS, I'M SURE YOU HAVE LOGIC CIRCUITS! ALLOW ME TO APPEAL TO THEM!

DECLARATION: TAKE US TO WHERE WE WANT TO GO OR THIS LARGE FELLOW OVER HERE IS GOING TO TURN YOU INTO SPARE PARTS!

NO TALK TRASH TO ME, MON! DIS GUY BE NO... :YIPE:

:HARRUMPH:- WHAT FLOOR WAS THAT AGAIN, SIR?

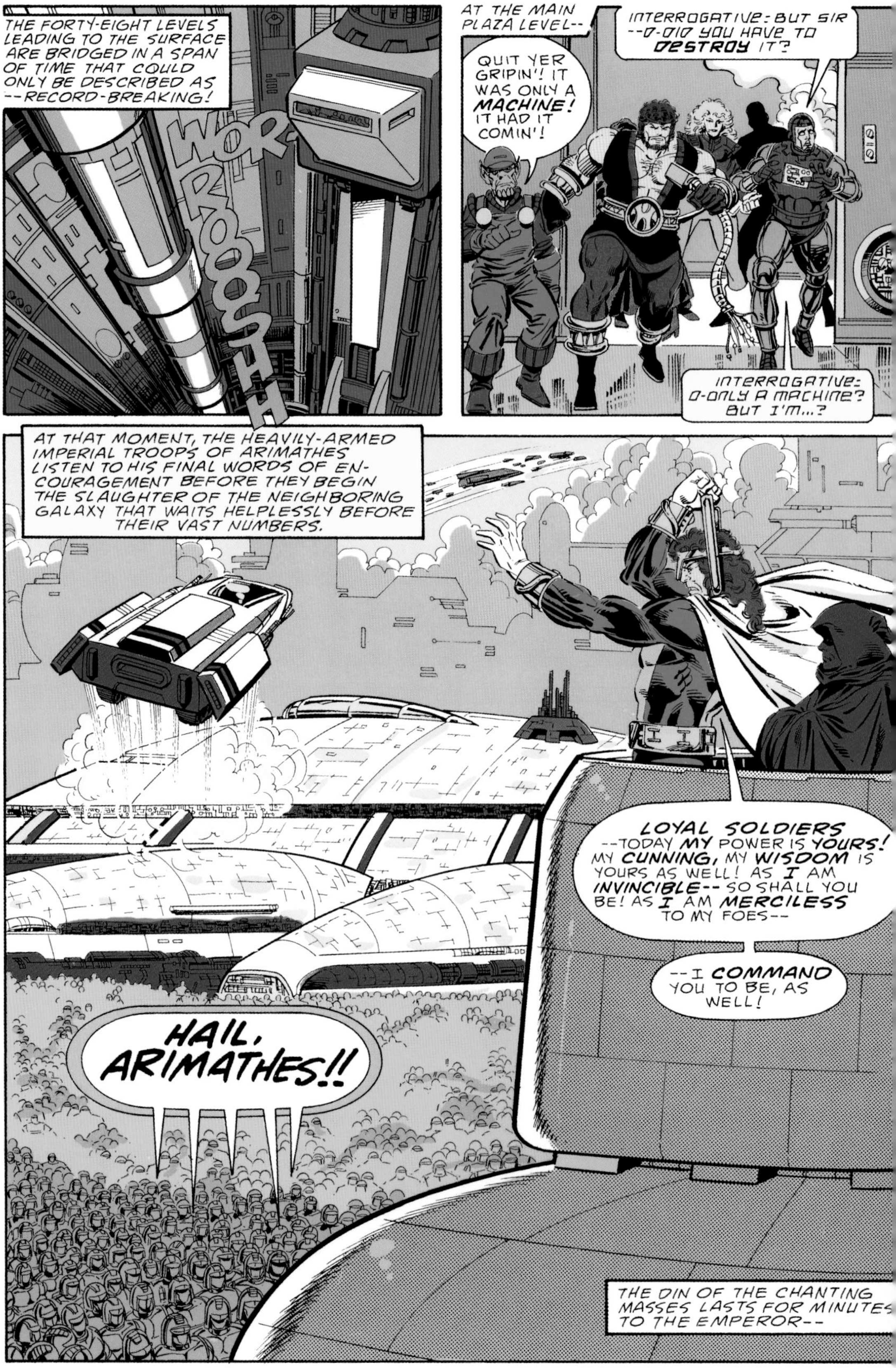
THE FORTY-EIGHT LEVELS LEADING TO THE SURFACE ARE BRIDGED IN A SPAN OF TIME THAT COULD ONLY BE DESCRIBED AS --RECORD-BREAKING!
WOR-ROOOSHH
AT THE MAIN PLAZA LEVEL--
QUIT YER GRIPIN'! IT WAS ONLY A MACHINE! IT HAD IT COMIN'!
INTERROGATIVE: BUT SIR --D-DID YOU HAVE TO DESTROY IT?
INTERROGATIVE: O-ONLY A MACHINE? BUT I'M...?
AT THAT MOMENT, THE HEAVILY-ARMED IMPERIAL TROOPS OF ARIMATHES LISTEN TO HIS FINAL WORDS OF ENCOURAGEMENT BEFORE THEY BEGIN THE SLAUGHTER OF THE NEIGHBORING GALAXY THAT WAITS HELPLESSLY BEFORE THEIR VAST NUMBERS.
LOYAL SOLDIERS --TODAY MY POWER IS YOURS! MY CUNNING, MY WISDOM IS YOURS AS WELL! AS I AM INVINCIBLE-- SO SHALL YOU BE! AS I AM MERCILESS TO MY FOES--
--I COMMAND YOU TO BE, AS WELL!
HAIL, ARIMATHES!!
THE DIN OF THE CHANTING MASSES LASTS FOR MINUTES TO THE EMPEROR--

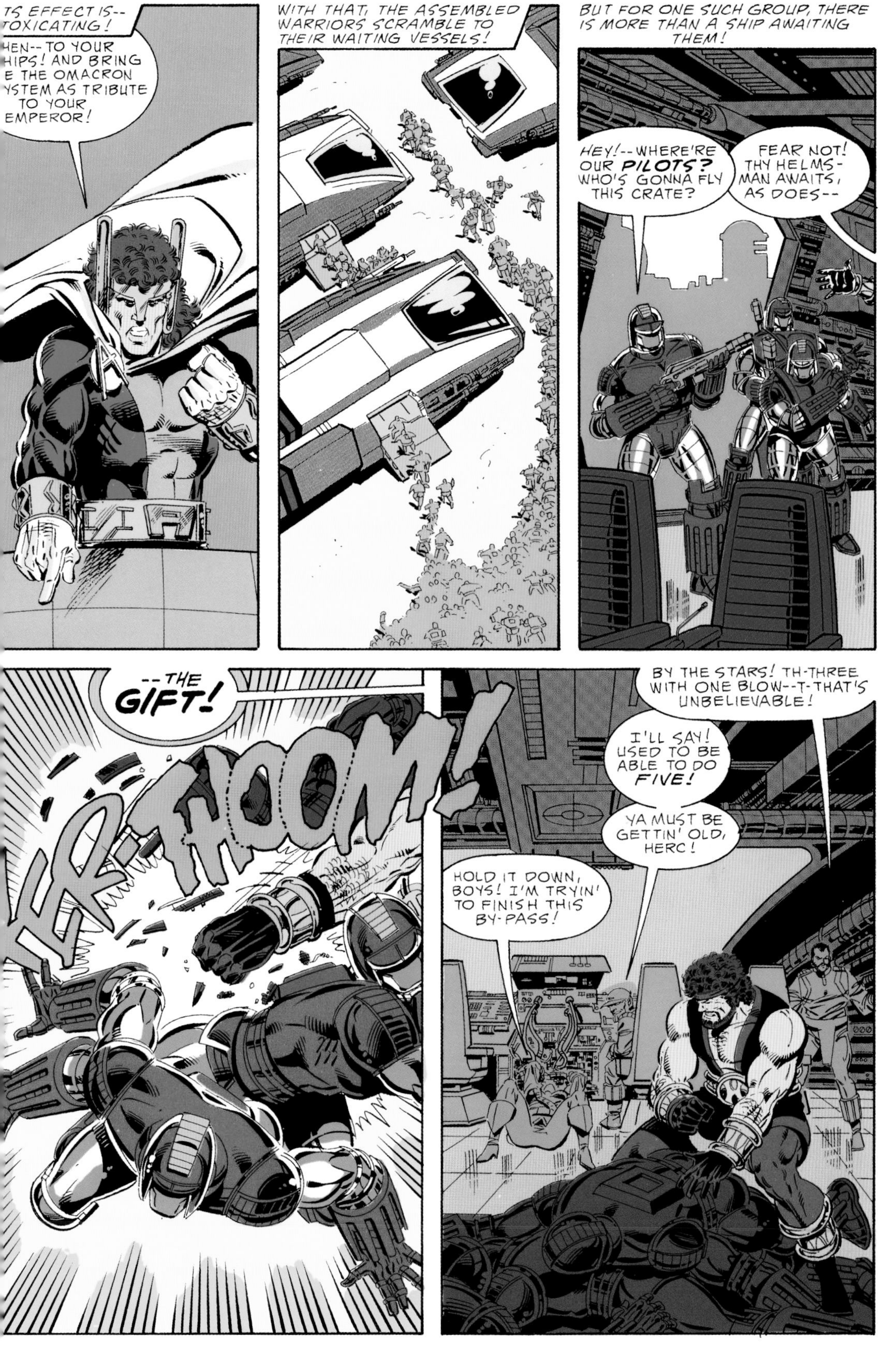

TS EFFECT IS--
TOXICATING!
HEN--TO YOUR
HIPS! AND BRING
E THE OMACRON
YSTEM AS TRIBUTE
TO YOUR
EMPEROR!
WITH THAT, THE ASSEMBLED WARRIORS SCRAMBLE TO THEIR WAITING VESSELS!
BUT FOR ONE SUCH GROUP, THERE IS MORE THAN A SHIP AWAITING THEM!
HEY!--WHERE'RE OUR PILOTS? WHO'S GONNA FLY THIS CRATE?
FEAR NOT! THY HELMSMAN AWAITS, AS DOES--
--THE GIFT!
KRR-THOOM!
BY THE STARS! TH-THREE WITH ONE BLOW--T-THAT'S UNBELIEVABLE!
I'LL SAY! USED TO BE ABLE TO DO FIVE!
YA MUST BE GETTIN' OLD, HERC!
HOLD IT DOWN, BOYS! I'M TRYIN' TO FINISH THIS BY-PASS!

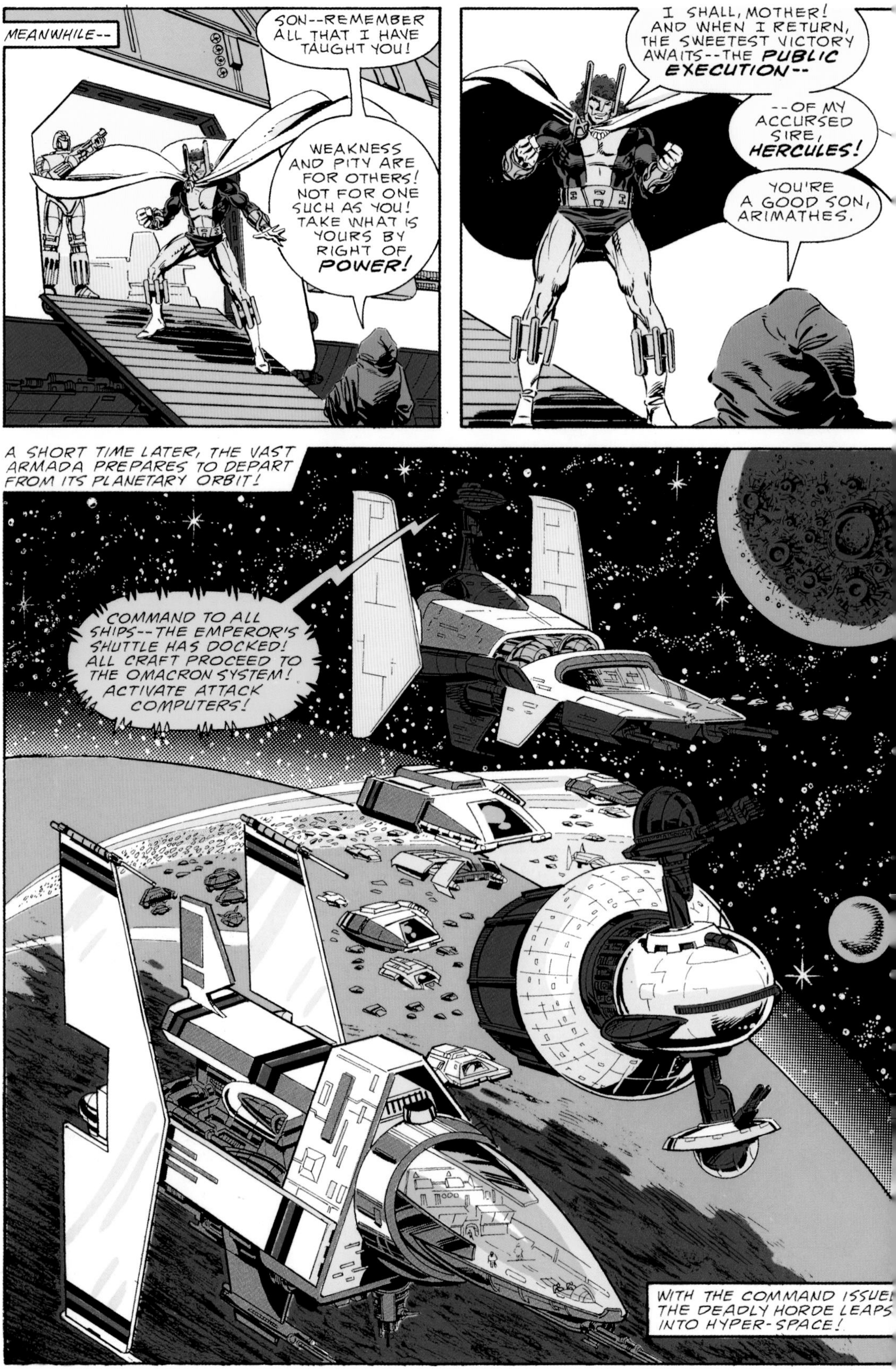
MEANWHILE--
SON--REMEMBER ALL THAT I HAVE TAUGHT YOU!
WEAKNESS AND PITY ARE FOR OTHERS! NOT FOR ONE SUCH AS YOU! TAKE WHAT IS YOURS BY RIGHT OF POWER!
I SHALL, MOTHER! AND WHEN I RETURN, THE SWEETEST VICTORY AWAITS--THE PUBLIC EXECUTION--
--OF MY ACCURSED SIRE, HERCULES!
YOU'RE A GOOD SON, ARIMATHES.
A SHORT TIME LATER, THE VAST ARMADA PREPARES TO DEPART FROM ITS PLANETARY ORBIT!
COMMAND TO ALL SHIPS--THE EMPEROR'S SHUTTLE HAS DOCKED! ALL CRAFT PROCEED TO THE OMACRON SYSTEM! ACTIVATE ATTACK COMPUTERS!
WITH THE COMMAND ISSUE! THE DEADLY HORDE LEAPS INTO HYPER-SPACE!

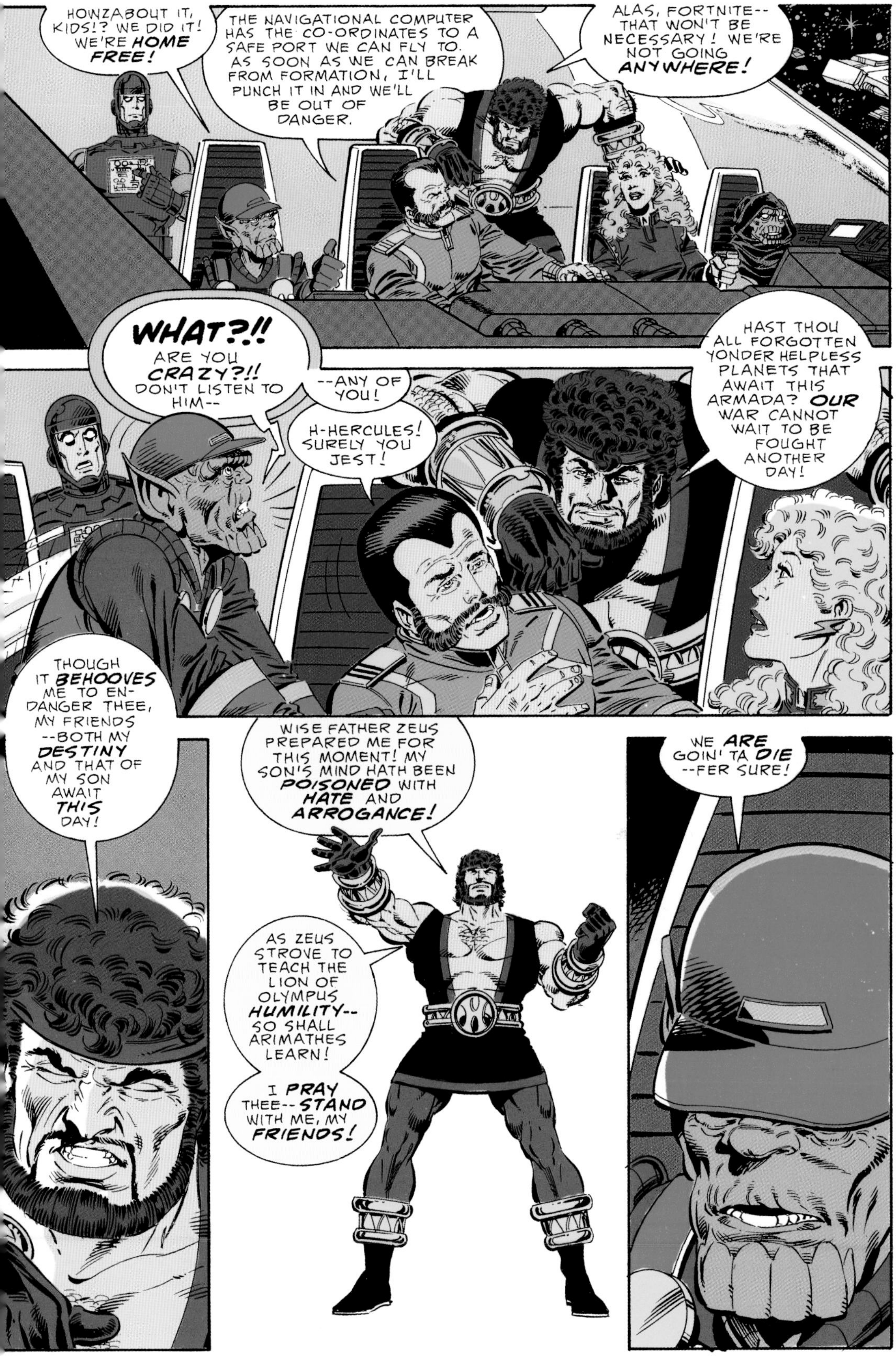

HOWZABOUT IT, KIDS!? WE DID IT! WE'RE HOME FREE!
THE NAVIGATIONAL COMPUTER HAS THE CO-ORDINATES TO A SAFE PORT WE CAN FLY TO. AS SOON AS WE CAN BREAK FROM FORMATION, I'LL PUNCH IT IN AND WE'LL BE OUT OF DANGER.
ALAS, FORTNITE-- THAT WON'T BE NECESSARY! WE'RE NOT GOING ANYWHERE!
WHAT?!! ARE YOU CRAZY?!! DON'T LISTEN TO HIM--
--ANY OF YOU!
H-HERCULES! SURELY YOU JEST!
HAST THOU ALL FORGOTTEN YONDER HELPLESS PLANETS THAT AWAIT THIS ARMADA? OUR WAR CANNOT WAIT TO BE FOUGHT ANOTHER DAY!
THOUGH IT BEHOOVES ME TO EN-DANGER THEE, MY FRIENDS --BOTH MY DESTINY AND THAT OF MY SON AWAIT THIS DAY!
WISE FATHER ZEUS PREPARED ME FOR THIS MOMENT! MY SON'S MIND HATH BEEN POISONED WITH HATE AND ARROGANCE!
AS ZEUS STROVE TO TEACH THE LION OF OLYMPUS HUMILITY-- SO SHALL ARIMATHES LEARN!
I PRAY THEE-- STAND WITH ME, MY FRIENDS!
WE ARE GOIN' TA DIE --FER SURE!

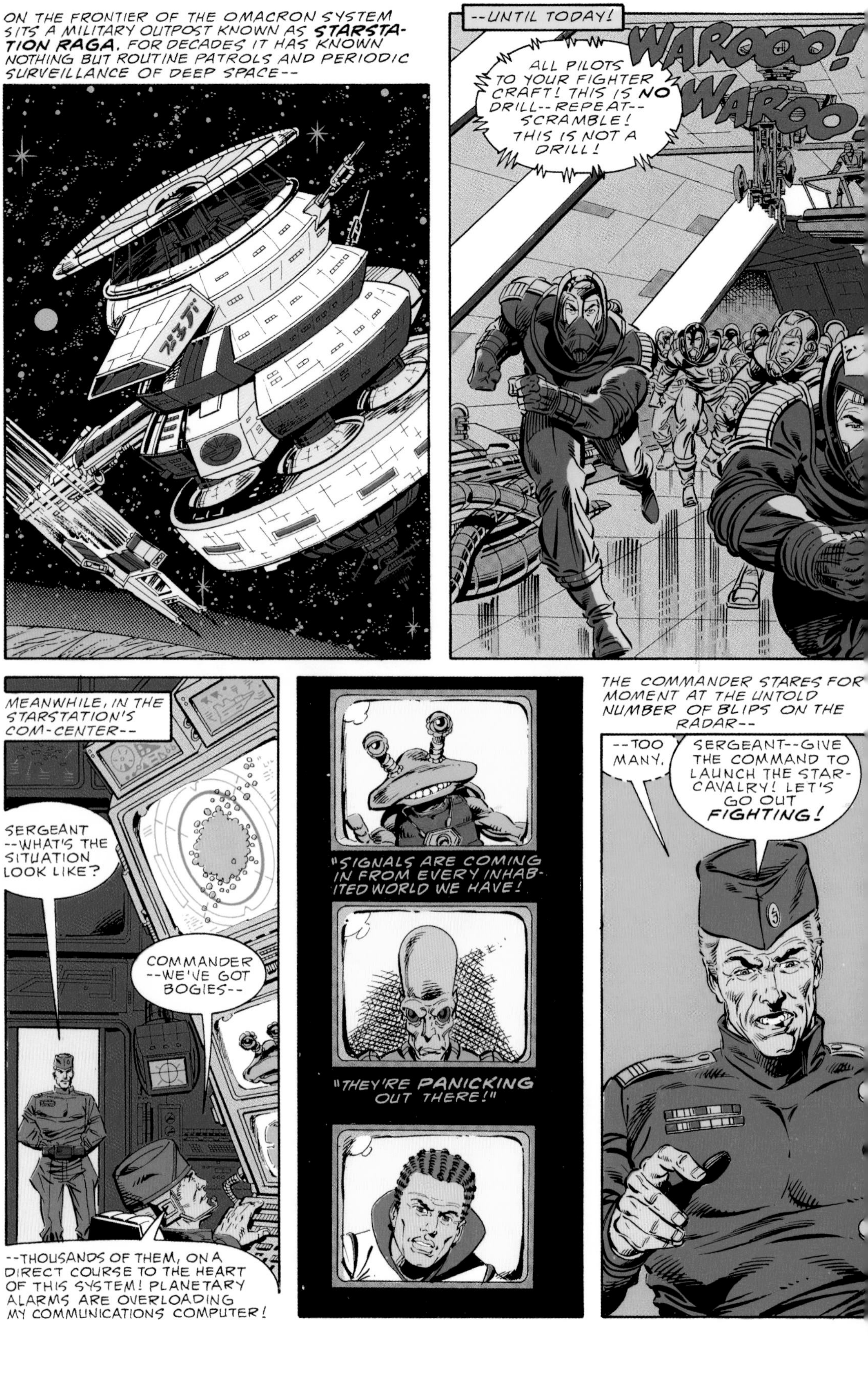

ON THE FRONTIER OF THE OMACRON SYSTEM SITS A MILITARY OUTPOST KNOWN AS STARSTATION RAGA. FOR DECADES IT HAS KNOWN NOTHING BUT ROUTINE PATROLS AND PERIODIC SURVEILLANCE OF DEEP SPACE--
--UNTIL TODAY!
WAROOO! WAROO!
ALL PILOTS TO YOUR FIGHTER CRAFT! THIS IS NO DRILL--REPEAT--SCRAMBLE! THIS IS NOT A DRILL!
MEANWHILE, IN THE STARSTATION'S COM-CENTER--
SERGEANT --WHAT'S THE SITUATION LOOK LIKE?
COMMANDER --WE'VE GOT BOGIES--
--THOUSANDS OF THEM, ON A DIRECT COURSE TO THE HEART OF THIS SYSTEM! PLANETARY ALARMS ARE OVERLOADING MY COMMUNICATIONS COMPUTER!
"SIGNALS ARE COMING IN FROM EVERY INHABITED WORLD WE HAVE!
"THEY'RE PANICKING OUT THERE!"
THE COMMANDER STARES FOR A MOMENT AT THE UNTOLD NUMBER OF BLIPS ON THE RADAR--
--TOO MANY.
SERGEANT--GIVE THE COMMAND TO LAUNCH THE STAR-CAVALRY! LET'S GO OUT FIGHTING!

WITH THE ORDER ISSUED, THE SQUADRONS PROPEL THEMSELVES INTO DEEP SPACE TOWARD A RENDEZVOUS WITH DOOM!

MEANWHILE, BACK WITH THE EMPEROR'S ARMADA...

IT'S NO USE, SWEETS! WE'RE NOT GOING TO BE ABLE TO BREAK RADIO SILENCE!

SHE'S RIGHT, STEROID-BREATH! WE'RE GONNA NEED THE ACCESS CODES FOR SHIP-TO-SHIP COMMUNICATIONS!

SO MUCH FOR YOUR PLAN, HERC!

WAIT A MINUTE-- LUCIE-BABY! WE'VE GOT THOSE SOLDIER-BOYS ON ICE IN THE HOLD-- RIGHT?

R//////GGHT! I LIKE THE WAY YOU THINK, GREENIE!

MOMENTS LATER--

WAKE UP, SOLDIER! IT'S TIME FOR YOUR MORNING EXERCISES!

W-WHAT DO YOU M-MEAN?

I MEAN-- YOU'RE GOIN' TO TAKE A VERY LONG WALK, GENERAL!

N-NO!! Y-YOU C-CAN'T D-DO THIS!

WANNA BET?
TELL YOU WHAT --YOU GIVE ME THE INTER-FLEET COM-CODES, AND I'LL EXCUSE YOU FROM YOUR LITTLE MARATHON SPACE-WALK!
BUT IF YOU DON'T WANNA TALK--
--I'LL BLAST YOUR BUTT ALL THE WAY BACK TO WILAMEAN!
WHAT'S IT GOING TO BE?
AT THAT MOMENT, BACK AT THE CONTROLS--
WE'RE IN DEEP FROPP NOW! THE FLEET IS ABOUT TEN MINUTES AWAY FROM EN-GAGING THE OMACRON STAR-CAVALRY!
AND--WE'VE GOT THEM HOPELESSLY OUTNUMBERED!
ETA 27
DON'T SWEAT IT, CREW! I GOT THE INFO WE'RE NEEDING!
WELL--QUIT WASTIN' TIME, SWEET-CHEEKS! PUNCH 'EM IN WHILE I MAKE A QUICK CHANGE!
THIRTY SECONDS LATER, AS EVERY COMMUNICATION PANEL IN THE FLEET ACTIVATES--
THIS IS EMPEROR ARIMATHES TO ALL SHIPS! STAND BY!
WHAT'S UP, I WONDER!?!
GOD--I HOPE IT'S NOT ANOTHER SPEECH!
THE FLEET WILL COME TO FULL STOP! YOU ARE NOT TO ENGAGE THE ENEMY STAR-CRAFT! REPEAT --DO NOT ENGAGE!
IS HE KIDDIN'?

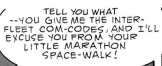

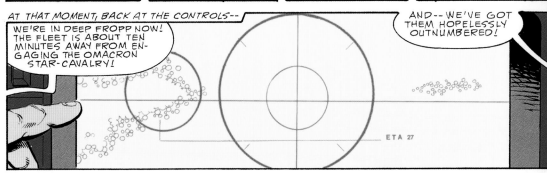

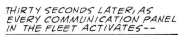

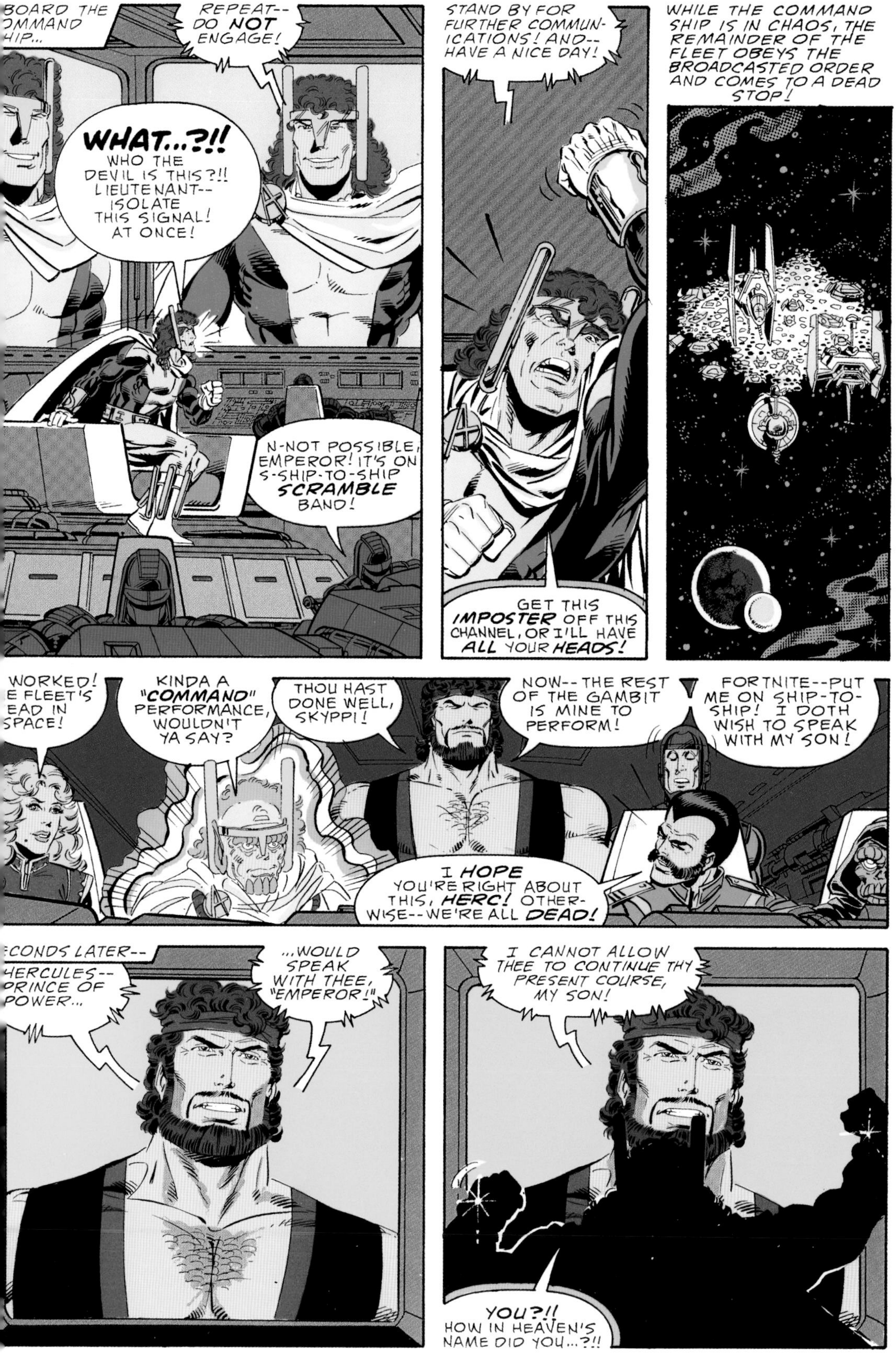
BOARD THE
OMMAND
HIP...
REPEAT--
DO NOT
ENGAGE!
WHAT...?!! WHO THE DEVIL IS THIS?!! LIEUTENANT-- ISOLATE THIS SIGNAL! AT ONCE!
N-NOT POSSIBLE, EMPEROR! IT'S ON S-SHIP-TO-SHIP SCRAMBLE BAND!
STAND BY FOR FURTHER COMMUNICATIONS! AND-- HAVE A NICE DAY!
GET THIS IMPOSTER OFF THIS CHANNEL, OR I'LL HAVE ALL YOUR HEADS!
WHILE THE COMMAND SHIP IS IN CHAOS, THE REMAINDER OF THE FLEET OBEYS THE BROADCASTED ORDER AND COMES TO A DEAD STOP!
WORKED! E FLEET'S EAD IN SPACE!
KINDA A "COMMAND" PERFORMANCE, WOULDN'T YA SAY?
THOU HAST DONE WELL, SKYPPI!
NOW-- THE REST OF THE GAMBIT IS MINE TO PERFORM!
FORTNITE--PUT ME ON SHIP-TO-SHIP! I DOTH WISH TO SPEAK WITH MY SON!
I HOPE YOU'RE RIGHT ABOUT THIS, HERC! OTHERWISE-- WE'RE ALL DEAD!
ECONDS LATER--
HERCULES-- PRINCE OF POWER...
...WOULD SPEAK WITH THEE, "EMPEROR!"
I CANNOT ALLOW THEE TO CONTINUE THY PRESENT COURSE, MY SON!
YOU?!! HOW IN HEAVEN'S NAME DID YOU...?!!

I DON'T KNOW HOW YOU ESCAPED, BUT I'LL FIND YOU--

--IF I HAVE TO DESTROY EVERY SHIP IN THE FLEET!

THAT WOULD SEEM A COWARDLY ACT FOR ONE WHO FANCIES HIMSELF--A KING!

IF THOU HAST A SCORE TO SETTLE WITH ME-- YOU SHAN'T ACCOMPLISH THAT BY SLAYING INNOCENTS!

SHOW YOUR-SELF, FEEBLE OLD MAN, AND I'LL MAKE YOUR ENDING SWIFT!

AYE--AND WITH THAT, THE TRUTH OF THINGS WILL DIE AS SWIFTLY!

WHAT'S GOIN' ON HERE?

BEATS THE FROPP OUTTA ME!

WHAT WOULD YO KNOW OF TRUTH "FATHER?!" YOU A THE MASTER OF DECEPTION!

IT'S TIME FOR THE CLINCHER HERC! LET 'IM HAVE IT!

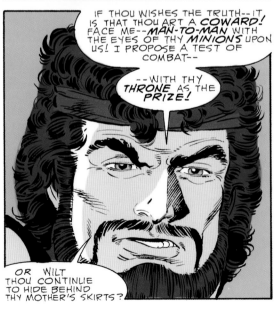

IF THOU WISHES THE TRUTH--IT IS THAT THOU ART A COWARD! FACE ME--MAN-TO-MAN WITH THE EYES OF THY MINIONS UPON US! I PROPOSE A TEST OF COMBAT--

--WITH THY THRONE AS THE PRIZE!

OR WILT THOU CONTINUE TO HIDE BEHIND THY MOTHER'S SKIRTS?

YOU DARE CALL ME A COWARD!! BLAST YOU!! I ACCEPT YOUR CHALLENGE!

MEET ME ON THE LARGEST PLANETOID THAT LIES AHEAD-- IN ONE HOUR! AND BEFORE THE EYES OF MY SUBJECTS--

--I'LL GRIND YOUR BONES INTO POWDER!

EMPEROR-- A SHIP IS BREAKING FORMATION!

70

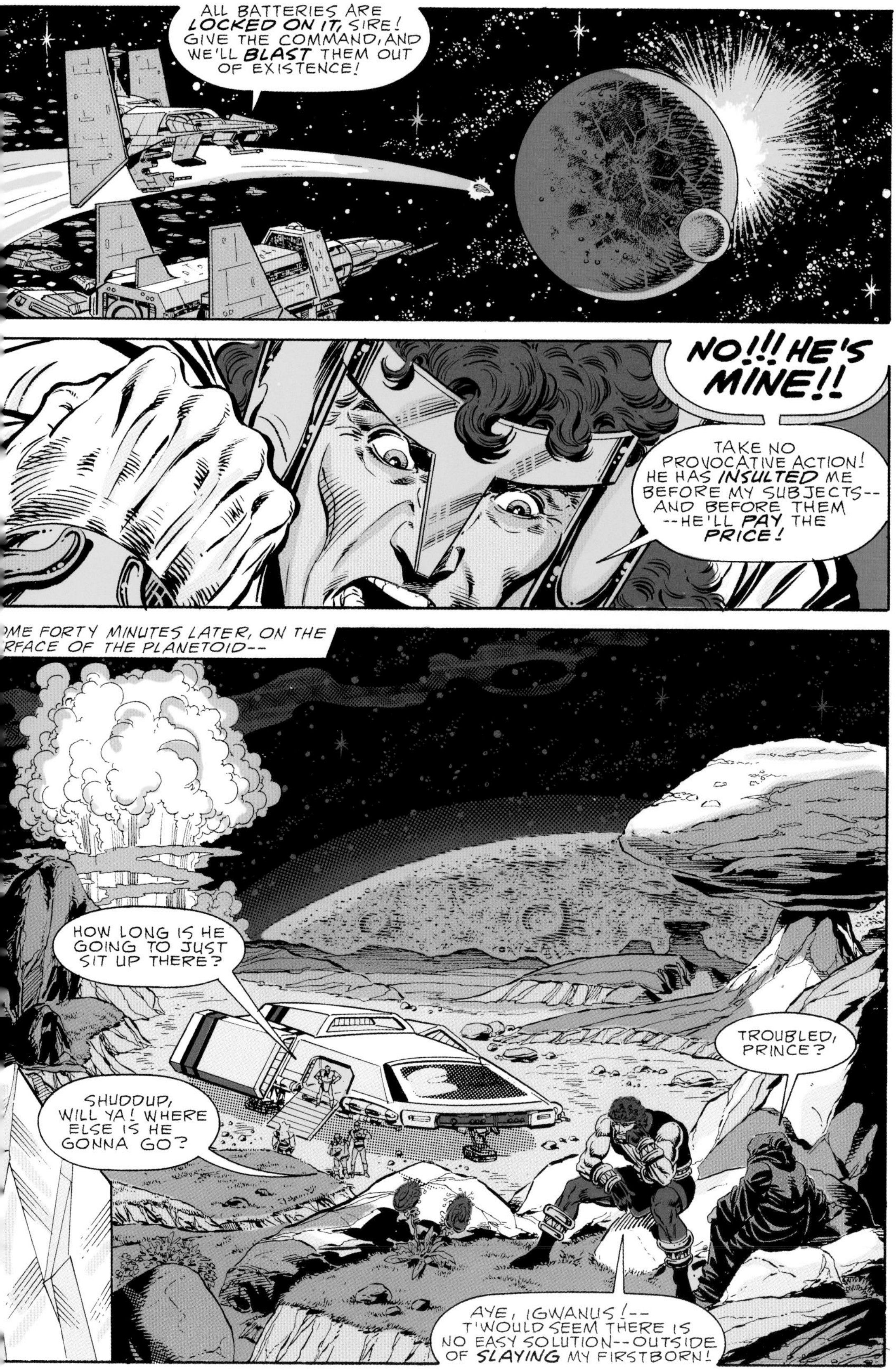
ALL BATTERIES ARE LOCKED ON IT, SIRE! GIVE THE COMMAND, AND WE'LL BLAST THEM OUT OF EXISTENCE!
NO!!! HE'S MINE!!
TAKE NO PROVOCATIVE ACTION! HE HAS INSULTED ME BEFORE MY SUBJECTS-- AND BEFORE THEM --HE'LL PAY THE PRICE!
ME FORTY MINUTES LATER, ON THE RFACE OF THE PLANETOID--
HOW LONG IS HE GOING TO JUST SIT UP THERE?
SHUDDUP, WILL YA! WHERE ELSE IS HE GONNA GO?
TROUBLED, PRINCE?
AYE, IGWANUS!-- T'WOULD SEEM THERE IS NO EASY SOLUTION--OUTSIDE OF SLAYING MY FIRSTBORN!

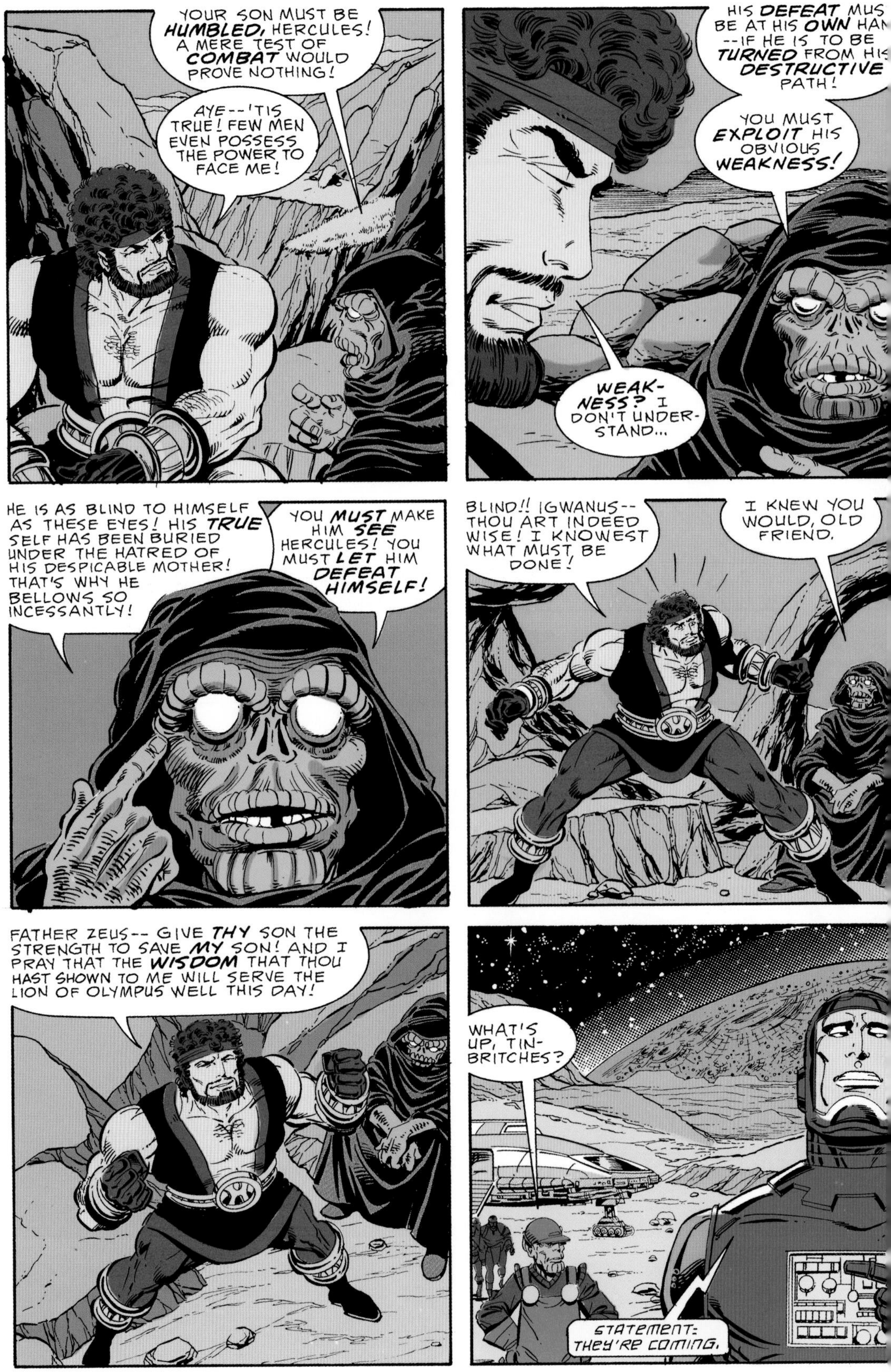
YOUR SON MUST BE HUMBLED, HERCULES! A MERE TEST OF COMBAT WOULD PROVE NOTHING!
AYE--'TIS TRUE! FEW MEN EVEN POSSESS THE POWER TO FACE ME!
HIS DEFEAT MUS BE AT HIS OWN HAN --IF HE IS TO BE TURNED FROM HIS DESTRUCTIVE PATH!
YOU MUST EXPLOIT HIS OBVIOUS WEAKNESS!
WEAK-NESS? I DON'T UNDER-STAND...
HE IS AS BLIND TO HIMSELF AS THESE EYES! HIS TRUE SELF HAS BEEN BURIED UNDER THE HATRED OF HIS DESPICABLE MOTHER! THAT'S WHY HE BELLOWS SO INCESSANTLY!
YOU MUST MAKE HIM SEE HERCULES! YOU MUST LET HIM DEFEAT HIMSELF!
BLIND!! IGWANUS-- THOU ART INDEED WISE! I KNOWEST WHAT MUST BE DONE!
I KNEW YOU WOULD, OLD FRIEND.
FATHER ZEUS-- GIVE THY SON THE STRENGTH TO SAVE MY SON! AND I PRAY THAT THE WISDOM THAT THOU HAST SHOWN TO ME WILL SERVE THE LION OF OLYMPUS WELL THIS DAY!
WHAT'S UP, TIN-BRITCHES?
STATEMENT: THEY'RE COMING.

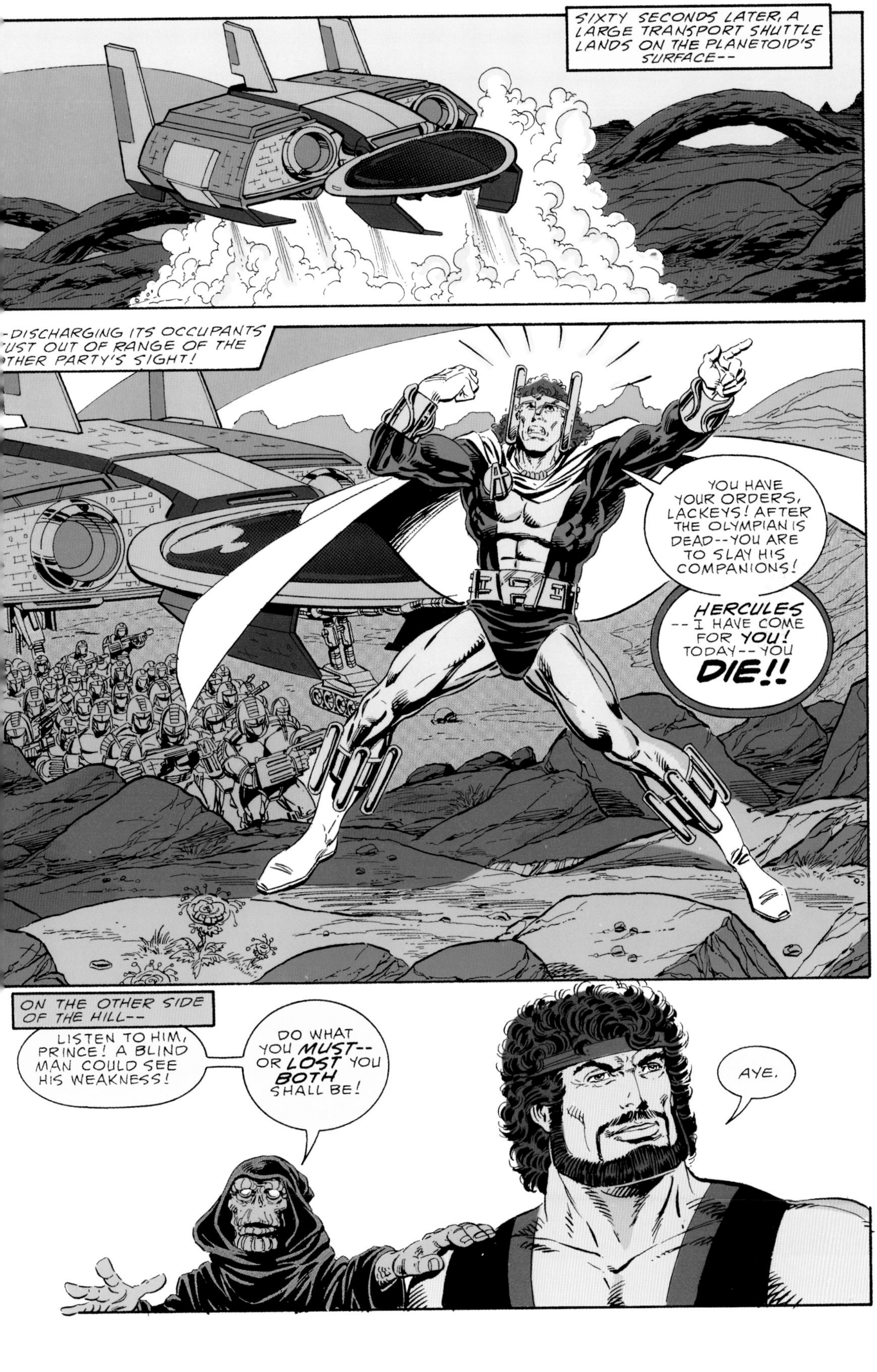
SIXTY SECONDS LATER, A LARGE TRANSPORT SHUTTLE LANDS ON THE PLANETOID'S SURFACE--
--DISCHARGING ITS OCCUPANTS JUST OUT OF RANGE OF THE OTHER PARTY'S SIGHT!
YOU HAVE YOUR ORDERS, LACKEYS! AFTER THE OLYMPIAN IS DEAD--YOU ARE TO SLAY HIS COMPANIONS!
HERCULES --I HAVE COME FOR YOU! TODAY--YOU DIE!!
ON THE OTHER SIDE OF THE HILL--
LISTEN TO HIM, PRINCE! A BLIND MAN COULD SEE HIS WEAKNESS!
DO WHAT YOU MUST-- OR LOST YOU BOTH SHALL BE!
AYE.

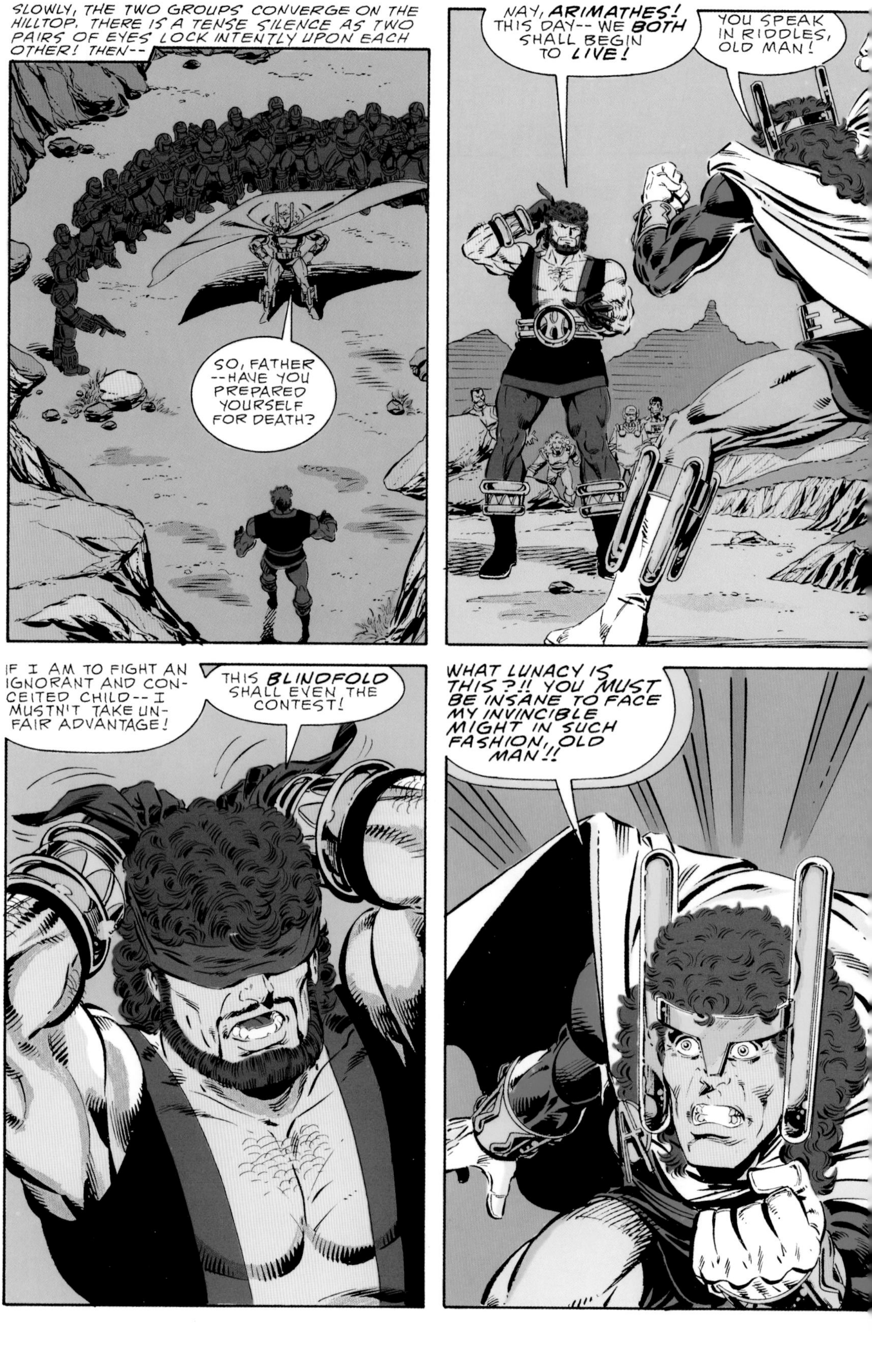

SLOWLY, THE TWO GROUPS CONVERGE ON THE HILLTOP. THERE IS A TENSE SILENCE AS TWO PAIRS OF EYES LOCK INTENTLY UPON EACH OTHER! THEN--
SO, FATHER --HAVE YOU PREPARED YOURSELF FOR DEATH?
NAY, ARIMATHES! THIS DAY-- WE BOTH SHALL BEGIN TO LIVE!
YOU SPEAK IN RIDDLES, OLD MAN!
IF I AM TO FIGHT AN IGNORANT AND CONCEITED CHILD-- I MUSTN'T TAKE UNFAIR ADVANTAGE!
THIS BLINDFOLD SHALL EVEN THE CONTEST!
WHAT LUNACY IS THIS?!! YOU MUST BE INSANE TO FACE MY INVINCIBLE MIGHT IN SUCH FASHION, OLD MAN!!

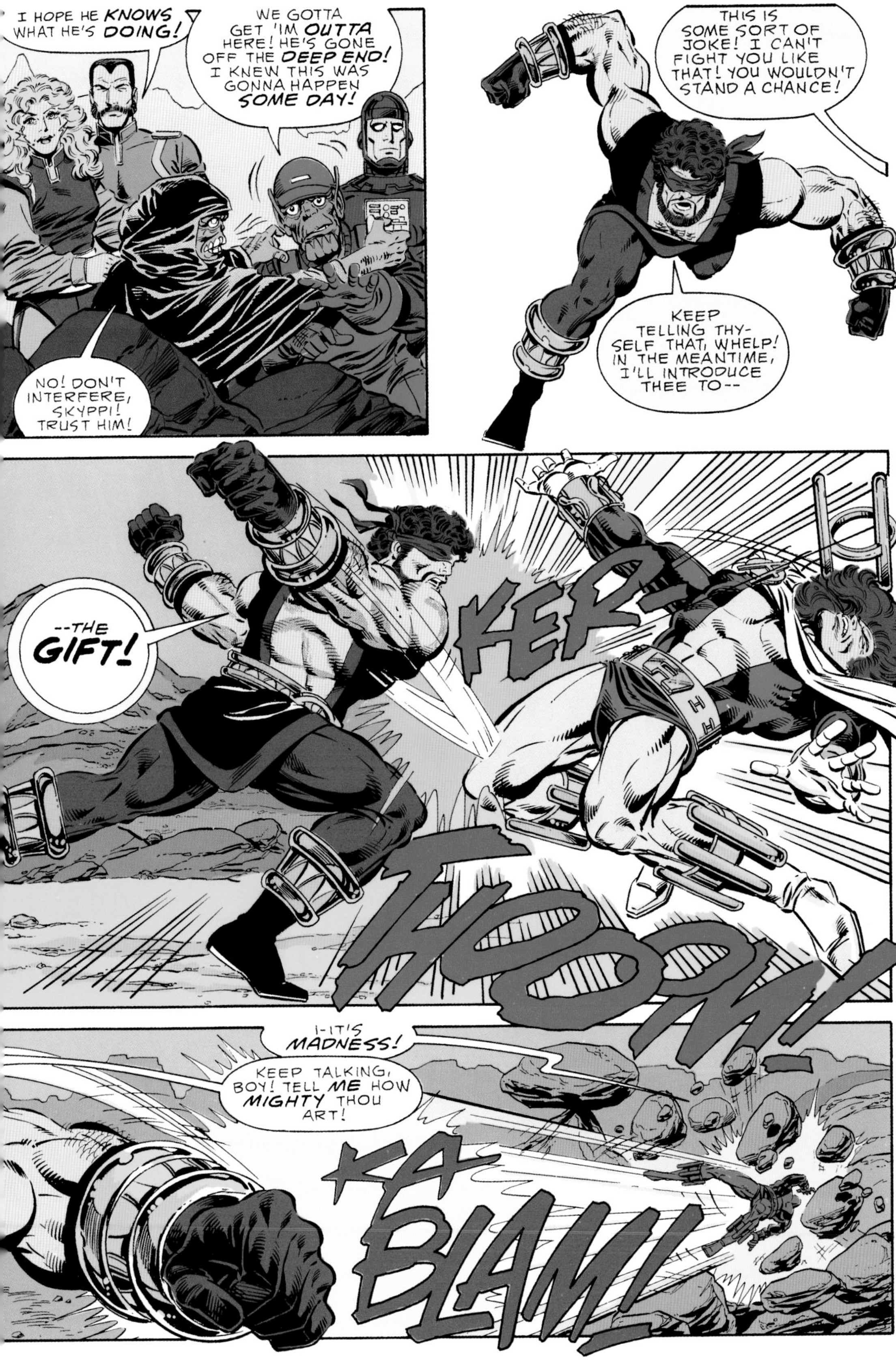
I HOPE HE KNOWS WHAT HE'S DOING!
WE GOTTA GET 'IM OUTTA HERE! HE'S GONE OFF THE DEEP END! I KNEW THIS WAS GONNA HAPPEN SOME DAY!
NO! DON'T INTERFERE, SKYPPI! TRUST HIM!
THIS IS SOME SORT OF JOKE! I CAN'T FIGHT YOU LIKE THAT! YOU WOULDN'T STAND A CHANCE!
KEEP TELLING THY-SELF THAT, WHELP! IN THE MEANTIME, I'LL INTRODUCE THEE TO--
--THE GIFT!
KER-THOOM!
I-IT'S MADNESS!
KEEP TALKING, BOY! TELL ME HOW MIGHTY THOU ART!
KA BLAM!

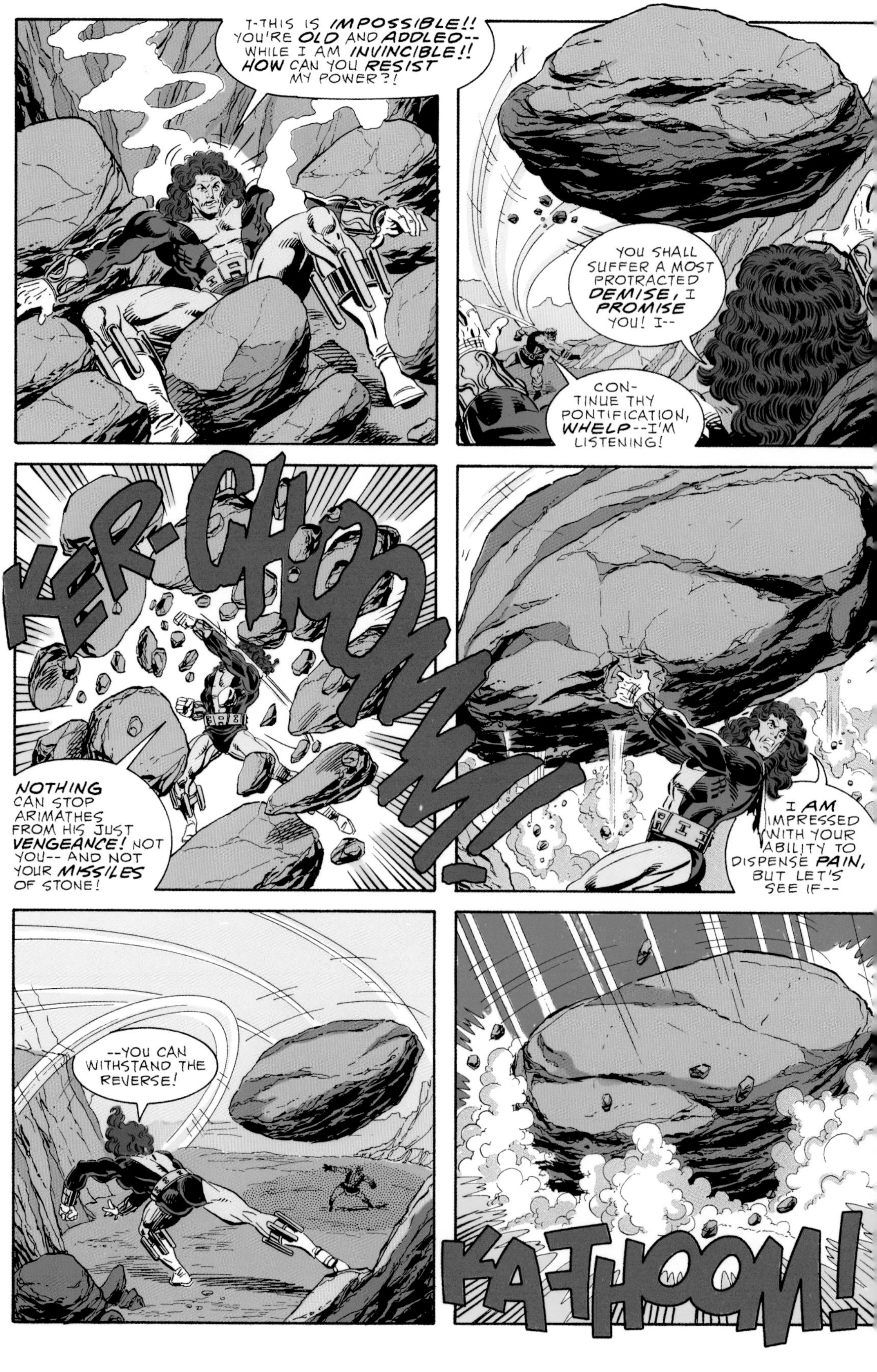
T-THIS IS IMPOSSIBLE!! YOU'RE OLD AND ADDLED-- WHILE I AM INVINCIBLE!! HOW CAN YOU RESIST MY POWER?!
YOU SHALL SUFFER A MOST PROTRACTED DEMISE, I PROMISE YOU! I--
CON-TINUE THY PONTIFICATION, WHELP--I'M LISTENING!
KER-CHOOMM!
NOTHING CAN STOP ARIMATHES FROM HIS JUST VENGEANCE! NOT YOU-- AND NOT YOUR MISSILES OF STONE!
I AM IMPRESSED WITH YOUR ABILITY TO DISPENSE PAIN, BUT LET'S SEE IF--
--YOU CAN WITHSTAND THE REVERSE!
KA-THOOM!

AFTER THE DUST OF THE IMPACT SETTLES--

...T ALL PAY HEED-- JUST AS THE LIFE OF MY ACCURSED FATHER HAS BEEN SNUFFED OUT--

RUMBLE RUMBLE!

--SO WILL BE THAT OF ANYONE WHO DARES PIT HIMSELF AGAINST THE UNCONQUERABLE MIGHT OF ARIMATHES!

BLE RUM BLE!

B-BY MY CROWN...!

KOKA-CHOOMM!

CON-CEITED BOY--!

THROUGH ALL THE AGES I HAVE LIVED-- NEVER HAVE I MET ONE SO PITIFUL AS THEE! THOU USES THY MIGHT TO SUBJUGATE THE WEAK!

NEVER HAST THOU FACED A FOE OF EQUAL MIGHT-- UNTIL THIS DAY!

I-I'M THROUGH TOYING WITH YOU, OLD MAN!

NOW YOU SHALL LEARN WHY I AM EMPEROR!

KER- BLAM!

THE SON OF HERCULES STRIKES WITH A BLOW THAT WOULD REND A MOUNTAIN ASUNDER!

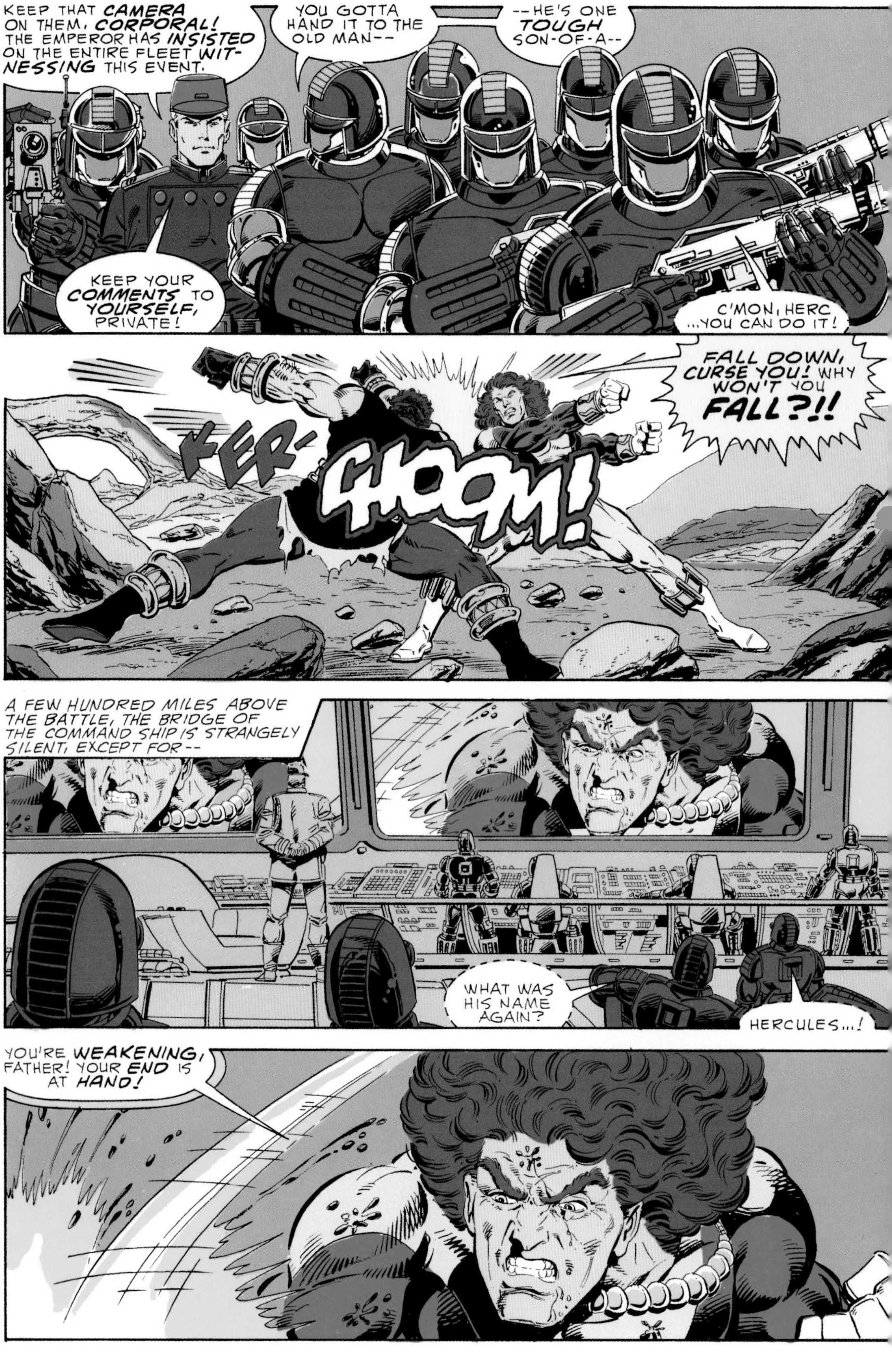

KEEP THAT CAMERA ON THEM, CORPORAL! THE EMPEROR HAS INSISTED ON THE ENTIRE FLEET WITNESSING THIS EVENT.
YOU GOTTA HAND IT TO THE OLD MAN--
--HE'S ONE TOUGH SON-OF-A--
KEEP YOUR COMMENTS TO YOURSELF, PRIVATE!
C'MON, HERC ...YOU CAN DO IT!
FALL DOWN, CURSE YOU! WHY WON'T YOU FALL?!!
KER-CHOOM!
A FEW HUNDRED MILES ABOVE THE BATTLE, THE BRIDGE OF THE COMMAND SHIP IS STRANGELY SILENT, EXCEPT FOR--
WHAT WAS HIS NAME AGAIN?
HERCULES...!
YOU'RE WEAKENING, FATHER! YOUR END IS AT HAND!

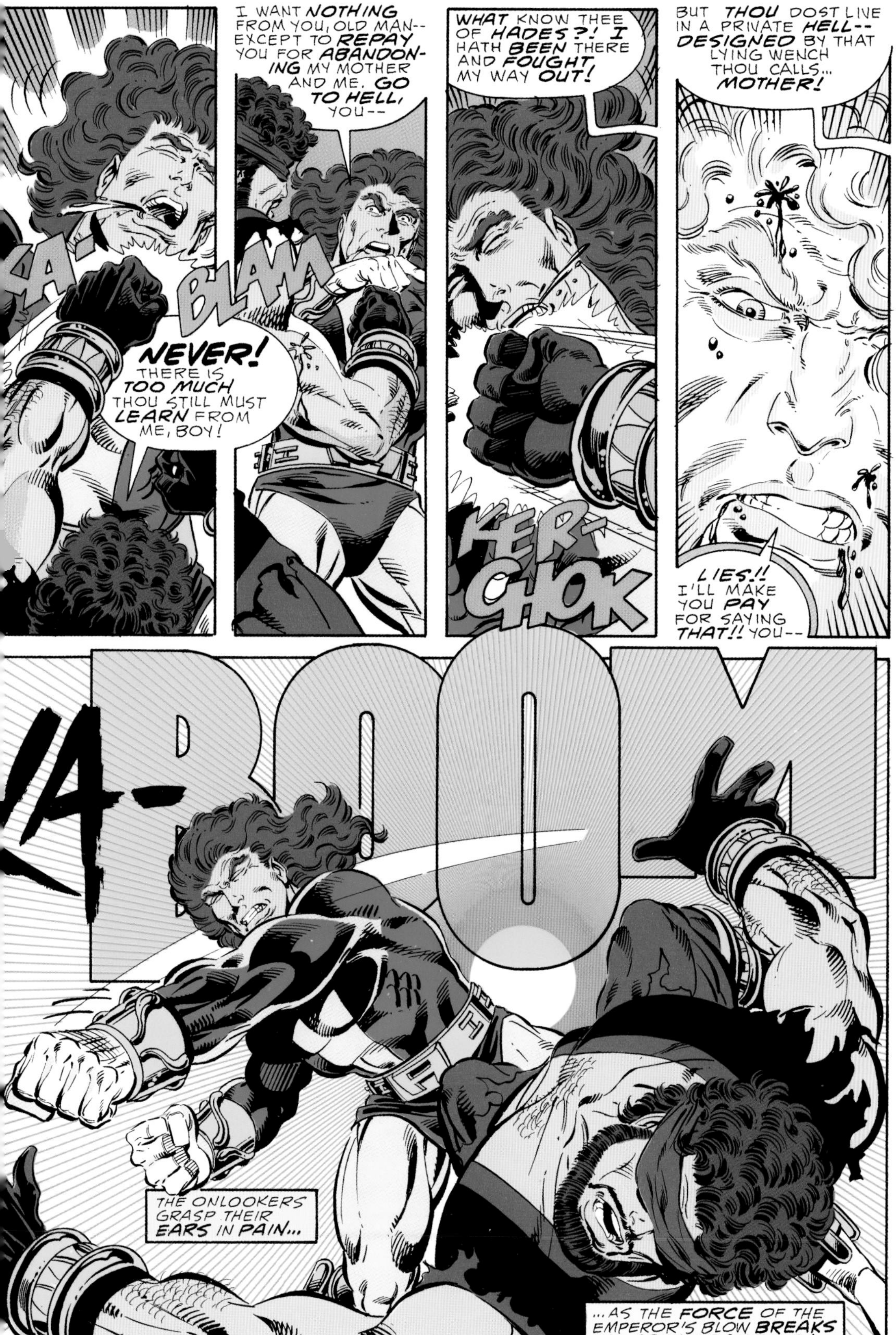
I WANT NOTHING FROM YOU, OLD MAN-- EXCEPT TO REPAY YOU FOR ABANDONING MY MOTHER AND ME. GO TO HELL, YOU--
BLAM
NEVER! THERE IS TOO MUCH THOU STILL MUST LEARN FROM ME, BOY!
WHAT KNOW THEE OF HADES?! I HATH BEEN THERE AND FOUGHT MY WAY OUT!
KER-CHOK
BUT THOU DOST LIVE IN A PRIVATE HELL-- DESIGNED BY THAT LYING WENCH THOU CALLS... MOTHER!
LIES!! I'LL MAKE YOU PAY FOR SAYING THAT!! YOU--
BOOM
THE ONLOOKERS GRASP THEIR EARS IN PAIN...
...AS THE FORCE OF THE EMPEROR'S BLOW BREAKS THE SOUND BARRIER!

SHE *LOVED* YOU! SHE LOVED YOU! --AND *YOU* SOLD HER TO THE *GEGKU!*

YOU *COULDN'T* BE *BURDENED* BY A *WOMAN* AND BASTARD *CHILD* --COULD YOU?!

KER-*CHOOOMMM!*

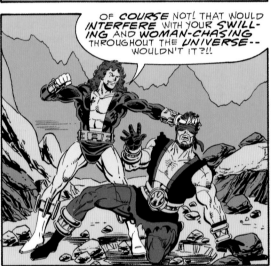

OF *COURSE* NOT! THAT WOULD *INTERFERE* WITH YOUR *SWILL-ING* AND *WOMAN-CHASING* THROUGHOUT THE *UNIVERSE*-- WOULDN'T IT?!!

SHE TOLD ME, OLD MAN! AND NOW--

--YOU'LL *PAY* FOR YOUR *TRANS-GRES-SIONS!*

KA-*BLAM!*

IT'S *OVER*-- AND *I* HAVE *WON!*

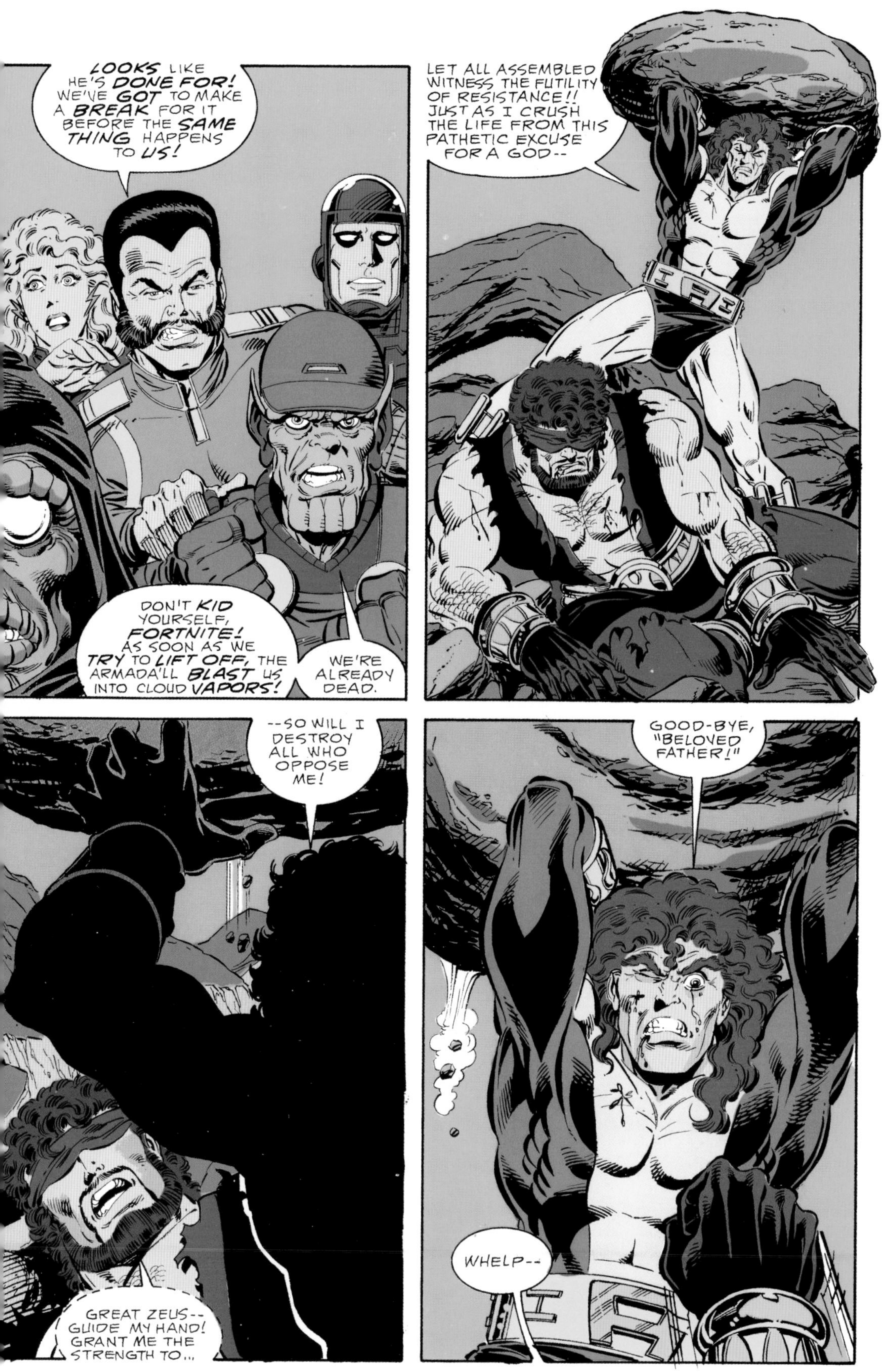
LOOKS LIKE HE'S DONE FOR! WE'VE GOT TO MAKE A BREAK FOR IT BEFORE THE SAME THING HAPPENS TO US!
DON'T KID YOURSELF, FORTNITE! AS SOON AS WE TRY TO LIFT OFF, THE ARMADA'LL BLAST US INTO CLOUD VAPORS!
WE'RE ALREADY DEAD.
LET ALL ASSEMBLED WITNESS THE FUTILITY OF RESISTANCE!! JUST AS I CRUSH THE LIFE FROM THIS PATHETIC EXCUSE FOR A GOD--
--SO WILL I DESTROY ALL WHO OPPOSE ME!
GREAT ZEUS-- GUIDE MY HAND! GRANT ME THE STRENGTH TO...
GOOD-BYE, "BELOVED FATHER!"
WHELP--

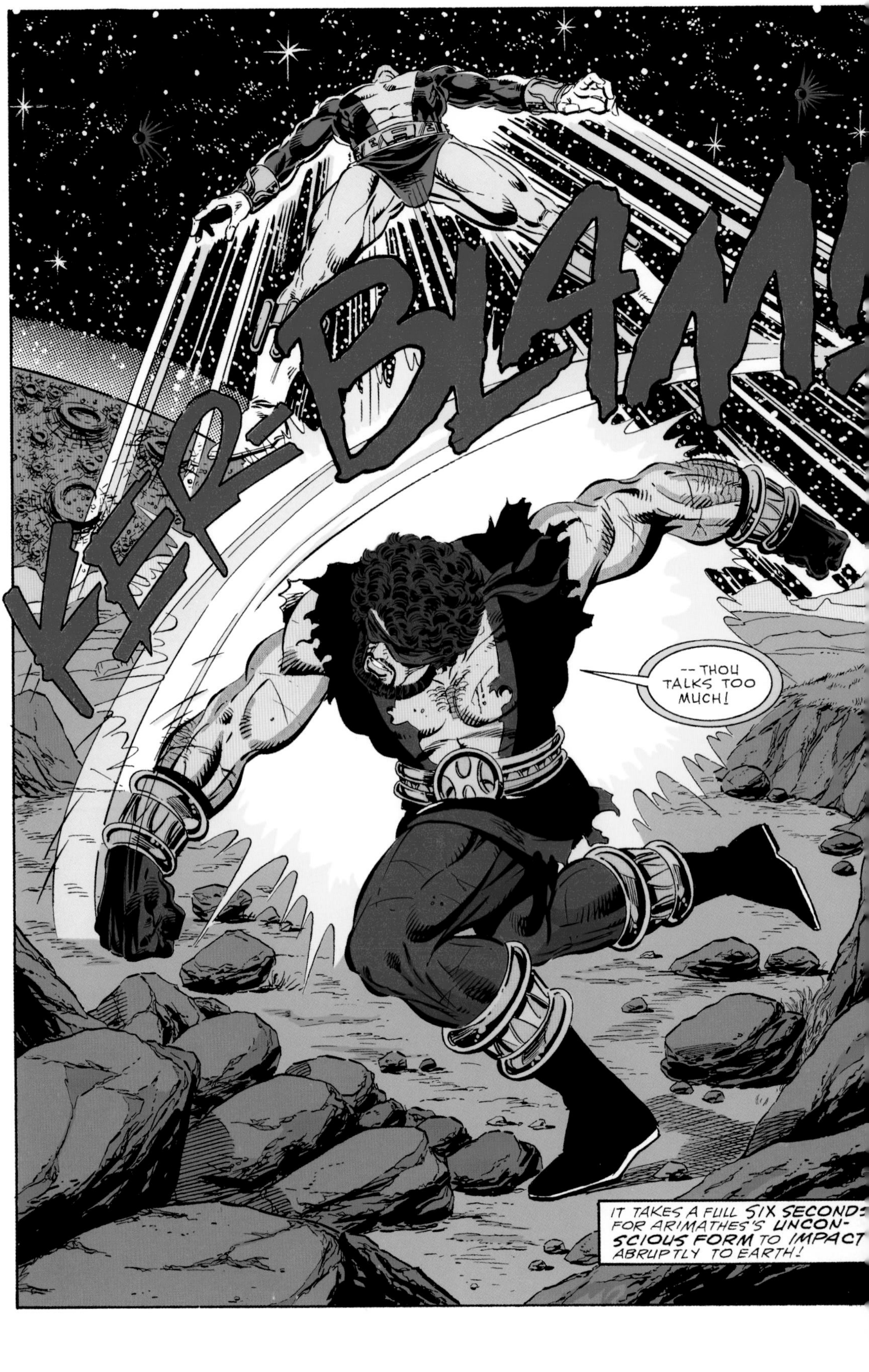
KER-BLAM!
--THOU TALKS TOO MUCH!
IT TAKES A FULL SIX SECONDS FOR ARIMATHES'S UNCONSCIOUS FORM TO IMPACT ABRUPTLY TO EARTH!

BLEEDING AND BATTERED, THE LION OF OLYMPUS FINDS HIS WAY TO THE INERT BODY OF HIS ONLY SON! HE IS OBLIVIOUS TO THE SOUND OF PRIMATHES'S SOLDIERS CHANTING HIS NAME!

--BY THE GODS!--

--'TIS A BITTER VICTORY, INDEED.

NO MATTER--THE BOY IS RETURNING TO CONSCIOUSNESS! I MUST ACT OUT THE FINAL SCENE OF THIS TRAGIC PLAY!

TO ALL ASSEMBLED --THE TRIAL BY COMBAT IS OVER. THE SPOILS OF VICTORY BE MINE! DOTH ANYONE CONTEST THIS JUDGEMENT?

ALL HAIL-- HERCULES!! HAIL! HAIL-- EMPEROR!!

NAY!!

SILENCE!

THIS BATTLE WAS NOT FOUGHT FOR POSSESSION OF SOME MEANINGLESS THRONE! NAY-- THE STAKES WERE MUCH HIGHER, INDEED!

ARISE, MY SON! MAYHAP NOW, THOU MIGHT HEAR THY FATHER OUT! THOU HAST LOST ALL THIS DAY, BUT-- THOU MAY YET GAIN A HUNDRED-FOLD BEFORE ITS END!

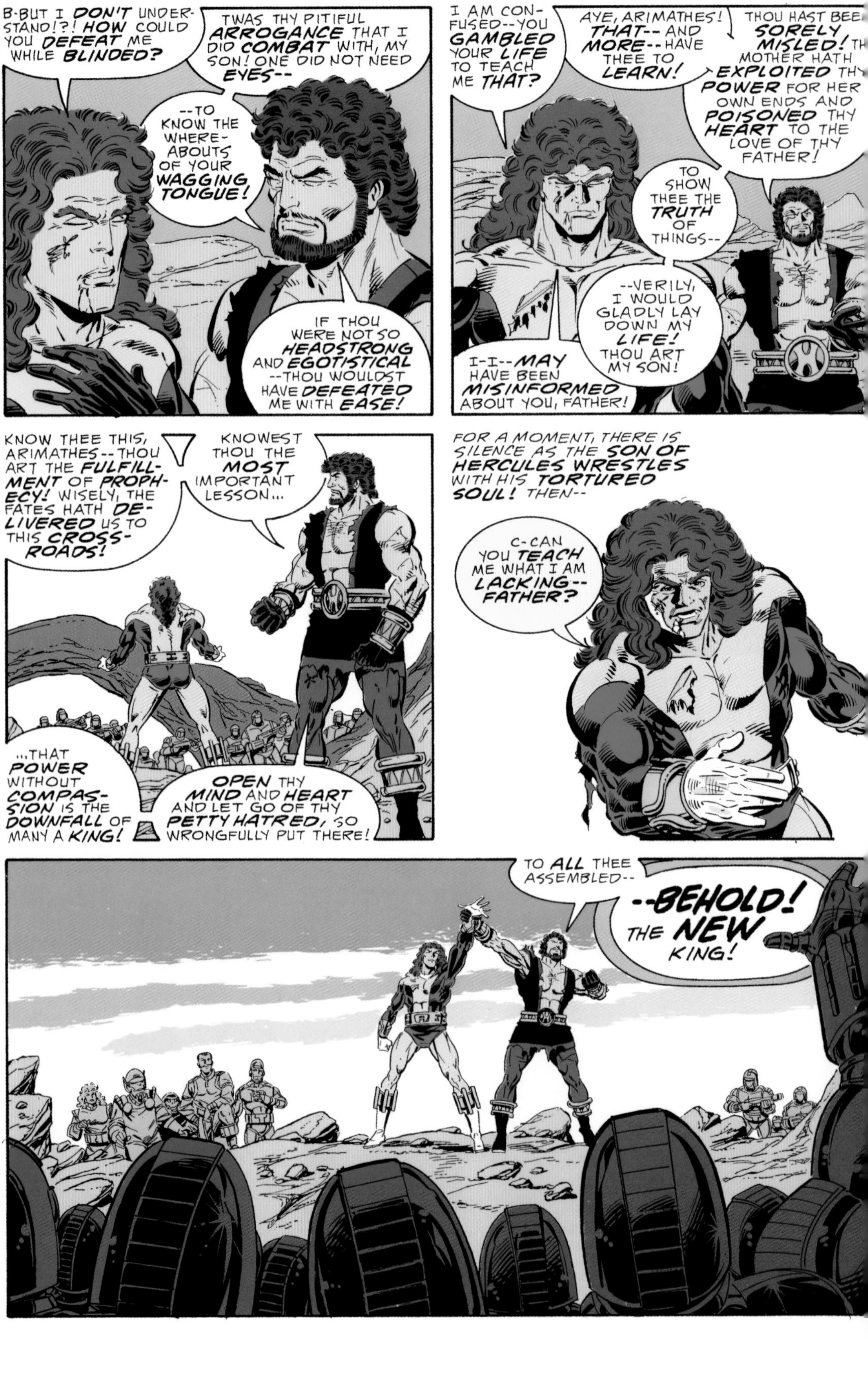
B-BUT I DON'T UNDERSTAND!?! HOW COULD YOU DEFEAT ME WHILE BLINDED?
TWAS THY PITIFUL ARROGANCE THAT I DID COMBAT WITH, MY SON! ONE DID NOT NEED EYES--
--TO KNOW THE WHEREABOUTS OF YOUR WAGGING TONGUE!
IF THOU WERE NOT SO HEADSTRONG AND EGOTISTICAL --THOU WOULDST HAVE DEFEATED ME WITH EASE!
I AM CONFUSED--YOU GAMBLED YOUR LIFE TO TEACH ME THAT?
AYE, ARIMATHES! THAT-- AND MORE-- HAVE THEE TO LEARN!
THOU HAST BEEN SORELY MISLED! TH MOTHER HATH EXPLOITED THY POWER FOR HER OWN ENDS AND POISONED THY HEART TO THE LOVE OF THY FATHER!
TO SHOW THEE THE TRUTH OF THINGS--
--VERILY, I WOULD GLADLY LAY DOWN MY LIFE! THOU ART MY SON!
I-I--MAY HAVE BEEN MISINFORMED ABOUT YOU, FATHER!
KNOW THEE THIS, ARIMATHES--THOU ART THE FULFILLMENT OF PROPHECY! WISELY, THE FATES HATH DELIVERED US TO THIS CROSSROADS!
KNOWEST THOU THE MOST IMPORTANT LESSON...
...THAT POWER WITHOUT COMPASSION IS THE DOWNFALL OF MANY A KING!
OPEN THY MIND AND HEART AND LET GO OF THY PETTY HATRED, SO WRONGFULLY PUT THERE!
FOR A MOMENT, THERE IS SILENCE AS THE SON OF HERCULES WRESTLES WITH HIS TORTURED SOUL! THEN--
C-CAN YOU TEACH ME WHAT I AM LACKING-- FATHER?
TO ALL THEE ASSEMBLED--
--BEHOLD! THE NEW KING!

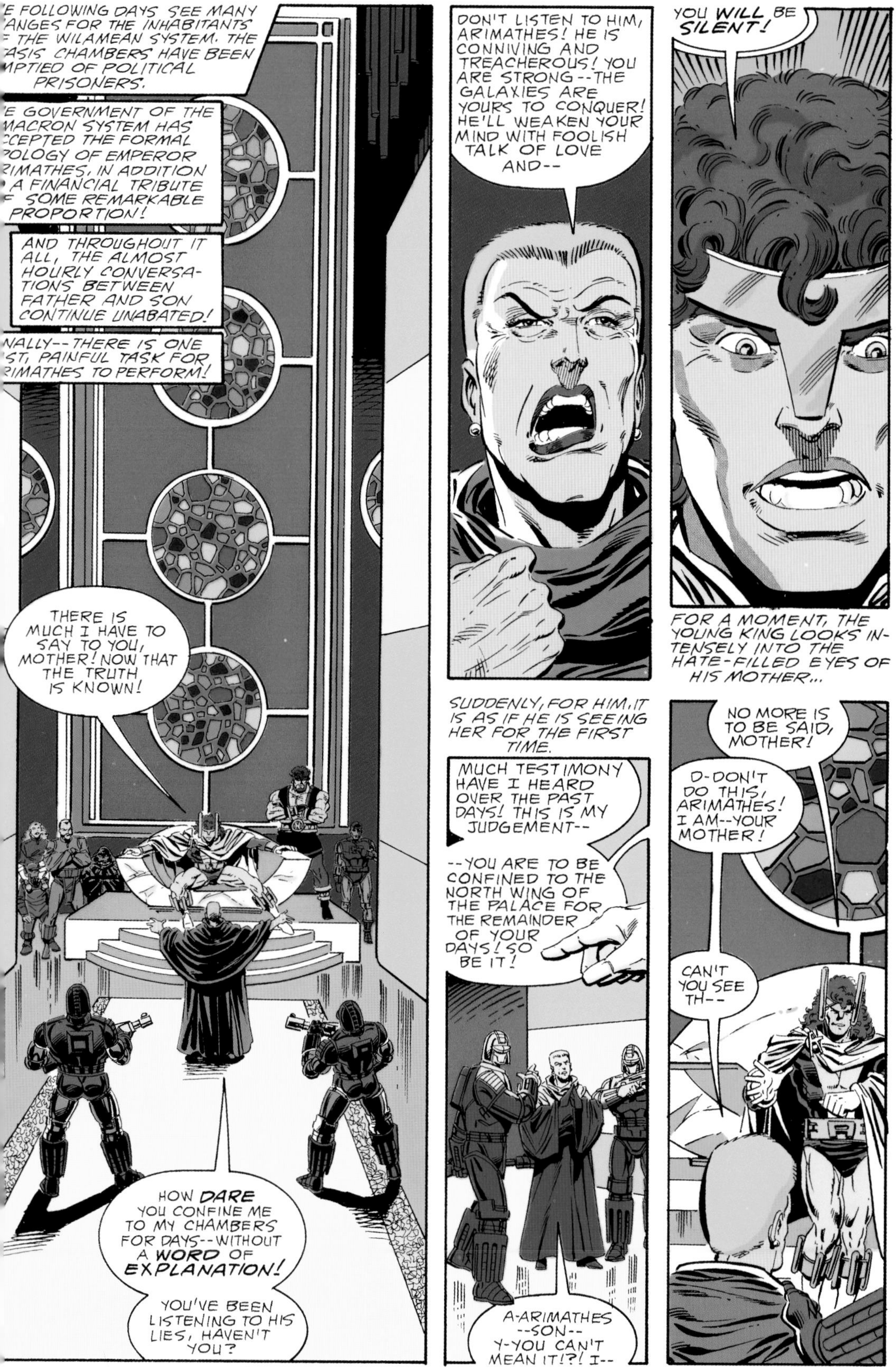
E FOLLOWING DAYS SEE MANY ANGES FOR THE INHABITANTS F THE WILAMEAN SYSTEM. THE ASIS CHAMBERS HAVE BEEN MPTIED OF POLITICAL PRISONERS.
E GOVERNMENT OF THE MACRON SYSTEM HAS CCEPTED THE FORMAL POLOGY OF EMPEROR RIMATHES, IN ADDITION A FINANCIAL TRIBUTE F SOME REMARKABLE PROPORTION!
AND THROUGHOUT IT ALL, THE ALMOST HOURLY CONVERSATIONS BETWEEN FATHER AND SON CONTINUE UNABATED!
NALLY--THERE IS ONE ST, PAINFUL TASK FOR RIMATHES TO PERFORM!
THERE IS MUCH I HAVE TO SAY TO YOU, MOTHER! NOW THAT THE TRUTH IS KNOWN!
HOW DARE YOU CONFINE ME TO MY CHAMBERS FOR DAYS--WITHOUT A WORD OF EXPLANATION!
YOU'VE BEEN LISTENING TO HIS LIES, HAVEN'T YOU?
DON'T LISTEN TO HIM, ARIMATHES! HE IS CONNIVING AND TREACHEROUS! YOU ARE STRONG--THE GALAXIES ARE YOURS TO CONQUER! HE'LL WEAKEN YOUR MIND WITH FOOLISH TALK OF LOVE AND--
YOU WILL BE SILENT!
FOR A MOMENT, THE YOUNG KING LOOKS INTENSELY INTO THE HATE-FILLED EYES OF HIS MOTHER...
SUDDENLY, FOR HIM, IT IS AS IF HE IS SEEING HER FOR THE FIRST TIME.
MUCH TESTIMONY HAVE I HEARD OVER THE PAST DAYS! THIS IS MY JUDGEMENT--
--YOU ARE TO BE CONFINED TO THE NORTH WING OF THE PALACE FOR THE REMAINDER OF YOUR DAYS! SO BE IT!
A-ARIMATHES --SON-- Y-YOU CAN'T MEAN IT!?! I--
NO MORE IS TO BE SAID, MOTHER!
D-DON'T DO THIS, ARIMATHES! I AM--YOUR MOTHER!
CAN'T YOU SEE TH--

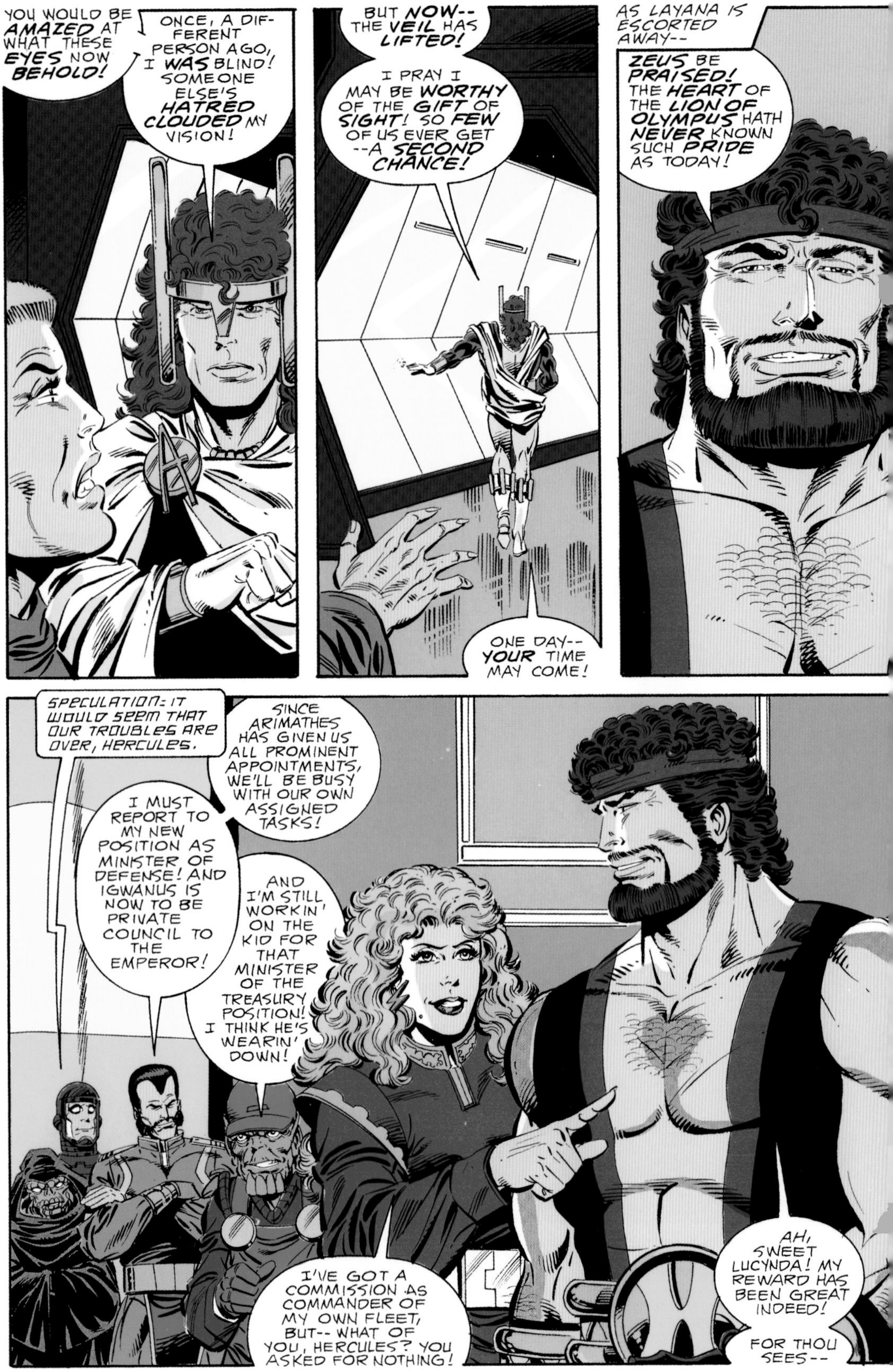
YOU WOULD BE AMAZED AT WHAT THESE EYES NOW BEHOLD!
ONCE, A DIF-FERENT PERSON AGO, I WAS BLIND! SOMEONE ELSE'S HATRED CLOUDED MY VISION!
BUT NOW-- THE VEIL HAS LIFTED!
I PRAY I MAY BE WORTHY OF THE GIFT OF SIGHT! SO FEW OF US EVER GET --A SECOND CHANCE!
ONE DAY-- YOUR TIME MAY COME!
AS LAYANA IS ESCORTED AWAY--
ZEUS BE PRAISED! THE HEART OF THE LION OF OLYMPUS HATH NEVER KNOWN SUCH PRIDE AS TODAY!
SPECULATION: IT WOULD SEEM THAT OUR TROUBLES ARE OVER, HERCULES.
SINCE ARIMATHES HAS GIVEN US ALL PROMINENT APPOINTMENTS, WE'LL BE BUSY WITH OUR OWN ASSIGNED TASKS!
I MUST REPORT TO MY NEW POSITION AS MINISTER OF DEFENSE! AND IGWANUS IS NOW TO BE PRIVATE COUNCIL TO THE EMPEROR!
AND I'M STILL WORKIN' ON THE KID FOR THAT MINISTER OF THE TREASURY POSITION! I THINK HE'S WEARIN' DOWN!
I'VE GOT A COMMISSION AS COMMANDER OF MY OWN FLEET, BUT-- WHAT OF YOU, HERCULES? YOU ASKED FOR NOTHING!
AH, SWEET LUCYNDA! MY REWARD HAS BEEN GREAT INDEED!
FOR THOU SEES--

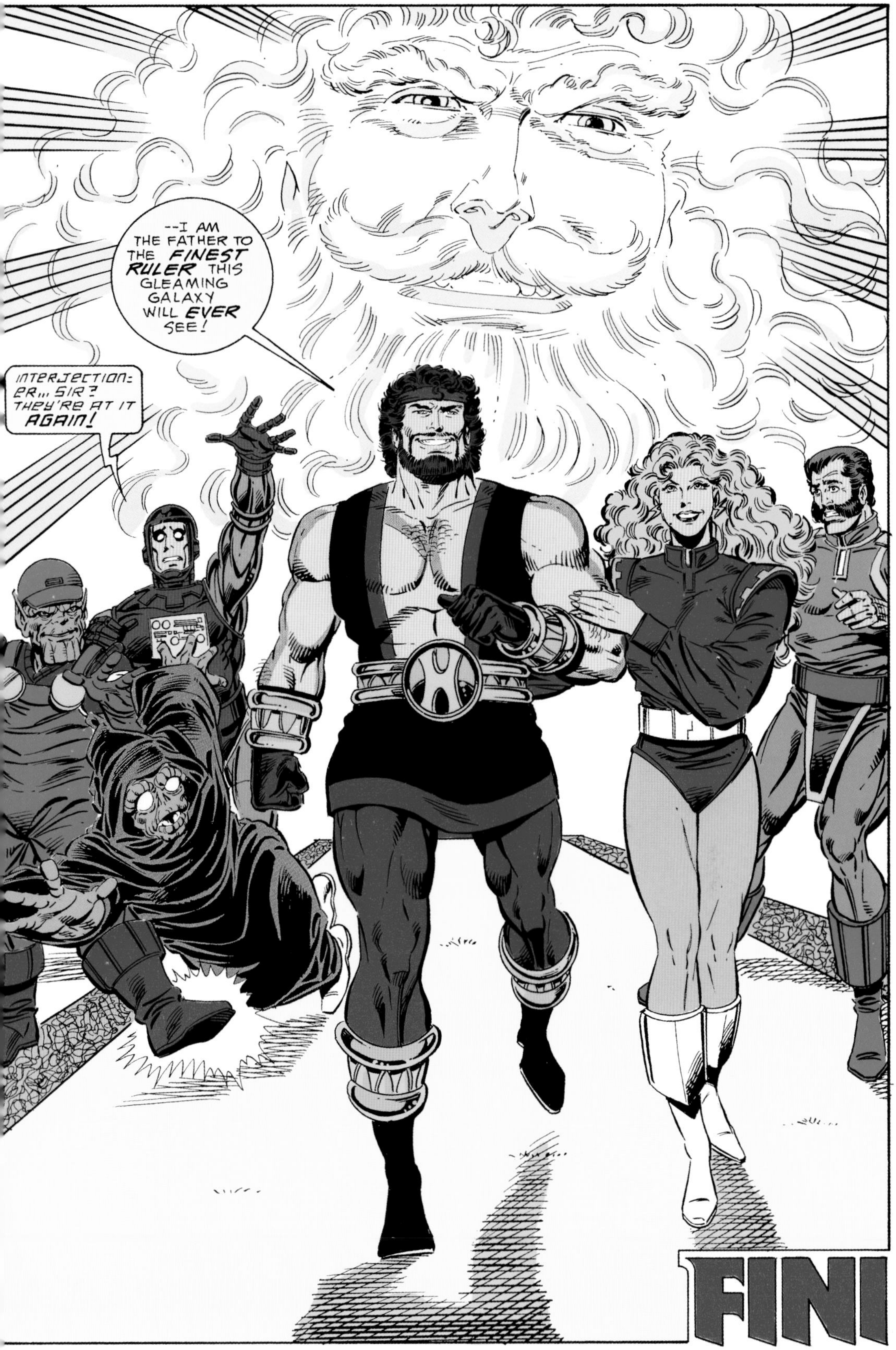
--I AM THE FATHER TO THE FINEST RULER THIS GLEAMING GALAXY WILL EVER SEE!
INTERJECTION: ER... SIR? THEY'RE AT IT AGAIN!
FINI

AFTERWORD

And so ends the future saga of the Prince of Power...for now. I would like to thank the following people for their support:

To Jim Shooter and David Michelinie, who believed when others scoffed.

To my artist's assistant, Donald Hudson, who is proving that the third time really is a charm.

To Jackson Guice, for the inflatable Galactus doll.

And to my wife Phyllis...to whom I, and all of you, who have enjoyed my work, owe a large debt of gratitude.

BOB LAYTON
3-28-88

US $6.95
Can. $9.25

[redacted]

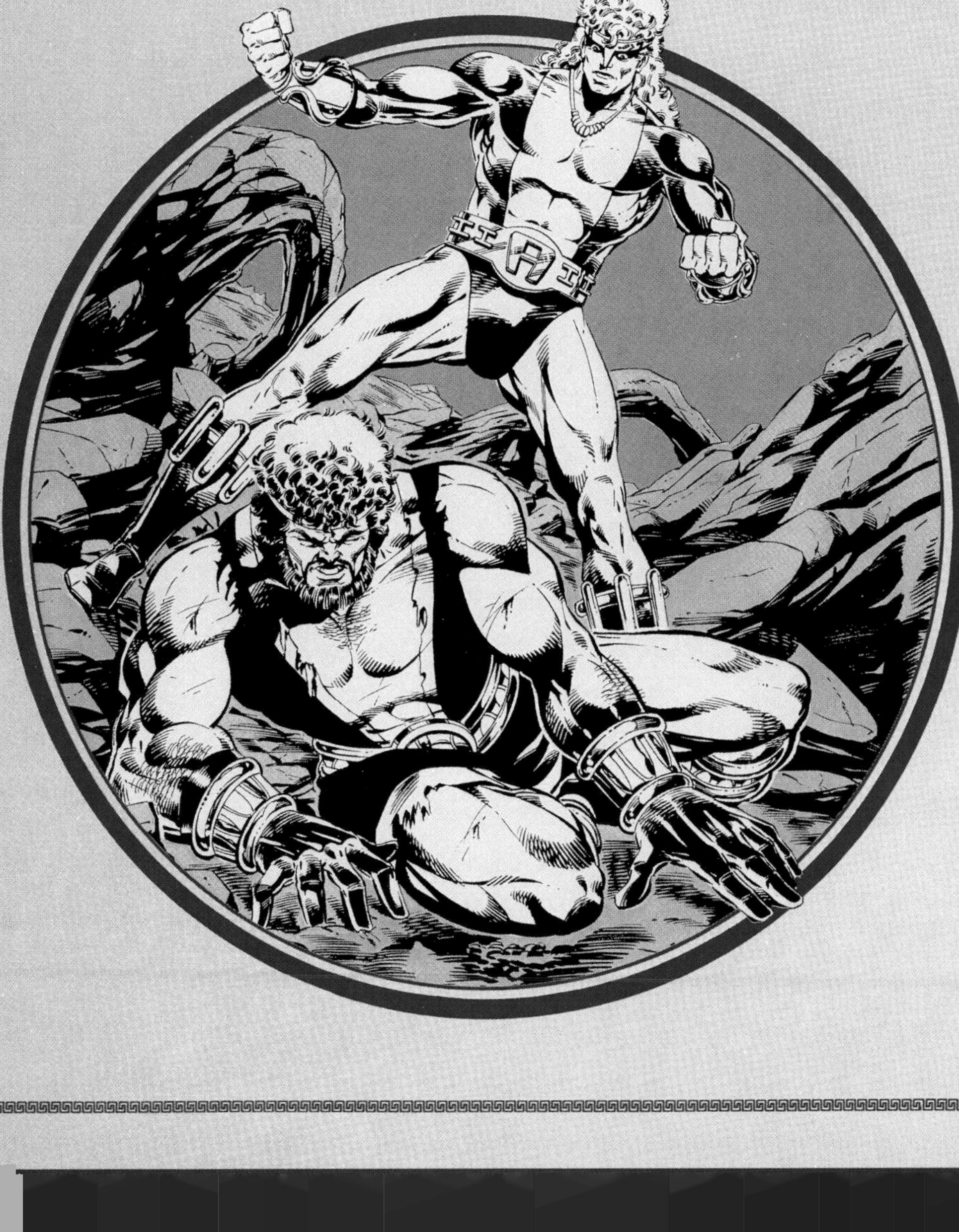

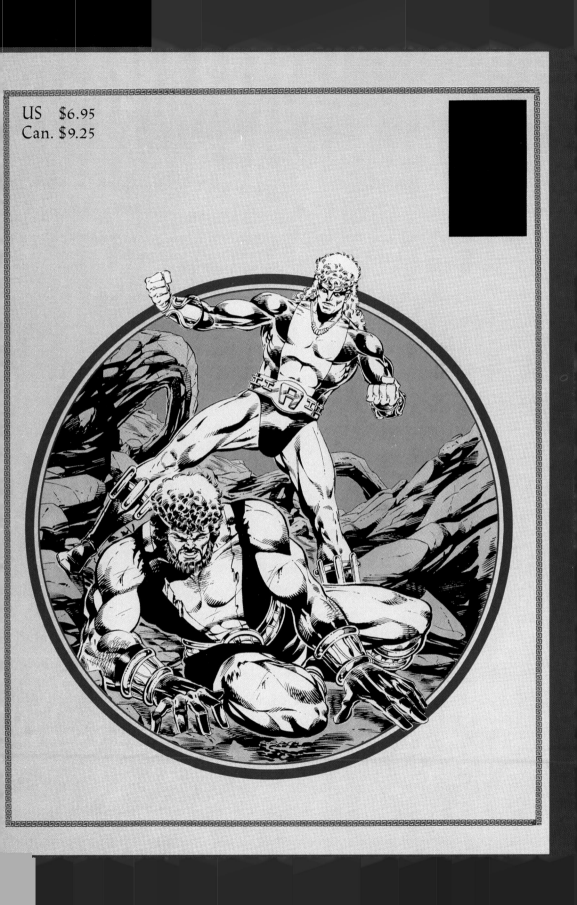

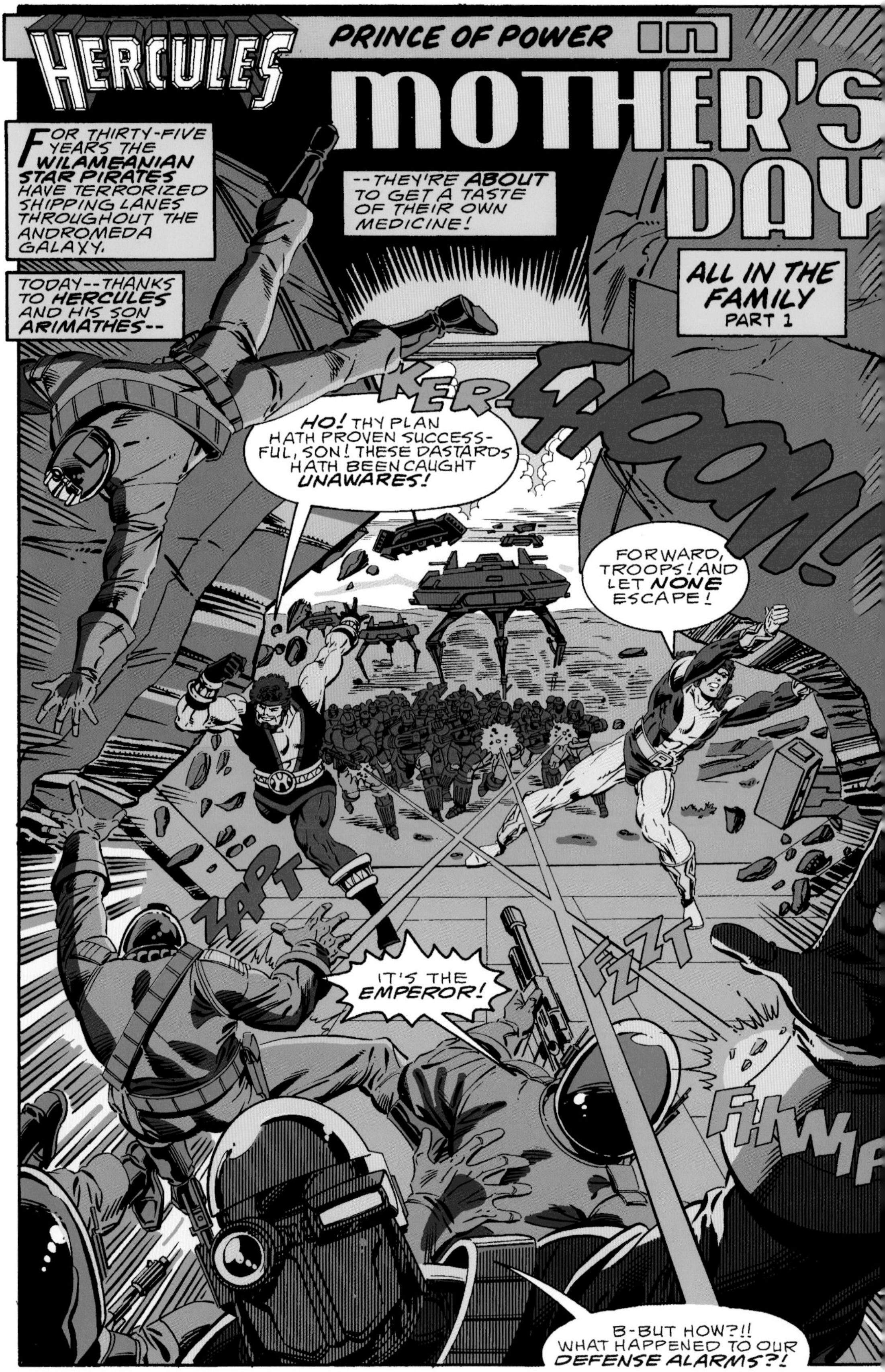
HERCULES
PRINCE OF POWER in
MOTHER'S DAY
FOR THIRTY-FIVE YEARS THE WILAMEANIAN STAR PIRATES HAVE TERRORIZED SHIPPING LANES THROUGHOUT THE ANDROMEDA GALAXY.
TODAY--THANKS TO HERCULES AND HIS SON ARIMATHES--
--THEY'RE ABOUT TO GET A TASTE OF THEIR OWN MEDICINE!
ALL IN THE FAMILY PART 1
KER-CHOOM!!
HO! THY PLAN HATH PROVEN SUCCESS-FUL, SON! THESE DASTARDS HATH BEEN CAUGHT UNAWARES!
FORWARD, TROOPS! AND LET NONE ESCAPE!
ZAPT
FZZT
IT'S THE EMPEROR!
FHWIP
B-BUT HOW?!! WHAT HAPPENED TO OUR DEFENSE ALARMS?!

ALL OUR MONTHS OF PLANNING HAVE BORNE FRUIT, FATHER!

I'VE WAITED A LONG TIME TO *REPAY* THESE SCUM FOR PREYING ON MY SUBJECTS!

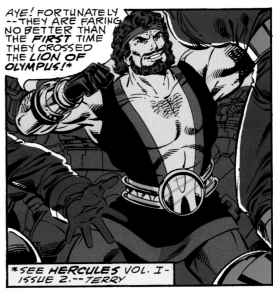

AYE! FORTUNATELY --THEY ARE FARING NO BETTER THAN THE *FIRST* TIME THEY CROSSED THE *LION OF OLYMPUS!**

**SEE HERCULES VOL. I- ISSUE 2.-- TERRY*

KER-

LET THIS BATTLE BE OUR *LAST!*

BA-BAMM!

THE CONFLICT *RAGES* ON UNTIL THE PIRATES' *NUMBERS* DWINDLE TO BUT A HANDFUL!

SURRENDER --OR PREPARE TO RECEIVE THE *GIFT!*

SOME THANKS I GET! SNEAK IN HERE --DEACTIVATE THE SECURITY SYSTEM, AND *YOU* WANT TO GIVE ME FREE DENTAL WORK! MY PAL, HERCULES!

W-WHOA! W-WAIT A MINUTE! I-IT'S *ME*, STEROID-BREATH!

SKYPPI...?

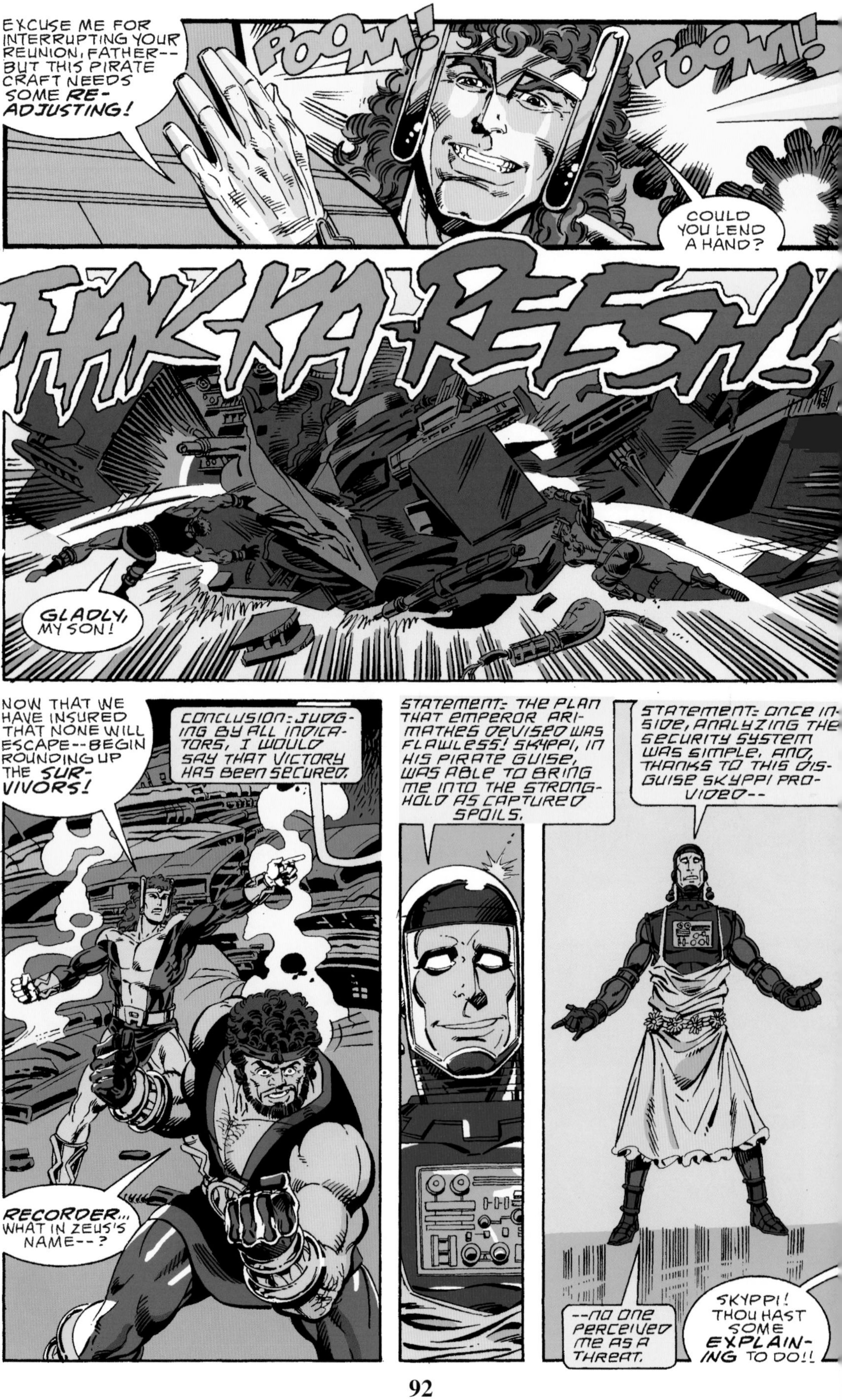
EXCUSE ME FOR INTERRUPTING YOUR REUNION, FATHER-- BUT THIS PIRATE CRAFT NEEDS SOME RE-ADJUSTING!
POOM!
POOM!
COULD YOU LEND A HAND?
THAK-KA-REESH!
GLADLY, MY SON!
NOW THAT WE HAVE INSURED THAT NONE WILL ESCAPE--BEGIN ROUNDING UP THE SURVIVORS!
CONCLUSION: JUDGING BY ALL INDICATORS, I WOULD SAY THAT VICTORY HAS BEEN SECURED.
RECORDER... WHAT IN ZEUS'S NAME--?
STATEMENT: THE PLAN THAT EMPEROR ARIMATHES DEVISED WAS FLAWLESS! SKYPPI, IN HIS PIRATE GUISE, WAS ABLE TO BRING ME INTO THE STRONGHOLD AS CAPTURED SPOILS.
STATEMENT: ONCE INSIDE, ANALYZING THE SECURITY SYSTEM WAS SIMPLE. AND, THANKS TO THIS DISGUISE SKYPPI PROVIDED--
--NO ONE PERCEIVED ME AS A THREAT.
SKYPPI! THOU HAST SOME EXPLAINING TO DO!!

A SHORT TIME LATER, AS THE PRISONERS ARE BEING PREPARED FOR TRANSPORT...

WHEN WE RETURN TO PORT ANTERIS, I'LL SEE TO IT THAT THESE PIRATE SCUM SUFFER PAINFULLY FOR THEIR TRANSGRESSIONS!

WHAT DOTH THOU PROPOSE? EAR-LOPPINGS? FLAILINGS? PERHAPS--PUBLIC EXECUTIONS?

WHY DO I HAVE THE FEELING I'M GOING TO RECEIVE ANOTHER "NOBILITY" LECTURE!

I MERELY SUGGEST THAT IF THE PIRATES LIVE TO TELL THE TALE, TODAY'S VICTORY MIGHT BETTER SERVE AS A WARNING TO OTHERS WHO MIGHT TRY LIKE FOLLY.

MERELY A SUGGESTION, "MY EMPEROR."

NOTED--"FAITHFUL SUBJECT." I WILL TAKE THE QUESTION OF JUST PUNISHMENT UNDER CONSIDERATION FOR A TIME. AFTER ALL, EVEN THESE PIRATES ARE MY SUBJECTS --EH?

A FEW DAYS HAVE PASSED SINCE EMPEROR ARIMATHES SENTENCED THE STAR-PIRATES TO A REHABILITATION COLONY. PEACE HAS BEEN RESTORED TO WILAMEAN. CALM RULES THE DAY--

--WITH THE EXCEPTION OF THE NORTH WING OF THE ROYAL PALACE. IT IS A PLACE THAT IS FORBIDDEN TO ALL BUT A SELECT FEW.

IT IS THE HOME OF THE EMPEROR'S EXILED MOTHER, LAYANA, AND FOR THE LAST TWELVE MONTHS, IT HAS BEEN A PLACE SEETHING WITH HATRED!

HE'S LATE-- AGAIN!

...WHERE IS HE --THE ROTTEN LITTLE CHEAT? HOW DARE HE KEEP ME WAITING!?

KEEP YOUR GIRDLE ON, MOMS! I'M COMIN'!

93

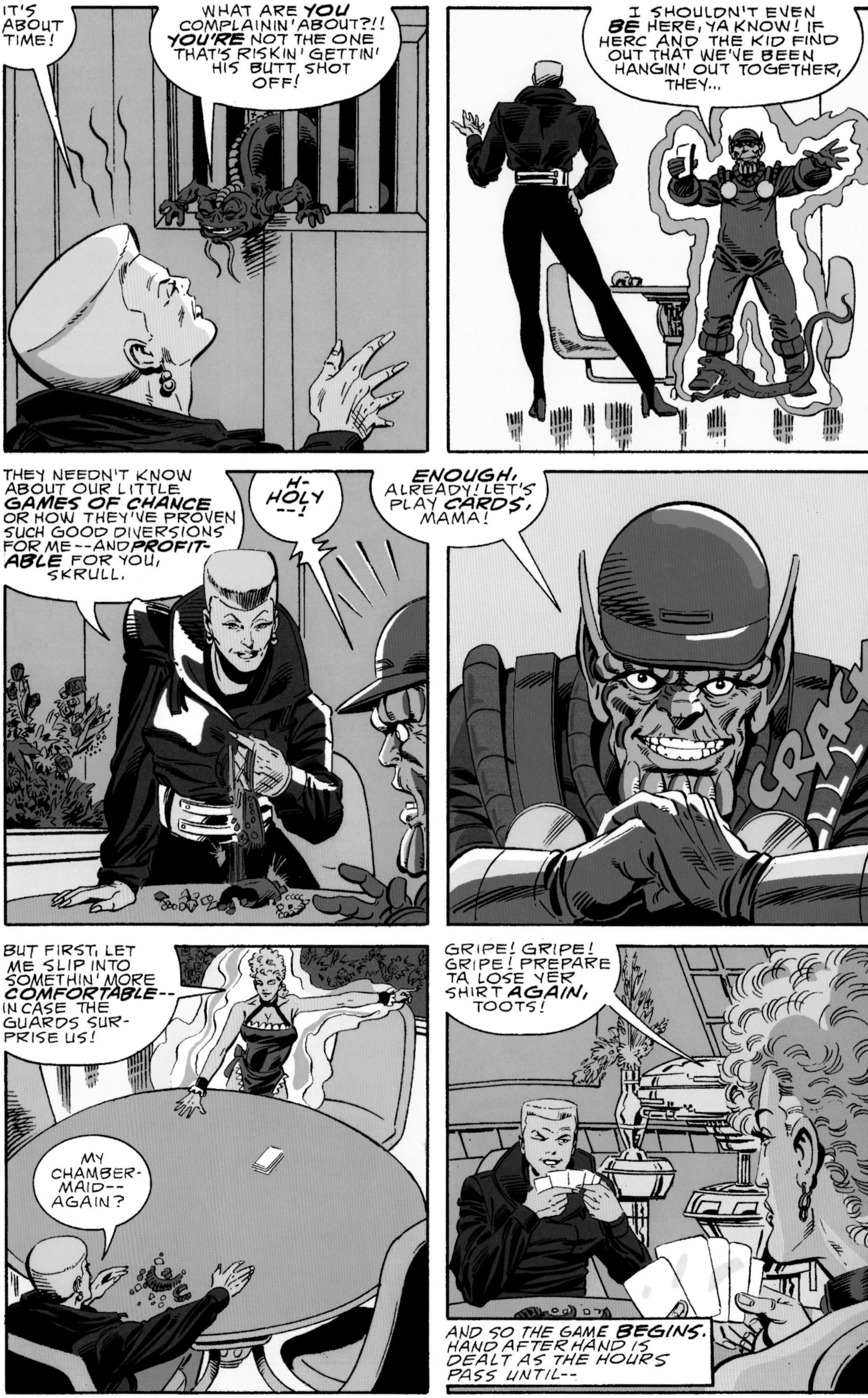

IT'S ABOUT TIME!
WHAT ARE YOU COMPLAININ' ABOUT?!! YOU'RE NOT THE ONE THAT'S RISKIN' GETTIN' HIS BUTT SHOT OFF!
I SHOULDN'T EVEN BE HERE, YA KNOW! IF HERC AND THE KID FIND OUT THAT WE'VE BEEN HANGIN' OUT TOGETHER, THEY...
THEY NEEDN'T KNOW ABOUT OUR LITTLE GAMES OF CHANCE OR HOW THEY'VE PROVEN SUCH GOOD DIVERSIONS FOR ME--AND PROFIT-ABLE FOR YOU, SKRULL.
H-HOLY--!
ENOUGH, ALREADY! LET'S PLAY CARDS, MAMA!
BUT FIRST, LET ME SLIP INTO SOMETHIN' MORE COMFORTABLE--IN CASE THE GUARDS SUR-PRISE US!
MY CHAMBER-MAID--AGAIN?
GRIPE! GRIPE! GRIPE! PREPARE TA LOSE YER SHIRT AGAIN, TOOTS!
AND SO THE GAME BEGINS. HAND AFTER HAND IS DEALT AS THE HOURS PASS UNTIL--

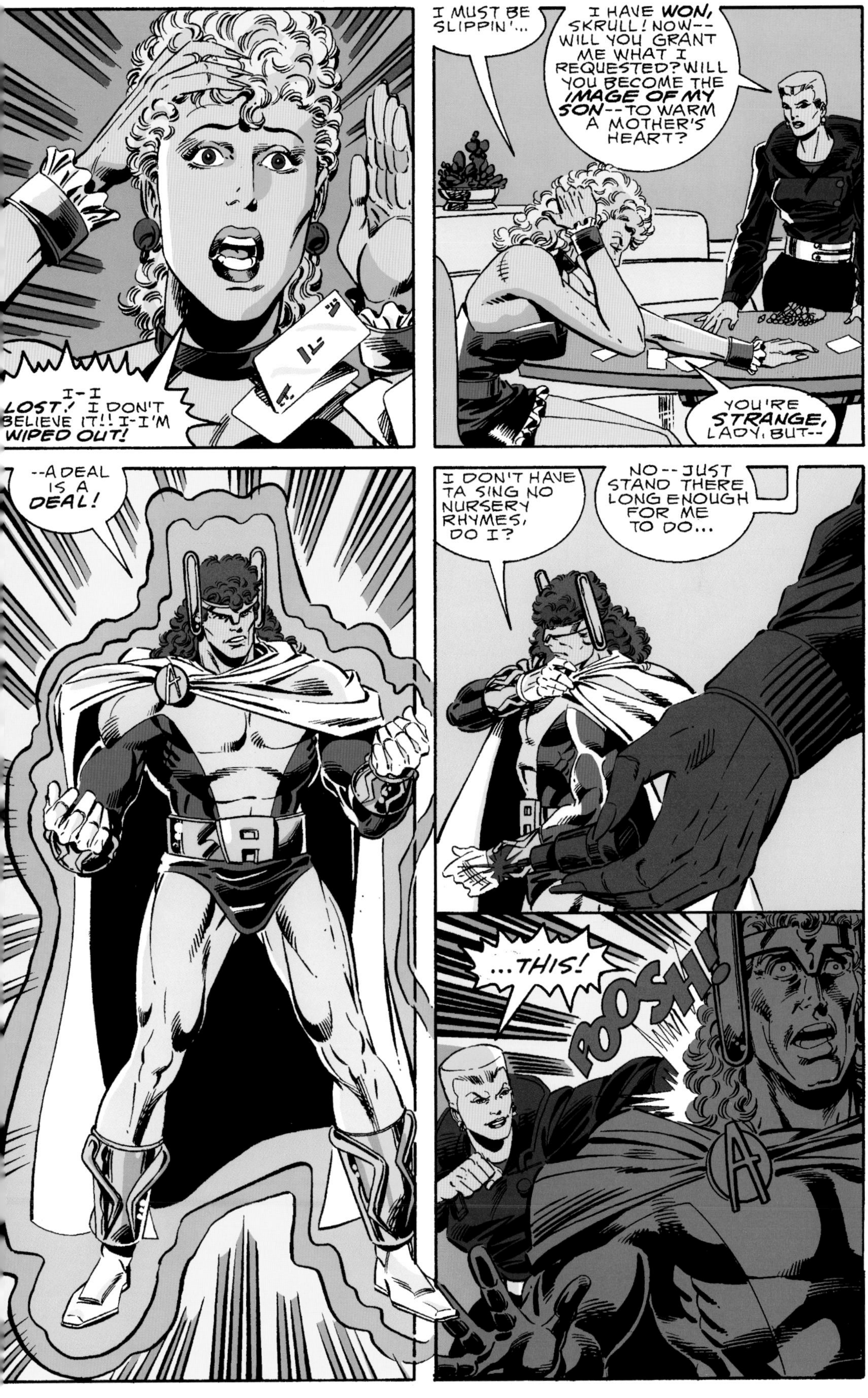
I-I LOST! I DON'T BELIEVE IT!! I-I'M WIPED OUT!
I MUST BE SLIPPIN'...
I HAVE WON, SKRULL! NOW-- WILL YOU GRANT ME WHAT I REQUESTED? WILL YOU BECOME THE IMAGE OF MY SON--TO WARM A MOTHER'S HEART?
YOU'RE STRANGE, LADY, BUT--
--A DEAL IS A DEAL!
I DON'T HAVE TA SING NO NURSERY RHYMES, DO I?
NO--JUST STAND THERE LONG ENOUGH FOR ME TO DO...
...THIS!
POOSH!

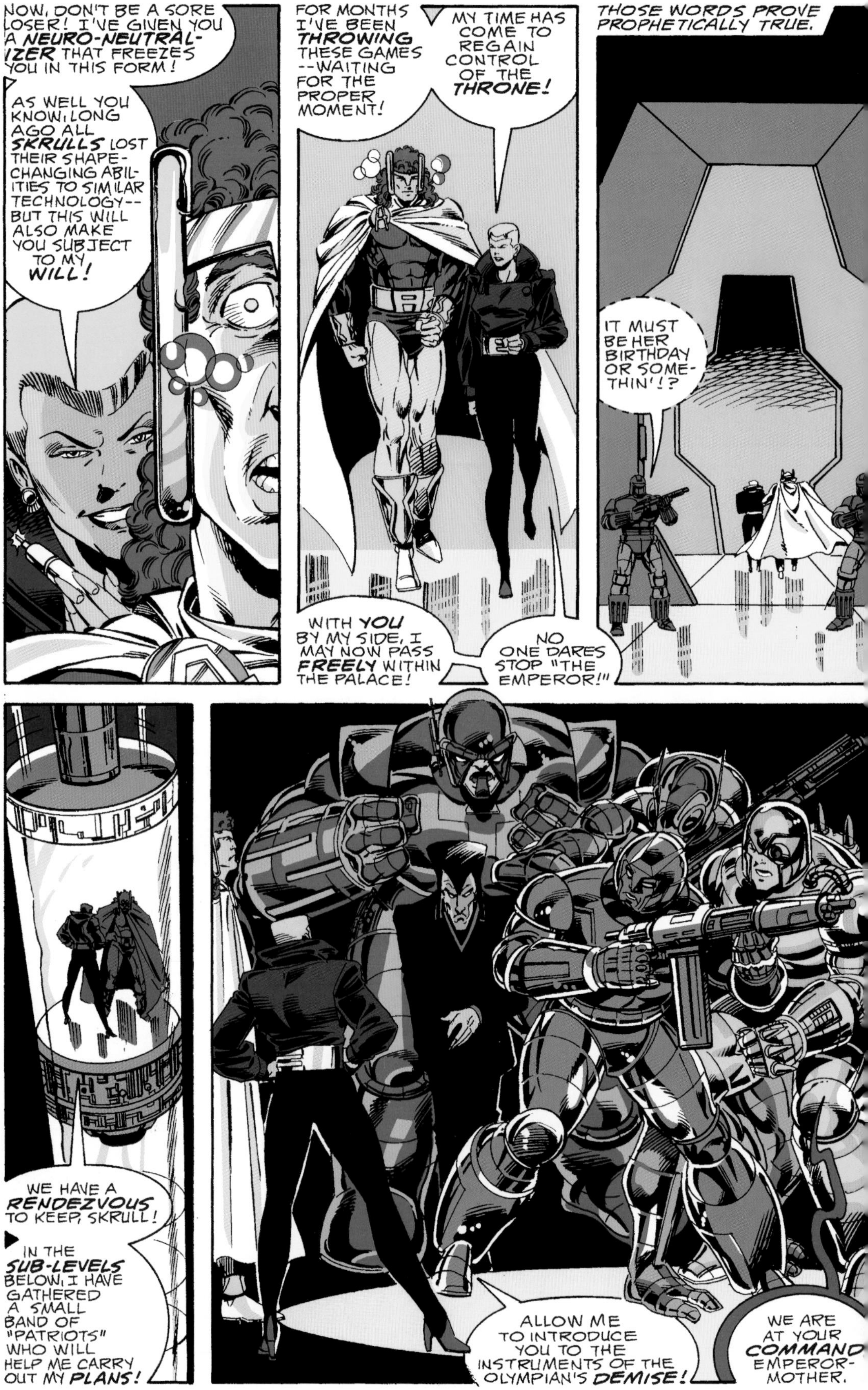
NOW, DON'T BE A SORE LOSER! I'VE GIVEN YOU A NEURO-NEUTRALIZER THAT FREEZES YOU IN THIS FORM!
AS WELL YOU KNOW, LONG AGO ALL SKRULLS LOST THEIR SHAPE-CHANGING ABILITIES TO SIMILAR TECHNOLOGY--BUT THIS WILL ALSO MAKE YOU SUBJECT TO MY WILL!
FOR MONTHS I'VE BEEN THROWING THESE GAMES --WAITING FOR THE PROPER MOMENT!
MY TIME HAS COME TO REGAIN CONTROL OF THE THRONE!
WITH YOU BY MY SIDE, I MAY NOW PASS FREELY WITHIN THE PALACE!
NO ONE DARES STOP "THE EMPEROR!"
THOSE WORDS PROVE PROPHETICALLY TRUE.
IT MUST BE HER BIRTHDAY OR SOMETHIN'!?
WE HAVE A RENDEZVOUS TO KEEP, SKRULL!
IN THE SUB-LEVELS BELOW, I HAVE GATHERED A SMALL BAND OF "PATRIOTS" WHO WILL HELP ME CARRY OUT MY PLANS!
ALLOW ME TO INTRODUCE YOU TO THE INSTRUMENTS OF THE OLYMPIAN'S DEMISE!
WE ARE AT YOUR COMMAND EMPEROR-MOTHER.

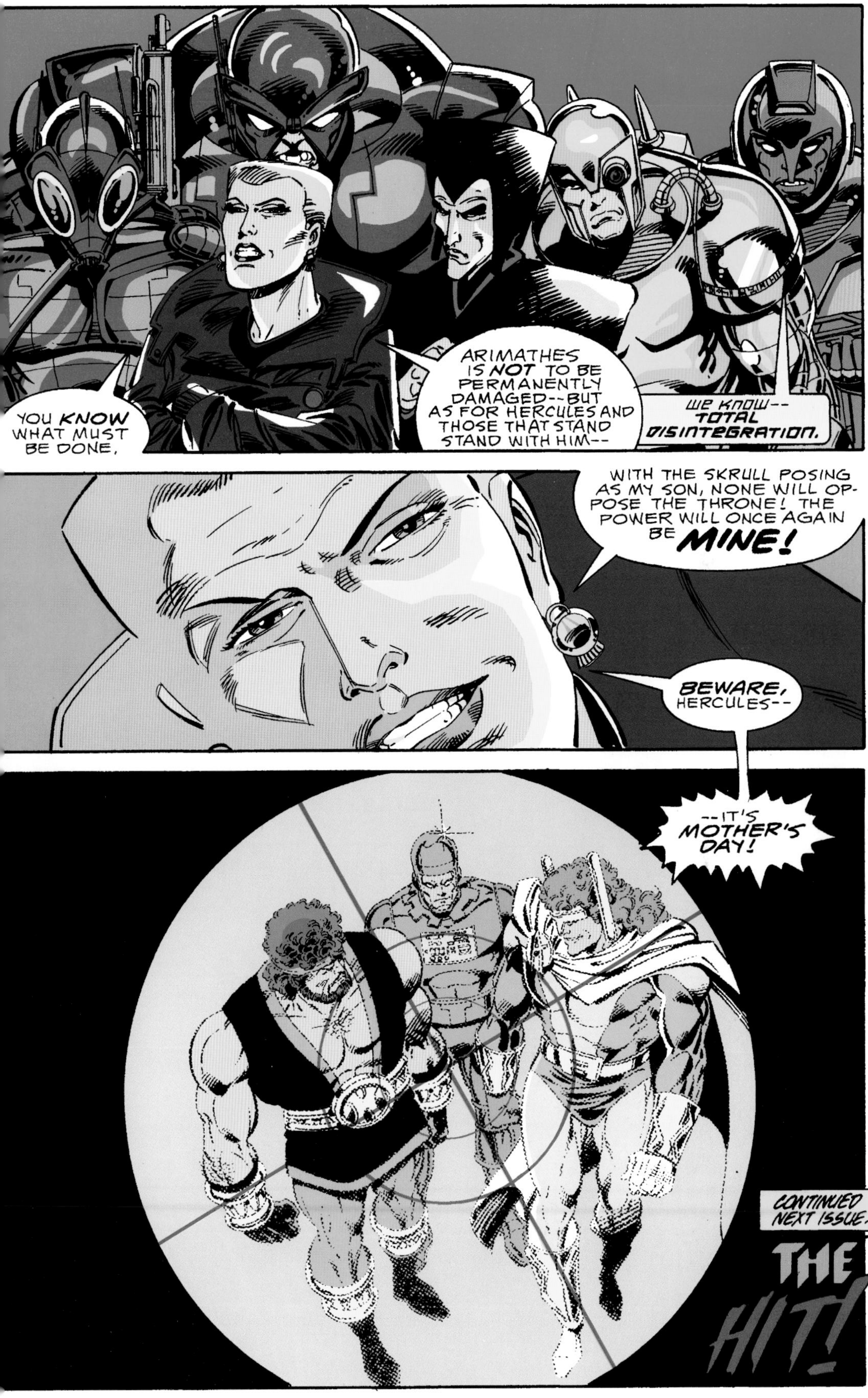

YOU KNOW WHAT MUST BE DONE.
ARIMATHES IS NOT TO BE PERMANENTLY DAMAGED--BUT AS FOR HERCULES AND THOSE THAT STAND STAND WITH HIM--
WE KNOW-- TOTAL DISINTEGRATION.
WITH THE SKRULL POSING AS MY SON, NONE WILL OPPOSE THE THRONE! THE POWER WILL ONCE AGAIN BE MINE!
BEWARE, HERCULES--
--IT'S MOTHER'S DAY!
CONTINUED NEXT ISSUE...
THE HIT!

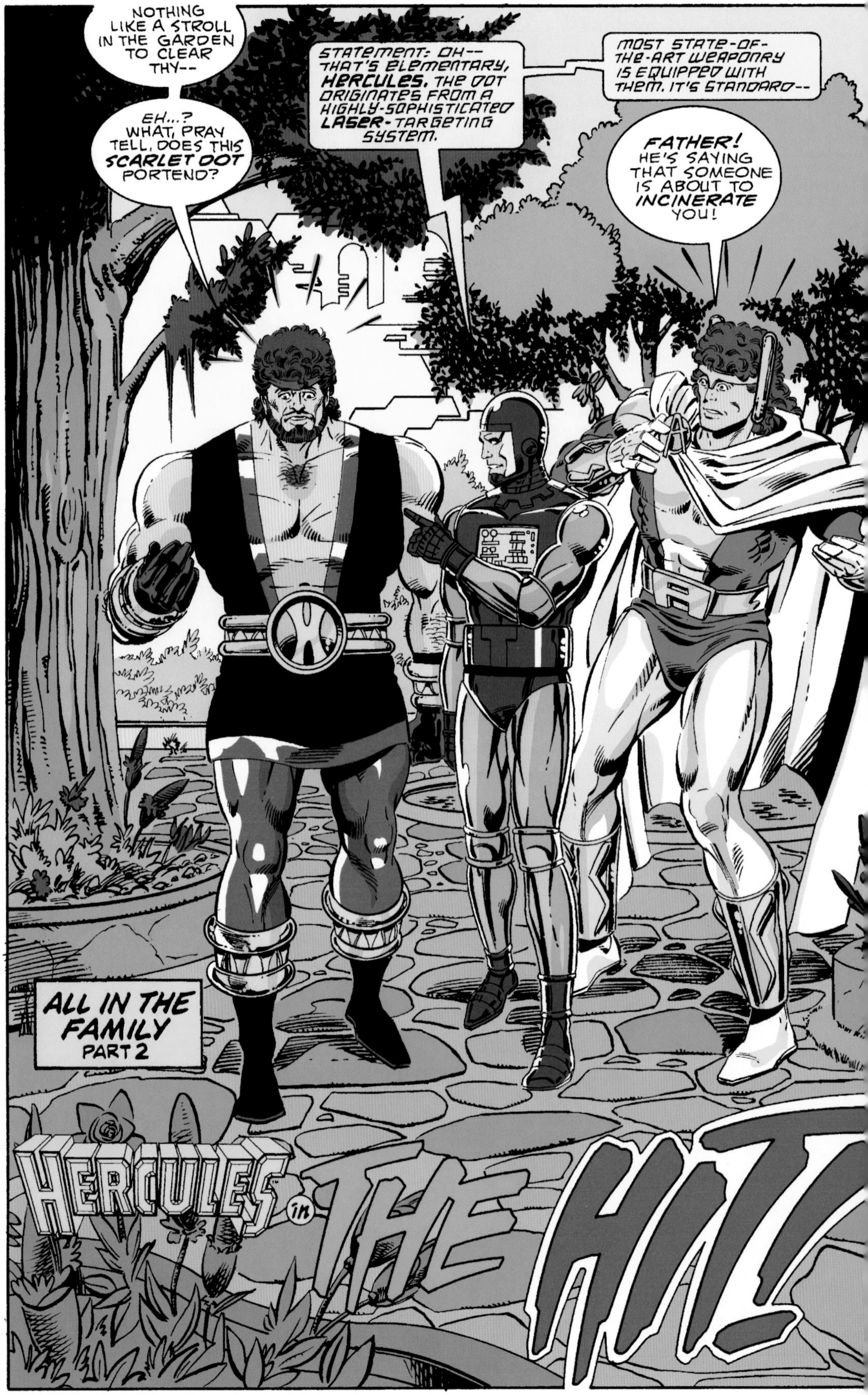
NOTHING LIKE A STROLL IN THE GARDEN TO CLEAR THY--
EH...? WHAT, PRAY TELL, DOES THIS SCARLET DOT PORTEND?
STATEMENT: OH-- THAT'S ELEMENTARY, HERCULES. THE DOT ORIGINATES FROM A HIGHLY-SOPHISTICATED LASER-TARGETING SYSTEM.
MOST STATE-OF-THE-ART WEAPONRY IS EQUIPPED WITH THEM. IT'S STANDARD--
FATHER! HE'S SAYING THAT SOMEONE IS ABOUT TO INCINERATE YOU!
ALL IN THE FAMILY PART 2
HERCULES in THE HIT!

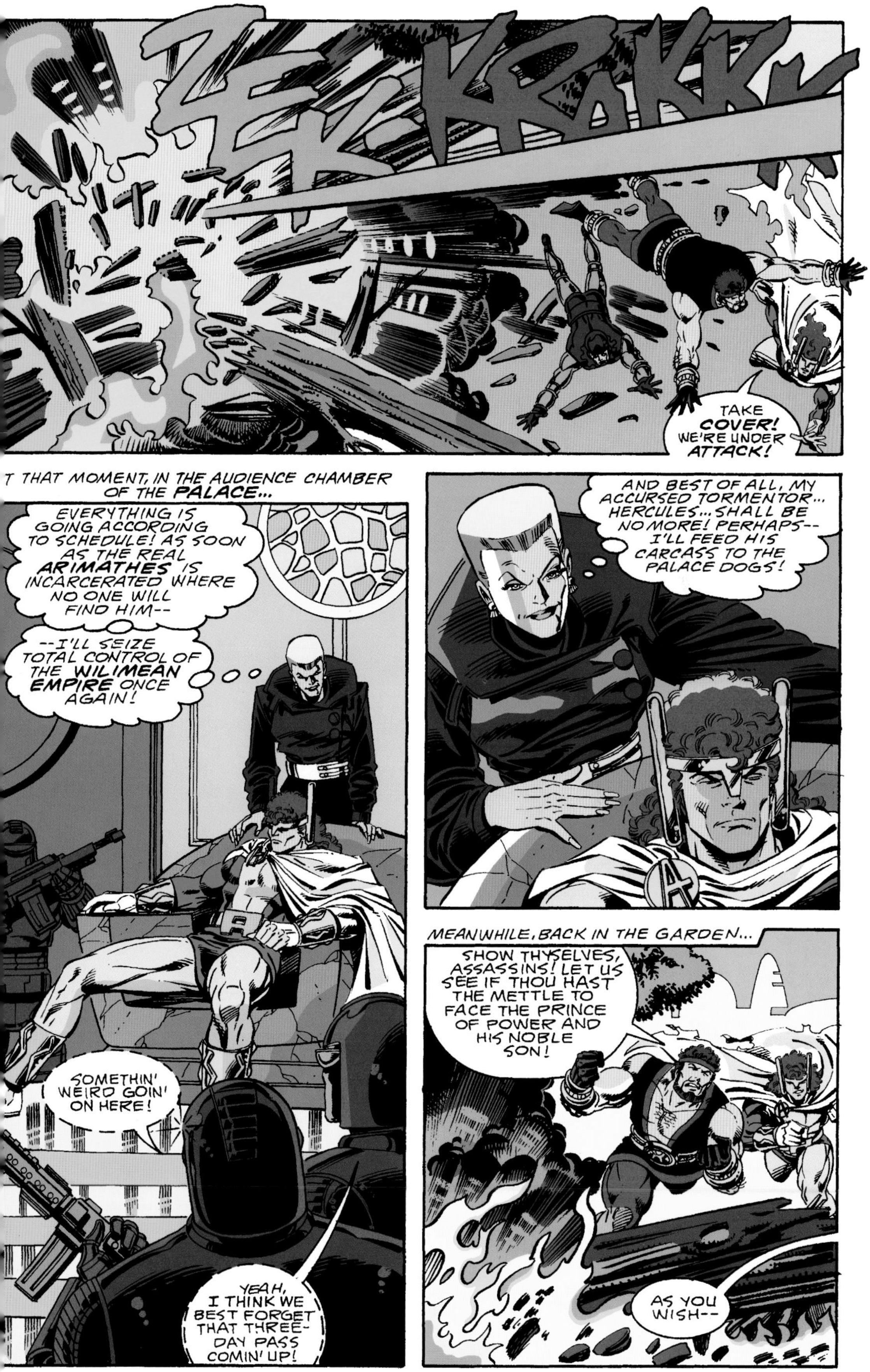
ZEKKRAKKK
TAKE COVER! WE'RE UNDER ATTACK!
T THAT MOMENT, IN THE AUDIENCE CHAMBER OF THE PALACE...
EVERYTHING IS GOING ACCORDING TO SCHEDULE! AS SOON AS THE REAL ARIMATHES IS INCARCERATED WHERE NO ONE WILL FIND HIM--
--I'LL SEIZE TOTAL CONTROL OF THE WILIMEAN EMPIRE ONCE AGAIN!
SOMETHIN' WEIRD GOIN' ON HERE!
YEAH, I THINK WE BEST FORGET THAT THREE-DAY PASS COMIN' UP!
AND BEST OF ALL, MY ACCURSED TORMENTOR... HERCULES... SHALL BE NO MORE! PERHAPS-- I'LL FEED HIS CARCASS TO THE PALACE DOGS!
MEANWHILE, BACK IN THE GARDEN...
SHOW THYSELVES, ASSASSINS! LET US SEE IF THOU HAST THE METTLE TO FACE THE PRINCE OF POWER AND HIS NOBLE SON!
AS YOU WISH--

-- SINCE YOU WON'T *LIVE* TO IDENTIFY US!

WE REPRESENT THE ELITE OF THE *ASSASSINS' GUILD!* YOU HAVE NO POSSIBLE HOPE OF VICTORY!

BUT I AM EMPOWERED TO OFFER YOU A BARGAIN, HERCULES! SURRENDER THE EMPEROR TO US AND--

--YOUR DEATH WILL BE SWIFT AND PAINLESS!

BASE COWARDS! THOU DOST BARGAIN TO PRESERVE THINE OWN HIDES!

NO MOTLEY BAND OF CUTTHROATS IS A MATCH FOR OUR GODLY MIGHT!

IT'S ME THEY WANT, FATHER! SO --

--LET'S GIVE THEM MORE THAN THEY BARGAINED FOR!

ARIMATHES-- WAIT! DON'T...

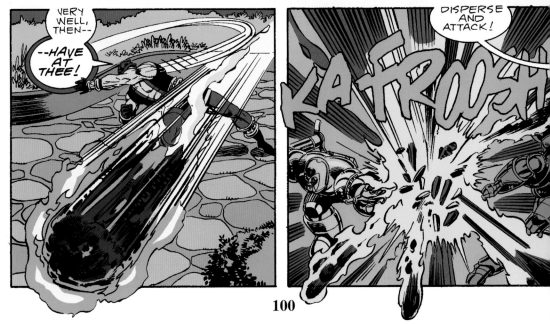

VERY WELL, THEN--

--HAVE AT THEE!

DISPERSE AND ATTACK!

KAFROOSH

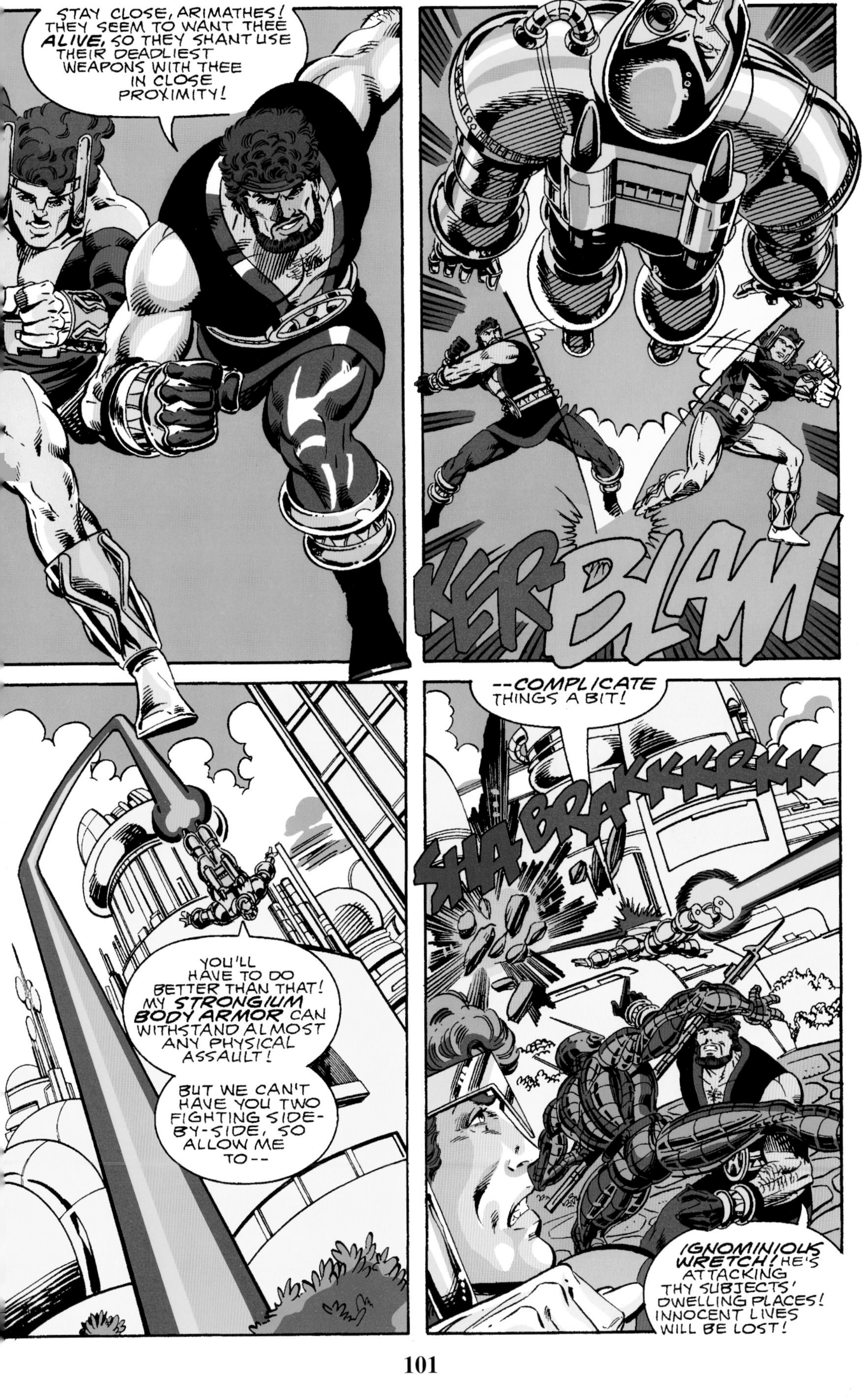
STAY CLOSE, ARIMATHES! THEY SEEM TO WANT THEE ALIVE, SO THEY SHANT USE THEIR DEADLIEST WEAPONS WITH THEE IN CLOSE PROXIMITY!
KER BLAM
YOU'LL HAVE TO DO BETTER THAN THAT! MY STRONGIUM BODY ARMOR CAN WITHSTAND ALMOST ANY PHYSICAL ASSAULT!
BUT WE CAN'T HAVE YOU TWO FIGHTING SIDE-BY-SIDE, SO ALLOW ME TO--
--COMPLICATE THINGS A BIT!
SHA BRAKKKRKK
IGNOMINIOUS WRETCH! HE'S ATTACKING THY SUBJECTS' DWELLING PLACES! INNOCENT LIVES WILL BE LOST!

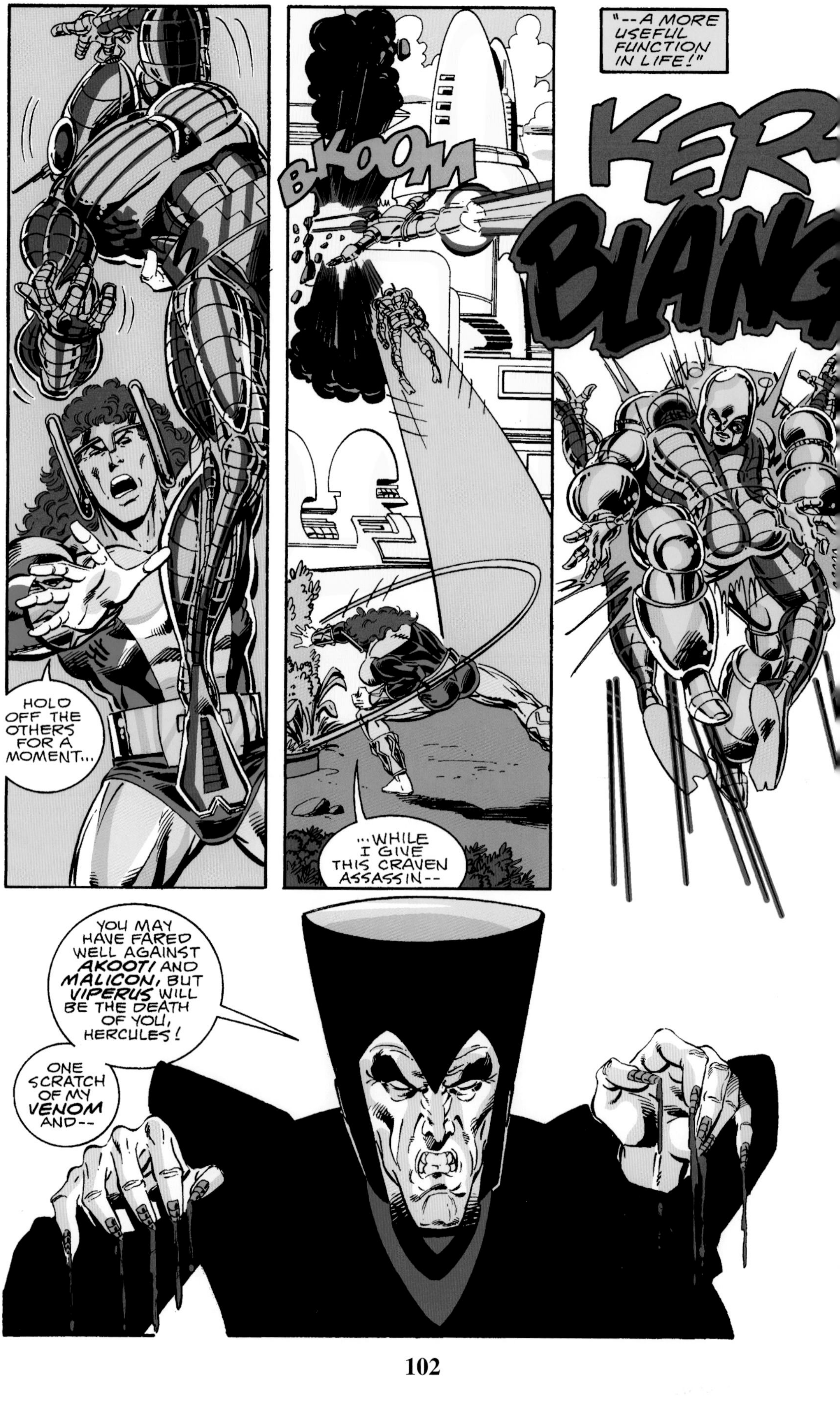
HOLD OFF THE OTHERS FOR A MOMENT...
BKOOM
...WHILE I GIVE THIS CRAVEN ASSASSIN--
"--A MORE USEFUL FUNCTION IN LIFE!"
KER BLANG
YOU MAY HAVE FARED WELL AGAINST AKOOTI AND MALICON, BUT VIPERUS WILL BE THE DEATH OF YOU, HERCULES!
ONE SCRATCH OF MY VENOM AND--

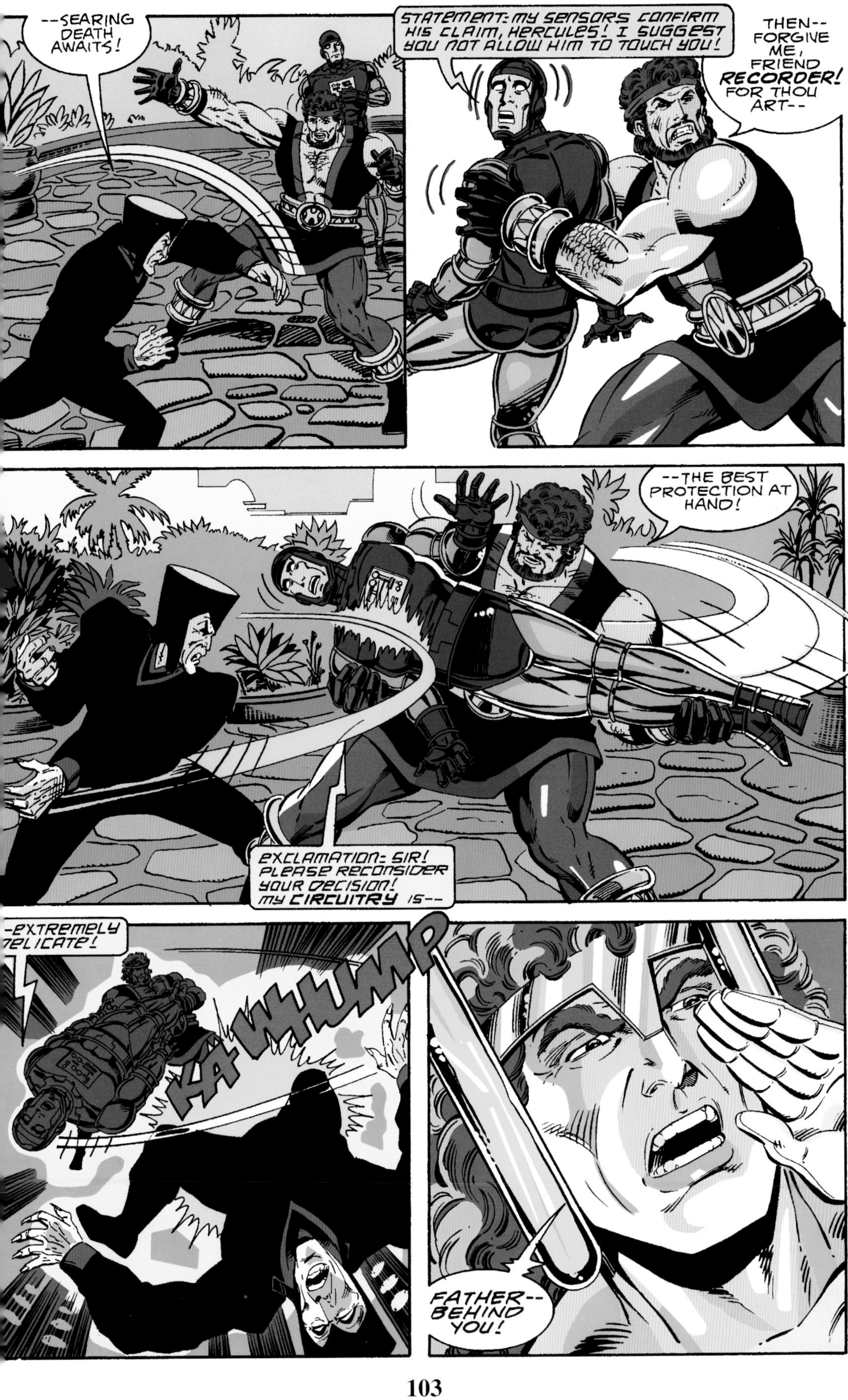
--SEARING DEATH AWAITS!
STATEMENT: MY SENSORS CONFIRM HIS CLAIM, HERCULES! I SUGGEST YOU NOT ALLOW HIM TO TOUCH YOU!
THEN--FORGIVE ME, FRIEND RECORDER! FOR THOU ART--
--THE BEST PROTECTION AT HAND!
EXCLAMATION: SIR! PLEASE RECONSIDER YOUR DECISION! MY CIRCUITRY IS--
-EXTREMELY DELICATE!
KA-WHUMP
FATHER--BEHIND YOU!

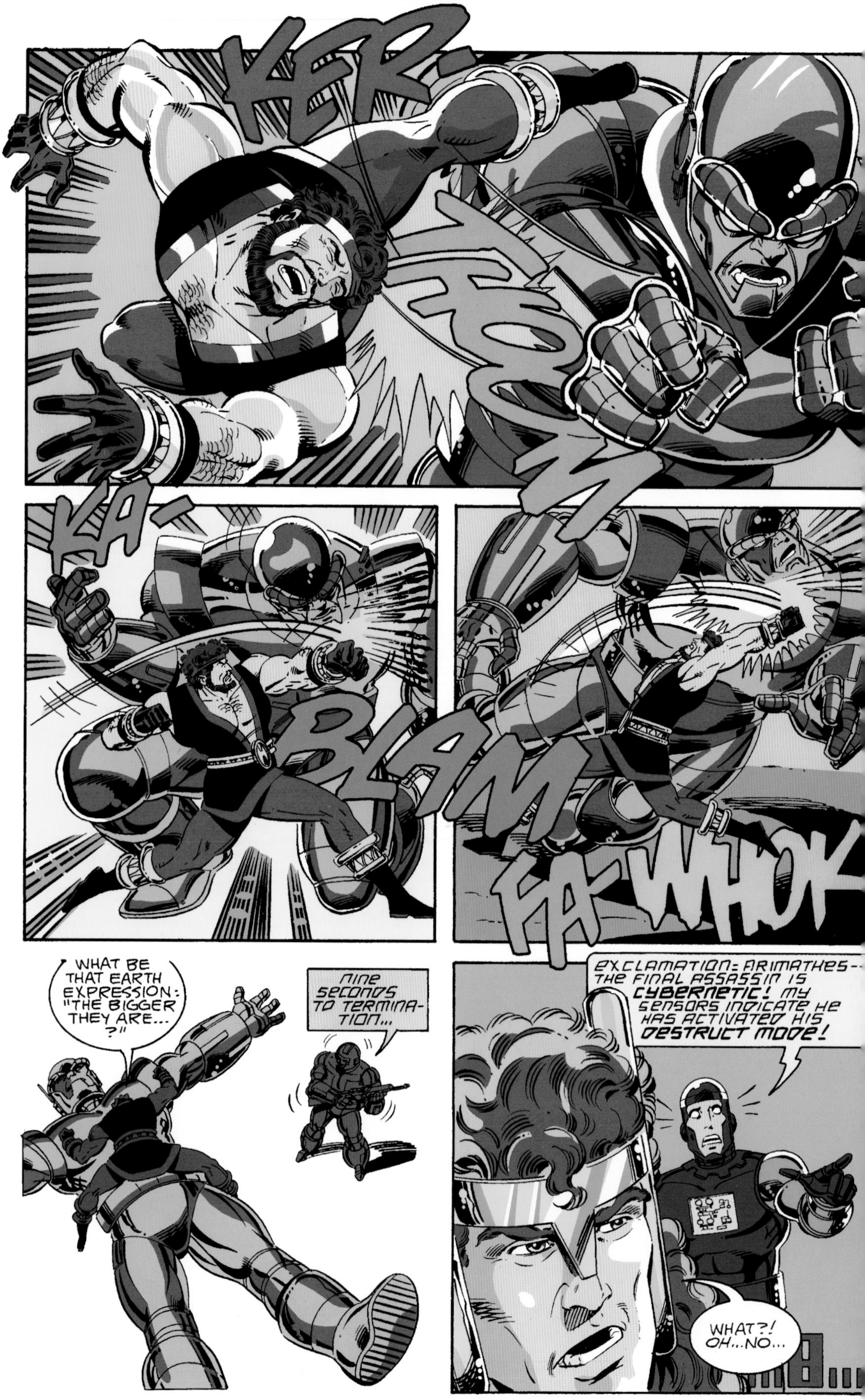
KER-THOOM
KA-BLAM
FA-WHOK
WHAT BE THAT EARTH EXPRESSION: "THE BIGGER THEY ARE...?"
NINE SECONDS TO TERMINATION...
EXCLAMATION: ARIMATHES-- THE FINAL ASSASSIN IS CYBERNETIC! MY SENSORS INDICATE HE HAS ACTIVATED HIS DESTRUCT MODE!
WHAT?! OH...NO...

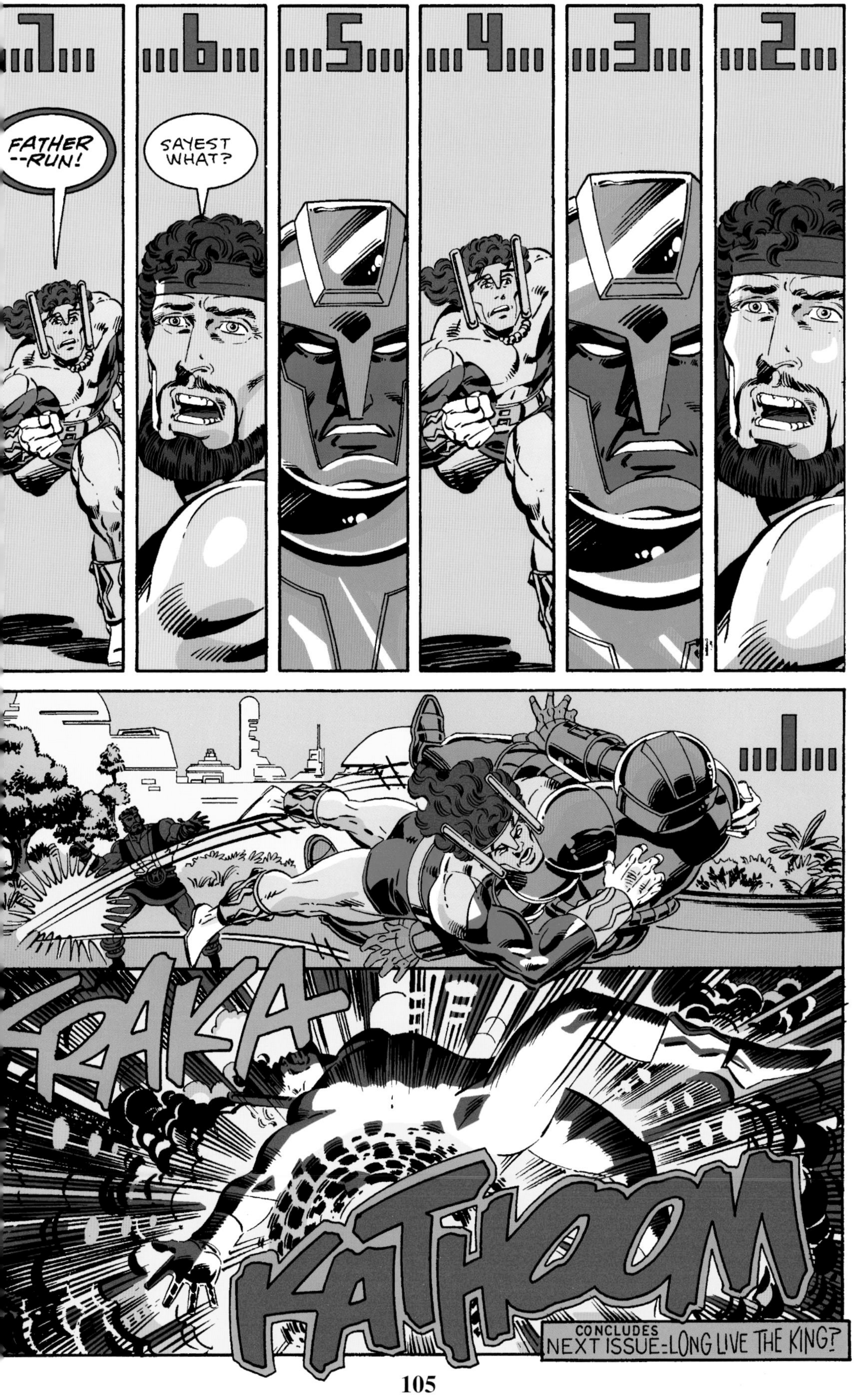
...7...
FATHER --RUN!
...6...
SAYEST WHAT?
...5...
...4...
...3...
...2...
...1...
KRAKA
KATHOOM
CONCLUDES NEXT ISSUE: LONG LIVE THE KING?

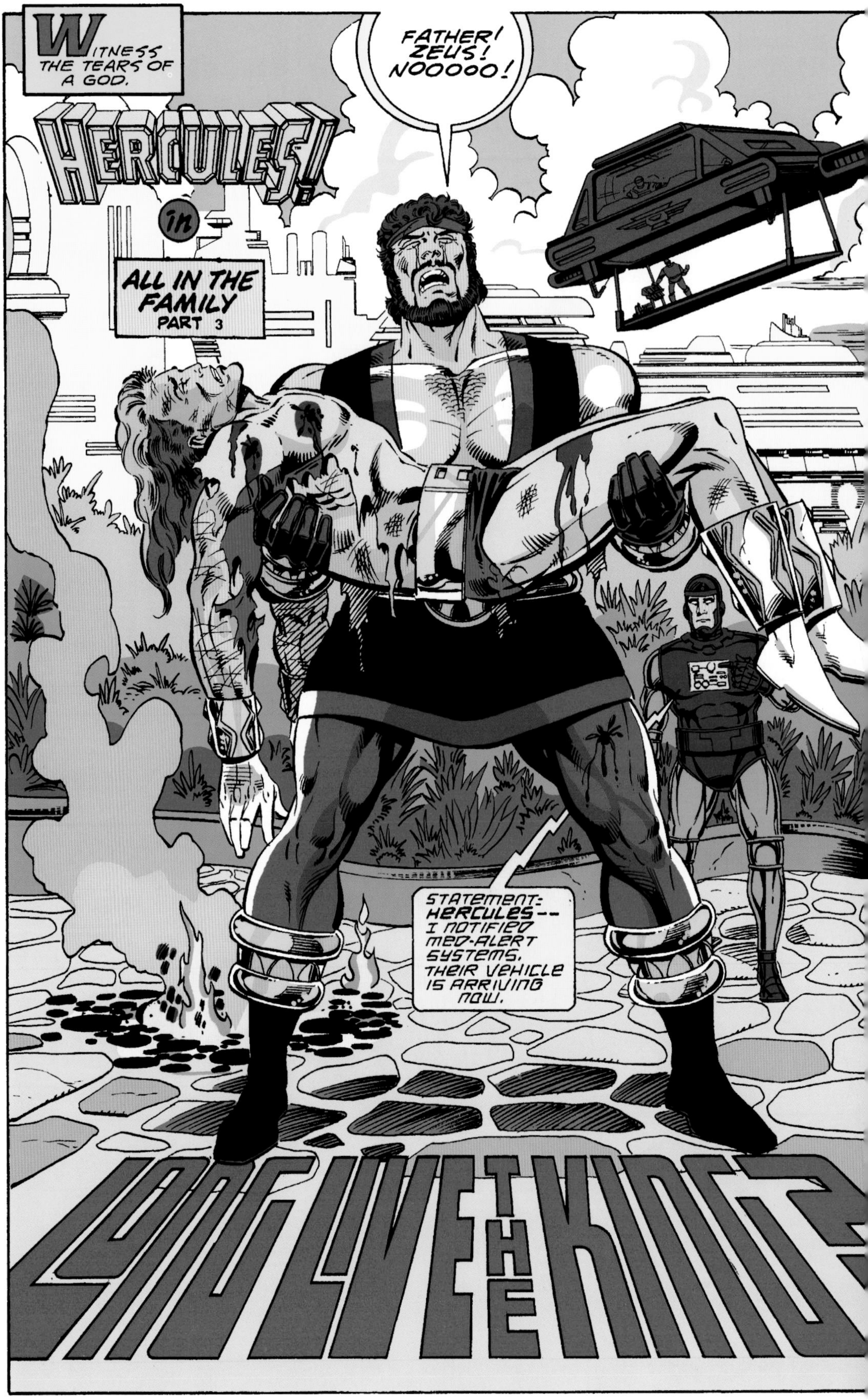
WITNESS THE TEARS OF A GOD.
HERCULES! in
ALL IN THE FAMILY PART 3
FATHER! ZEUS! NOOOOO!
STATEMENT: HERCULES-- I NOTIFIED MED-ALERT SYSTEMS. THEIR VEHICLE IS ARRIVING NOW.
LONG LIVE THE KING?

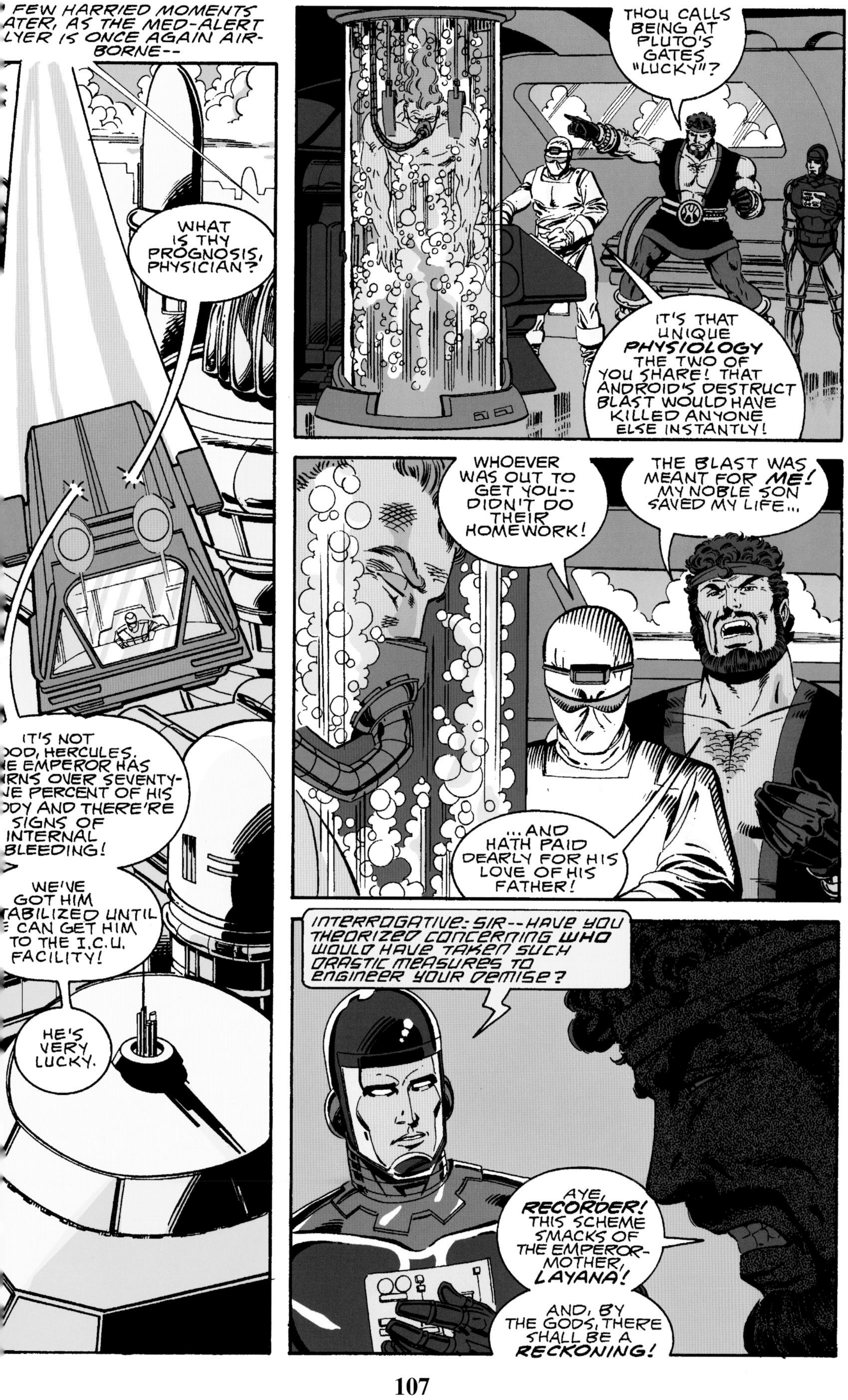

FEW HARRIED MOMENTS ATER, AS THE MED-ALERT LYER IS ONCE AGAIN AIR-BORNE--
WHAT IS THY PROGNOSIS, PHYSICIAN?
IT'S NOT OOD, HERCULES. E EMPEROR HAS RNS OVER SEVENTY- E PERCENT OF HIS ODY AND THERE'RE SIGNS OF INTERNAL BLEEDING!
WE'VE GOT HIM TABILIZED UNTIL E CAN GET HIM TO THE I.C.U. FACILITY!
HE'S VERY LUCKY.
THOU CALLS BEING AT PLUTO'S GATES "LUCKY"?
IT'S THAT UNIQUE PHYSIOLOGY THE TWO OF YOU SHARE! THAT ANDROID'S DESTRUCT BLAST WOULD HAVE KILLED ANYONE ELSE INSTANTLY!
WHOEVER WAS OUT TO GET YOU-- DIDN'T DO THEIR HOMEWORK!
THE BLAST WAS MEANT FOR ME! MY NOBLE SON SAVED MY LIFE...
...AND HATH PAID DEARLY FOR HIS LOVE OF HIS FATHER!
INTERROGATIVE: SIR--HAVE YOU THEORIZED CONCERNING WHO WOULD HAVE TAKEN SUCH DRASTIC MEASURES TO ENGINEER YOUR DEMISE?
AYE, RECORDER! THIS SCHEME SMACKS OF THE EMPEROR-MOTHER, LAYANA!
AND, BY THE GODS, THERE SHALL BE A RECKONING!

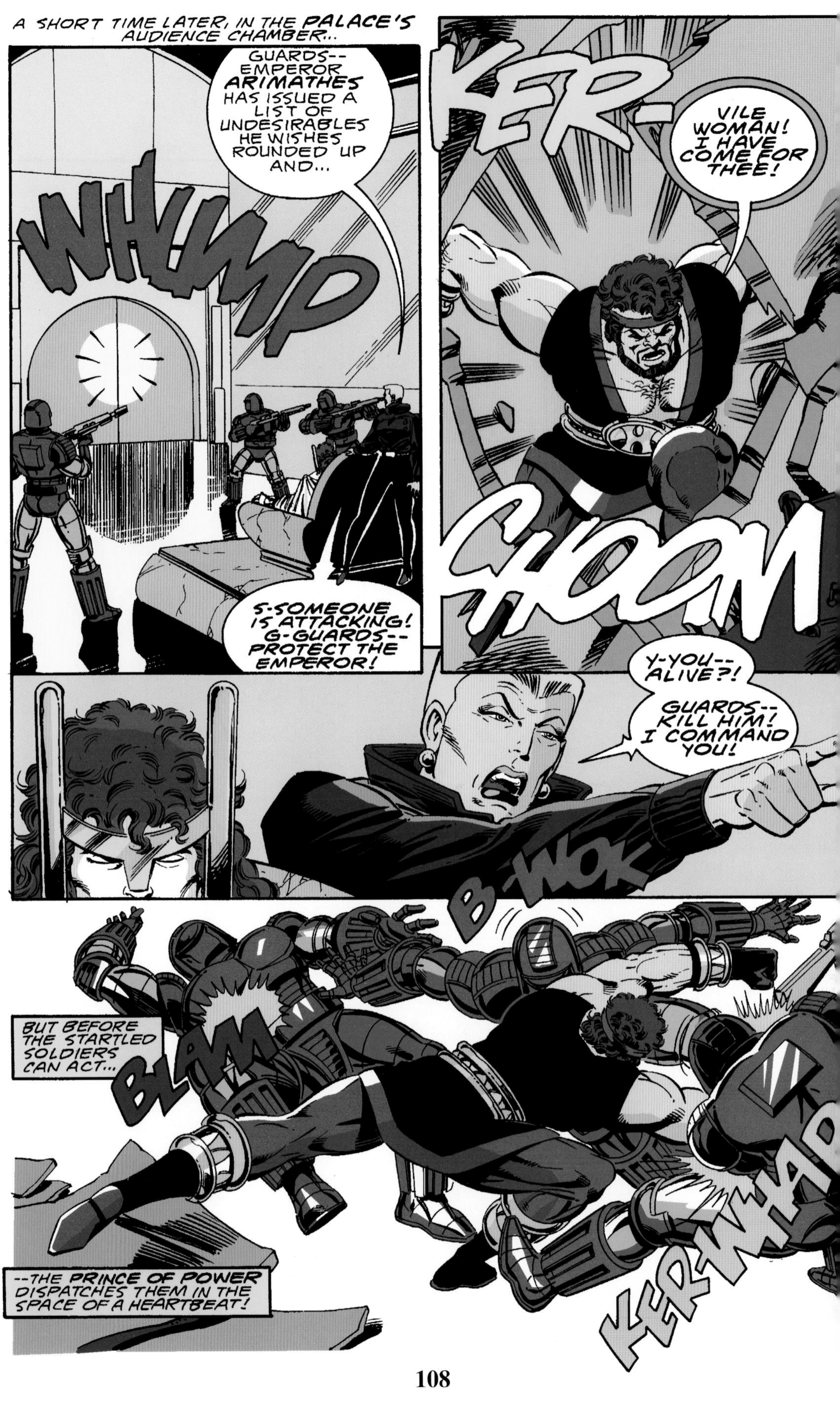
A SHORT TIME LATER, IN THE PALACE'S AUDIENCE CHAMBER..
GUARDS-- EMPEROR ARIMATHES HAS ISSUED A LIST OF UNDESIRABLES HE WISHES ROUNDED UP AND...
WHUMP
S-SOMEONE IS ATTACKING! G-GUARDS-- PROTECT THE EMPEROR!
KER-
VILE WOMAN! I HAVE COME FOR THEE!
CHOOM
Y-YOU-- ALIVE?!
GUARDS-- KILL HIM! I COMMAND YOU!
B-WOK
BUT BEFORE THE STARTLED SOLDIERS CAN ACT...
BLAM
--THE PRINCE OF POWER DISPATCHES THEM IN THE SPACE OF A HEARTBEAT!
KERWHAP

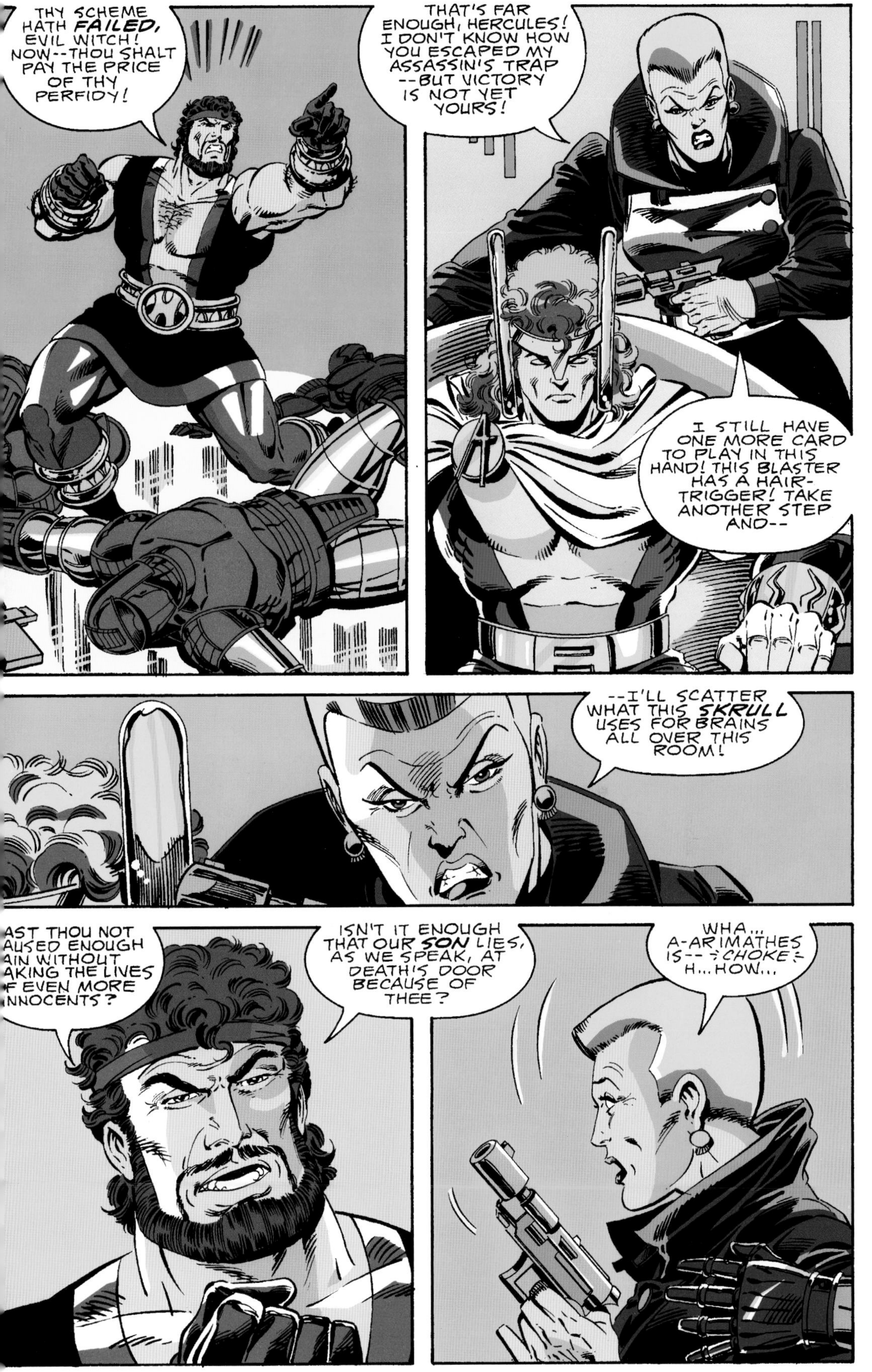
THY SCHEME HATH FAILED, EVIL WITCH! NOW--THOU SHALT PAY THE PRICE OF THY PERFIDY!
THAT'S FAR ENOUGH, HERCULES! I DON'T KNOW HOW YOU ESCAPED MY ASSASSIN'S TRAP --BUT VICTORY IS NOT YET YOURS!
I STILL HAVE ONE MORE CARD TO PLAY IN THIS HAND! THIS BLASTER HAS A HAIR-TRIGGER! TAKE ANOTHER STEP AND--
--I'LL SCATTER WHAT THIS SKRULL USES FOR BRAINS ALL OVER THIS ROOM!
AST THOU NOT AUSED ENOUGH AIN WITHOUT AKING THE LIVES F EVEN MORE NNOCENTS?
ISN'T IT ENOUGH THAT OUR SON LIES, AS WE SPEAK, AT DEATH'S DOOR BECAUSE OF THEE?
WHA... A-ARIMATHES IS-- CHOKE H...HOW...

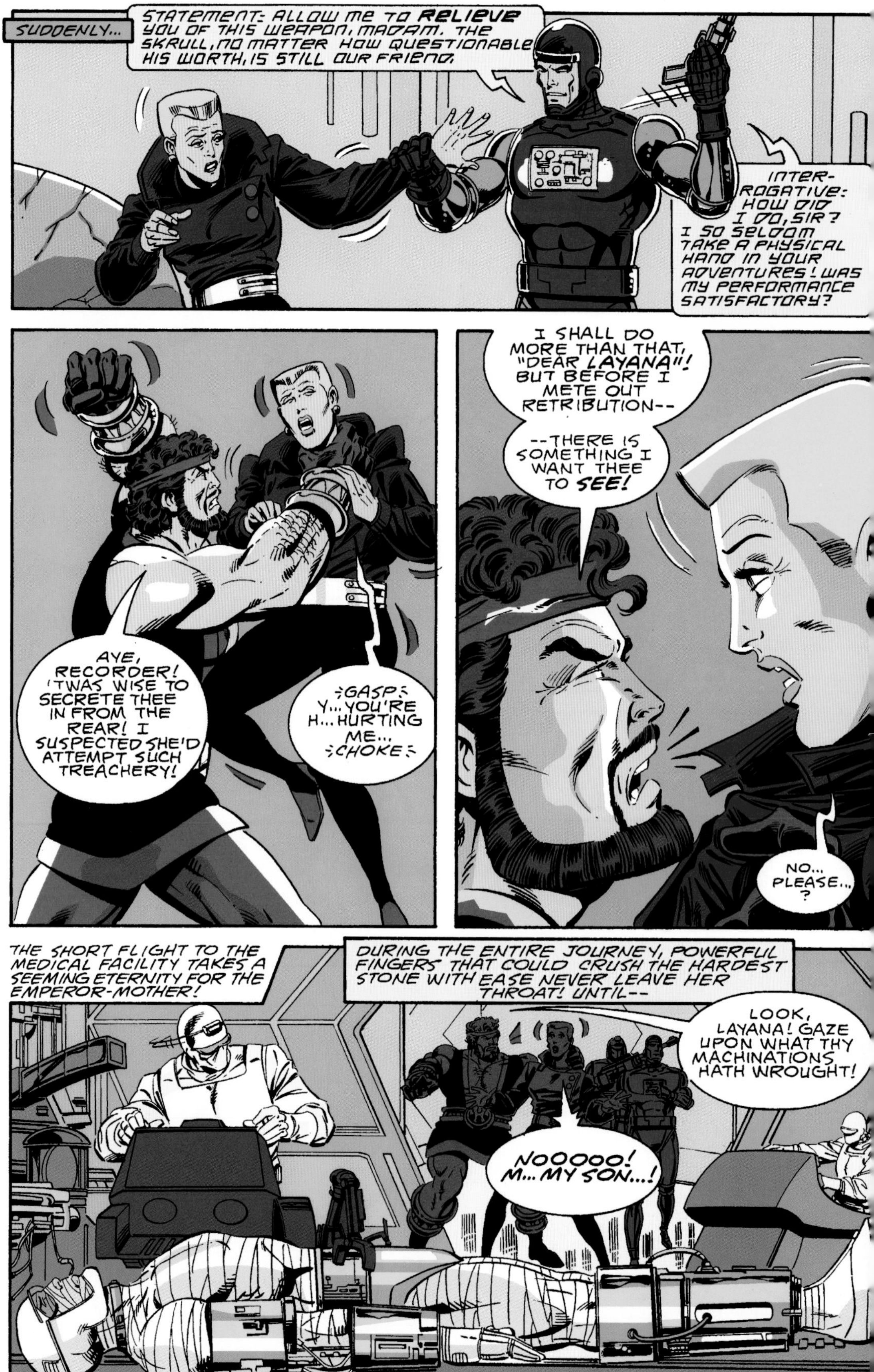
SUDDENLY...
STATEMENT: ALLOW ME TO RELIEVE YOU OF THIS WEAPON, MADAM. THE SKRULL, NO MATTER HOW QUESTIONABLE HIS WORTH, IS STILL OUR FRIEND.
INTERROGATIVE: HOW DID I DO, SIR? I SO SELDOM TAKE A PHYSICAL HAND IN YOUR ADVENTURES! WAS MY PERFORMANCE SATISFACTORY?
AYE, RECORDER! 'TWAS WISE TO SECRETE THEE IN FROM THE REAR! I SUSPECTED SHE'D ATTEMPT SUCH TREACHERY!
GASP Y... YOU'RE H... HURTING ME... CHOKE
I SHALL DO MORE THAN THAT, "DEAR LAYANA"! BUT BEFORE I METE OUT RETRIBUTION--
--THERE IS SOMETHING I WANT THEE TO SEE!
NO... PLEASE...?
THE SHORT FLIGHT TO THE MEDICAL FACILITY TAKES A SEEMING ETERNITY FOR THE EMPEROR-MOTHER!
DURING THE ENTIRE JOURNEY, POWERFUL FINGERS THAT COULD CRUSH THE HARDEST STONE WITH EASE NEVER LEAVE HER THROAT! UNTIL--
LOOK, LAYANA! GAZE UPON WHAT THY MACHINATIONS HATH WROUGHT!
NOOOOO! M... MY SON...!

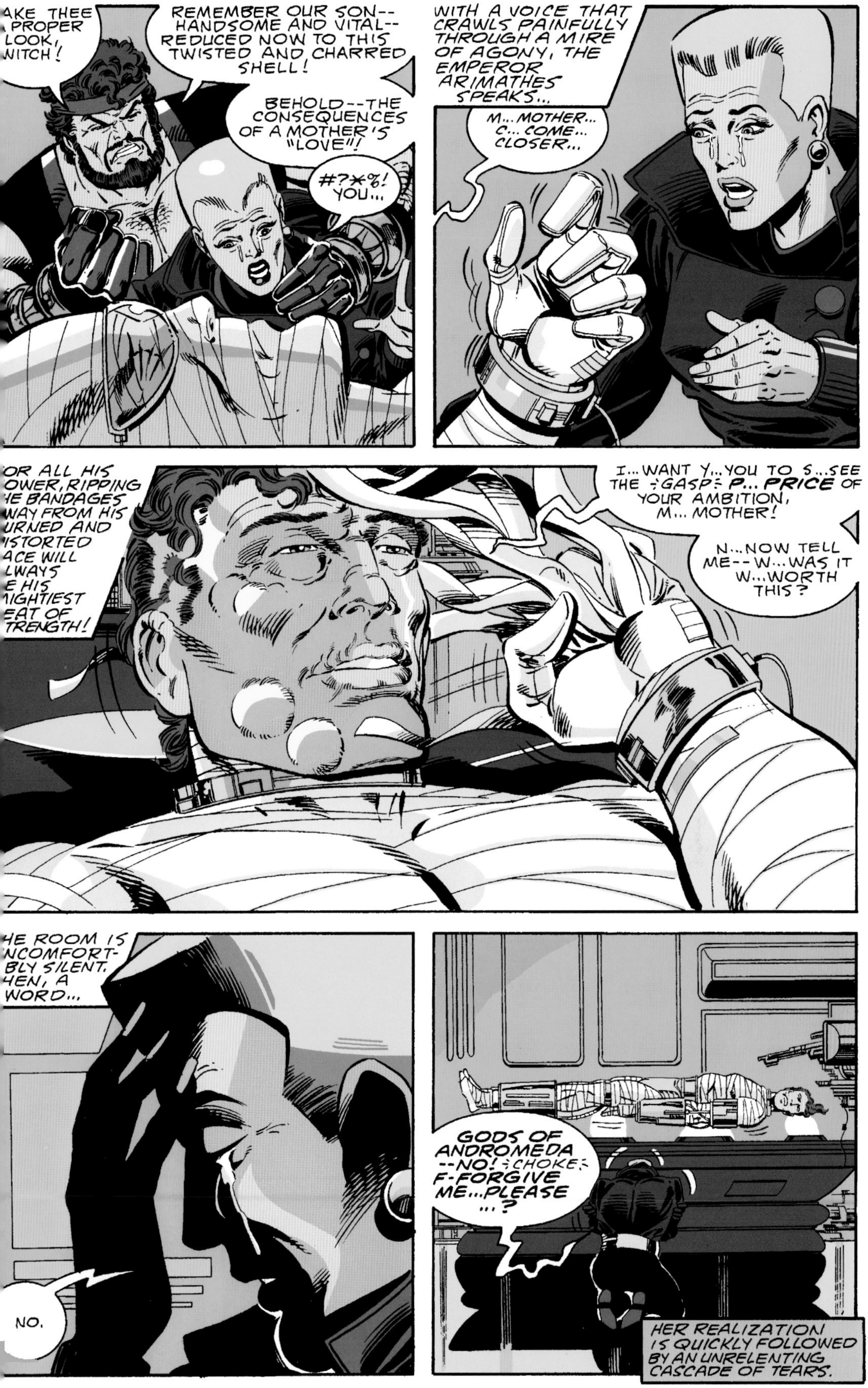
AKE THEE
PROPER
LOOK,
WITCH!
REMEMBER OUR SON--
HANDSOME AND VITAL--
REDUCED NOW TO THIS
TWISTED AND CHARRED
SHELL!
BEHOLD--THE
CONSEQUENCES
OF A MOTHER'S
"LOVE"!
#?*%!
YOU...
WITH A VOICE THAT
CRAWLS PAINFULLY
THROUGH A MIRE
OF AGONY, THE
EMPEROR
ARIMATHES
SPEAKS...
M...MOTHER...
C...COME...
CLOSER...
OR ALL HIS
OWER, RIPPING
HE BANDAGES
WAY FROM HIS
URNED AND
ISTORTED
ACE WILL
LWAYS
E HIS
MIGHTIEST
EAT OF
TRENGTH!
I...WANT Y...YOU TO S...SEE
THE ÷GASP÷ P...PRICE OF
YOUR AMBITION,
M...MOTHER!
N...NOW TELL
ME--W...WAS IT
W...WORTH
THIS?
HE ROOM IS
NCOMFORT-
BLY SILENT.
HEN, A
WORD...
NO.
GODS OF
ANDROMEDA
--NO! ÷CHOKE÷
F-FORGIVE
ME...PLEASE
...?
HER REALIZATION
IS QUICKLY FOLLOWED
BY AN UNRELENTING
CASCADE OF TEARS.

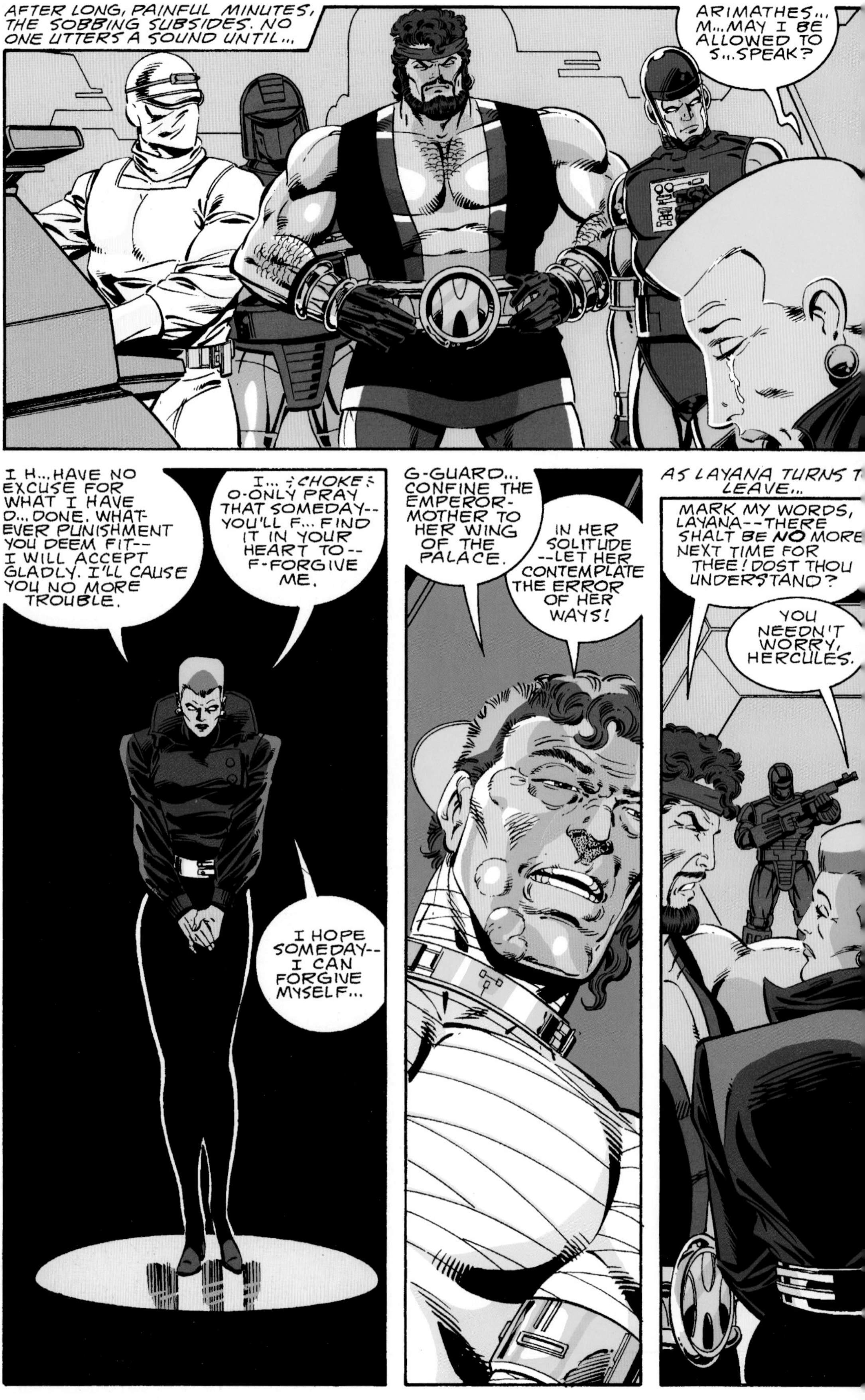
AFTER LONG, PAINFUL MINUTES, THE SOBBING SUBSIDES. NO ONE UTTERS A SOUND UNTIL...
ARIMATHES... M...MAY I BE ALLOWED TO S...SPEAK?
I H...HAVE NO EXCUSE FOR WHAT I HAVE D...DONE. WHATEVER PUNISHMENT YOU DEEM FIT-- I WILL ACCEPT GLADLY. I'LL CAUSE YOU NO MORE TROUBLE.
I... ;CHOKE; O-ONLY PRAY THAT SOMEDAY-- YOU'LL F... FIND IT IN YOUR HEART TO-- F-FORGIVE ME.
I HOPE SOMEDAY-- I CAN FORGIVE MYSELF...
G-GUARD... CONFINE THE EMPEROR-MOTHER TO HER WING OF THE PALACE.
IN HER SOLITUDE --LET HER CONTEMPLATE THE ERROR OF HER WAYS!
AS LAYANA TURNS T LEAVE...
MARK MY WORDS, LAYANA--THERE SHALT BE NO MORE NEXT TIME FOR THEE! DOST THOU UNDERSTAND?
YOU NEEDN'T WORRY, HERCULES.

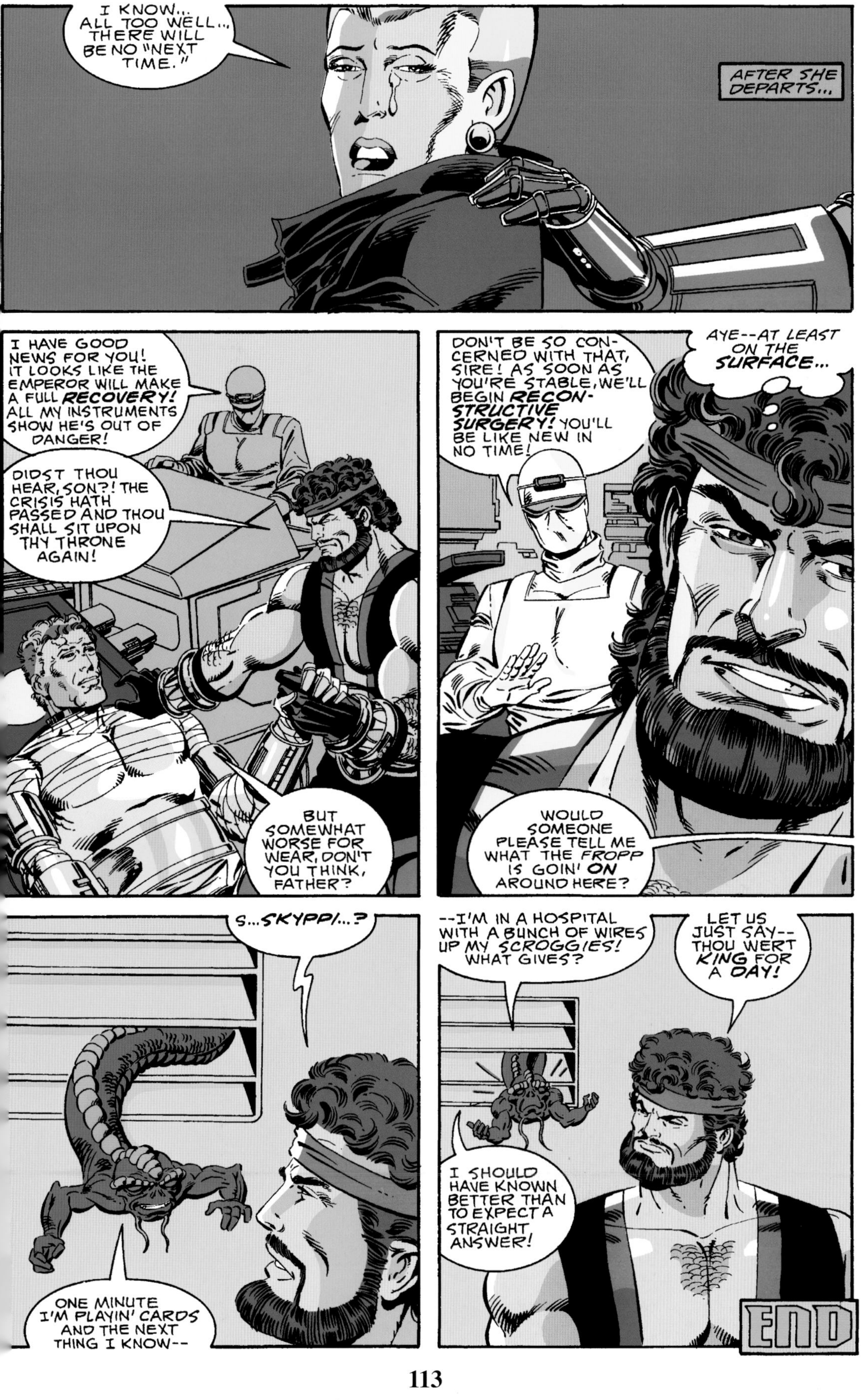
I KNOW... ALL TOO WELL... THERE WILL BE NO "NEXT TIME."
AFTER SHE DEPARTS...
I HAVE GOOD NEWS FOR YOU! IT LOOKS LIKE THE EMPEROR WILL MAKE A FULL RECOVERY! ALL MY INSTRUMENTS SHOW HE'S OUT OF DANGER!
DIDST THOU HEAR, SON?! THE CRISIS HATH PASSED AND THOU SHALL SIT UPON THY THRONE AGAIN!
BUT SOMEWHAT WORSE FOR WEAR, DON'T YOU THINK, FATHER?
DON'T BE SO CONCERNED WITH THAT, SIRE! AS SOON AS YOU'RE STABLE, WE'LL BEGIN RECONSTRUCTIVE SURGERY! YOU'LL BE LIKE NEW IN NO TIME!
AYE--AT LEAST ON THE SURFACE...
WOULD SOMEONE PLEASE TELL ME WHAT THE FROPP IS GOIN' ON AROUND HERE?
S...SKYPPI...?
ONE MINUTE I'M PLAYIN' CARDS AND THE NEXT THING I KNOW--
--I'M IN A HOSPITAL WITH A BUNCH OF WIRES UP MY SCROGGIES! WHAT GIVES?
LET US JUST SAY-- THOU WERT KING FOR A DAY!
I SHOULD HAVE KNOWN BETTER THAN TO EXPECT A STRAIGHT ANSWER!
END

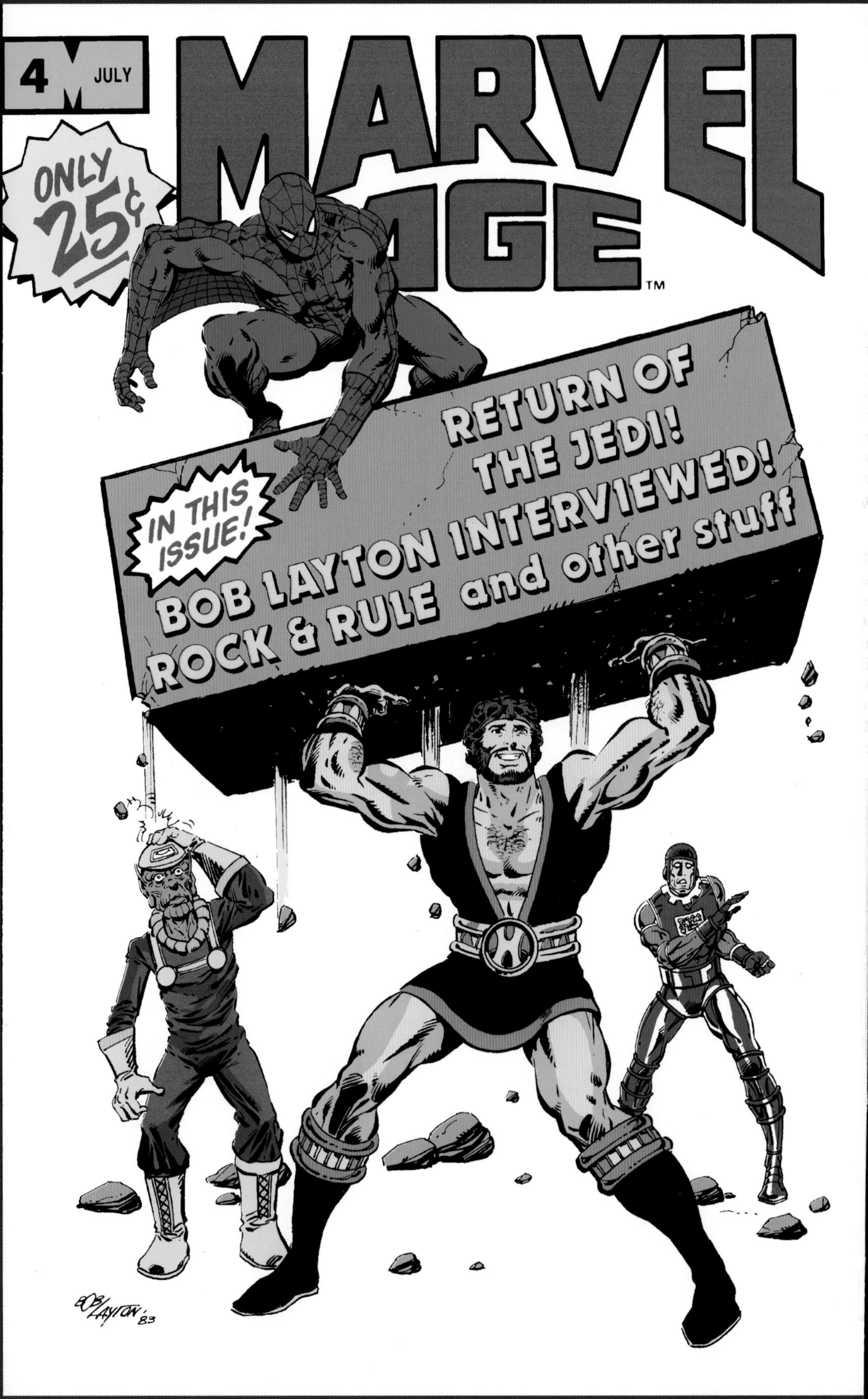

4
M
JULY
MARVEL AGE
TM
ONLY 25¢
IN THIS ISSUE!
RETURN OF THE JEDI!
BOB LAYTON INTERVIEWED!
ROCK & RULE and other stuff
BOB LAYTON '83

BABYFACED BOB LAYTON

by Steve Ringgenberg

In a relatively short span of time, Bob Layton went m being an assistant to artists such as Wally Wood and ck Giordano to become one of the industry's top inkers. llowing his first stint at Marvel, Layton worked for DC a year, then returned to Marvel to work as inker and co-iter on IRON MAN. After that, Layton turned to writ- and the result was last summer's Hercules mini-series, first mini-series to be successful enough to warrant a uel later this year. Layton will also be writing and draw- a new Spider-Man Graphic Novel.

ARVEL AGE: Why did you choose Spider-Man for a aphic Novel? Why Spider-Man of all the Marvel charac-s?

OB LAYTON: The particular story that I have; The ngs that I wanted to do with Peter Parker. It's not the d of story that would relate to, say, Captain America, or redevil — it's really exclusive to who Parker is as a per-, and why he can't seem to get his act together. Spider-n is not, was *never* one of my particular favorites, but I lly felt like this story was something that would really bring out a different side of him, and that would change his life to some degree.

MA: Will it involve radical changes in the character?

LAYTON: Not changes. Radical growth I imagine, to some degree. Some might think I'm wrong, but I see him as still being quite naive, especially when it comes to his personal life and dealing with other people, women in particular. And I wanted to get him into a situation that wasn't typically Spider-Man.

MA: Such as?

LAYTON: Well, Spider-Man undergoes a really traumatic event — he gets shot up really badly for the first time in his life. He's had colds and sprained his arm, that kind of thing. But here he's rescuing this woman who's the intended victim of a mob hit, and in a moment of decision, he makes a wrong move — he goes for his webs, and they're empty.

MA: After twenty years, he was about due to flub one.

LAYTON: Right. And he takes nine rounds of machine gun fire. So the woman he's just rescued gets him back to her house, and while he's being nursed back to health, he falls in love with her.

FOLLIES
BURLESK
SALE
cinerama
theatre
STEAKS
FORUM

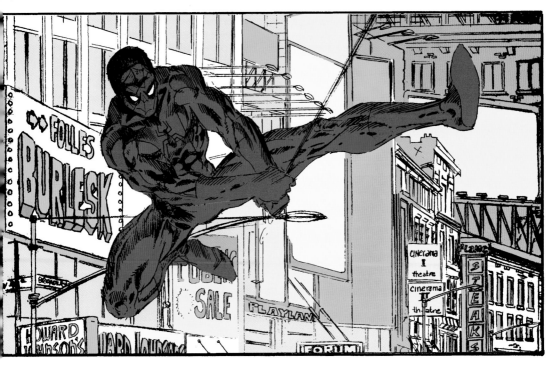

MA: And Spider-Man would be gun shy after the experience?

LAYTON: So why not just chuck Spider-Man altogether and live with this beautiful woman? Except, of course, that she's the wife of a gangland bigshot.

MA: He has an affair with a married woman?

LAYTON: Yeah, and that's all I'll say about it.

MA: I assume this takes place over some months. How does it fit into the continuity of the series?

LAYTON: There is no continuity in Graphic Novels. If you talk to Jim Shooter, I think he would tell you the same thing I'm going to tell you, that the Graphic Novels are supposed to be major events in the lives of the characters; not something beyond what *could* happen, or would even be allowed to happen in the regular series. When a story happens in a Graphic Novel, it should be something that is referred to for the rest of the character's existence. Yeah, this is going to change him a little bit, but I don't think in a radical way. I don't think he's going to come out of it with a total personality change. Other writers, of course have the option to refer to it or not, but I imagine they will.

MA: Are there going to be any super-villains in this book?

LAYTON: This is one of the reasons why I'm really particulary excited about this story, is that it could actually be a non-super-hero story, and still work.

MA: And you're going to be penciling, inking, and writing?

LAYTON: I'll be doing it all. Except for the coloring, I think Christie Scheele is coloring it.

MA: How much of an influence on your version of Spider-Man, artistically, that is, were the interpretation's of other artists?

LAYTON: I think it's natural to do the Spider-Man that everyone's come to know. I'm not going to get really outlandish with it. I mean, my Spider-Man will vary from Paul Smith's Spider-Man or John Romita Jr.'s Spider-Man. It just so happens that my style happens to be pretty close to what J.R. does anyway. I'm very influenced by him, having worked with him for so long on *Iron Man*. You know, you can't help but come off drawing a little bit like him. I hope I picked up some good things from him. I never really know what it's going to look like, though, until I ink it. Because many people say that, the guts of my drawing is in the inks, not the pencils, so the pencils are more concerned with storytelling. The drawing and the rendering and everything comes in later and that usually determines what the book's going to look like. I never really know. It's like with Herc, I really didn't know what kind of look the book would take until after I started inking it.

MA: You first started as an inker, right?

LAYTON: That's right, yeah.

MA: You were on *Iron Man*, I believe.

LAYTON: For Marvel, yeah, I think I did two stints at Marvel. I worked here in '75, and I went over to DC for a year.

MA: What did you do over there?

LAYTON: I did *All-Star Comics* and *Starhunters, Claw the Unconquered*. That's where I first teamed up with Dave Michelinie, and after a year at DC we came over here and did *Iron Man* together, so it was just like continuing our team-up that we had over at DC.

MA: When did you start writing?

LAYTON: I started writing last year, with *Hercules*, actually. Although I had co-plotted the 38 or so issues of *Iron Man* that I did with Dave. Dave was a tremendous learning experience; I think he is a really good writer. And he knows the technical aspects of writing better than anybody. And through the years of co-plotting with him, I got a little more confident as I went along and I felt like the time was right, and I always wanted to write, but I waited until such a time that I felt comfortable with the notion. Then I went to Jim with the Hercules concept and he said: "Take a chance, go out and do it."

MA: Well, it seems to have worked out really well.

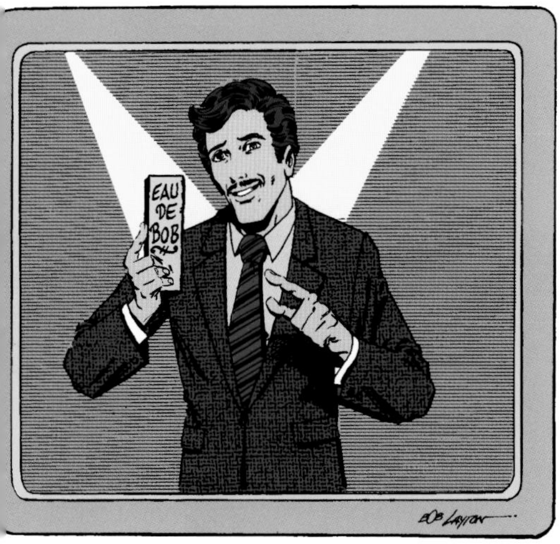
EAU DE BOB

AYTON: Oh, apparently it was tremendously success-l, yes.
[A: Were you surprised that it was that successful?
AYTON: I didn't do it as a success thing. I really thought was the kind of thing I wanted to write. I wanted to write rt of tongue in cheek, sort of James Bond kind of stories, d I wanted to do some fantasy, because Iron Man was avily entrenched in reality, with a lot of modern day stuff d modern dress and all that. I wanted to do something here I could create everything from the ground up. And, I as a little amazed that it sold as well as it did. I'm *glad*. nd I think that's what precipitated us doing the second ini-series. My understanding from Jim is that it was one the top-selling books of '82.
A: It was nice that you did do it with kind of a light touch stead of stony seriousness.
AYTON: I love the books here. I think all our books are scinating and completely well done. But, I feel that a lot them really take themselves too seriously, and I really anted to get into a frame of mind with the strip that it just nd of coasted along and everybody was having a good ne. That was the primary concern, and I was just having a od time with it, you know? And getting people maybe to en laugh out loud, which I think is rare when you're ading a comic. As I mentioned before, about James ond, which I think is a really good formula for doing mor: you have a straight, simple adventure story first. ond is fighting the bad guy, who's fighting over the ulti-ate whatchamadig, but they never resist the chance to row in a gag, throw in a laugh, although they keep the aight storyline going. Any chance they get to throw in mething humorous, to do a gag, they do. And I really felt e that's the approach that I wanted to take.
A: A lot of the humor was derived from the verbal ex-anges between Hercules and the other characters.
AYTON: Right, right. Well, you know, part of it is his akeup, too. The fact that Hercules is not what you would ll the most religious person in the world. And he is so im-ılsive that he will do something and think about the con-quences later, which I tried to bring out in that strip. That akes him a great character to use in any particular situa-on.
A: Are you going to use the same kind of approach in the xt mini-series?

LAYTON: More or less, although it takes a little more serious vein in the next one. The same formula that I used on the first series will be there in the second, but I'm introducing a second sidekick as well as the Recorder; there's a 400 year-old geriatric Skrull named Skyppi, who will be Herc's other sidekick... Actually he's going to be the Recorder's sidekick. The sidekick of the sidekick. But it will take a little more serious vein as it builds up towards the ending. It's going to have a galacitc, climactic ending. It's going to be a Greek version of Ragnarok. You know, something that really wasn't clear in the first mini-series was that it took place centuries in the future. In the new strip it's even further — four hundred years — and Herc finally returns to Olympus to find that practically all the gods are dead. Only he and Zeus are left, and Zeus has flipped out completely. So Herc has a final battle with Zeus to preserve his own immortality.
MA: And when is this supposed to be out?
LAYTON: Well, my understanding is that it has an October release. You know, after I finish the Graphic Novel, I'll start on Hercules, and I think the final release date is sometime in October.
MA: And the Graphic Novel is for next summer?
LAYTON: Next summer. I think the release date's in July.
MA: And what else are you working on besides the Hercules mini-series and the Spider-Man Graphic Novel?
LAYTON: That's pretty much it for the time being. That's enough, isn't it? You're talking about an immense load of work here. I talked with Tom DeFalco about the possibility of a Hercules Graphic Novel after I finish the mini-series; that's a possibility. If not, I'd like to get back onto a regular series, something I can write and draw. I may do another

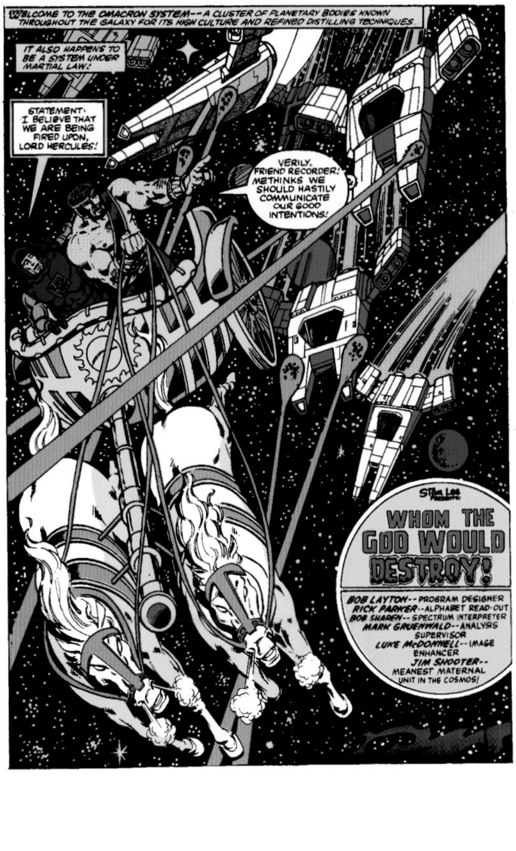
WELCOME TO THE OMACRON SYSTEM-- A CLUSTER OF PLANETARY BODIES KNOWN THROUGHOUT THE GALAXY FOR ITS HIGH CULTURE AND REFINED DISTILLING TECHNIQUES...
IT ALSO HAPPENS TO BE A SYSTEM UNDER MARTIAL LAW!
STATEMENT: I BELIEVE THAT WE ARE BEING FIRED UPON, LORD HERCULES!
VERILY, FRIEND RECORDER! METHINKS WE SHOULD HASTILY COMMUNICATE OUR GOOD INTENTIONS!
WHOM THE GOD WOULD DESTROY!
BOB LAYTON-- PROGRAM DESIGNER
RICK PARKER--ALPHABET READ-OUT
BOB SHAREN-- SPECTRUM INTERPRETER
MARK GRUENWALD-- ANALYSIS SUPERVISOR
LUKE McDONNELL-- IMAGE ENHANCER
JIM SHOOTER-- MEANEST MATERNAL UNIT IN THE COSMOS!

mini-series, I don't know... I like doing a regular book, though. I enjoyed Iron Man immensely, just because I had a chance to really grow with the character. And I did a *long* stint on that, and I wouldn't mind finding a character I really wanted to do up here and go with it...

MA: Any characters in particular?

LAYTON: Well, no. Not at the moment. The thing is, it's too far ahead for me to think about. I have an idea for a mini-series I want to do with Red Wolf, Marvel's Indian Western character...

MA: oh, yeah. He hasn't been used in ages.

LAYTON: I know. And I have this real affection for "third-rate" characters.

MA: That's what I was going to say. Hercules was always sort of a second-rater...

LAYTON: Not anymore. The thing is, that's what I'd like to do with Red Wolf. I'd like to just get my hands on him and totally revamp him. Maybe sometime in the future.

MA: Now how are you going to handle doing the Graphic Novel, are you going to sit down and do the script first and then break it down visually?

LAYTON: No. What I do is, I've already plotted it and I sat down and worked that out with DeFalco and we had a lot of wonderful arguments over it. Then I break it down in outline form; (since I'm drawing it myself, I don't really need to go into big descriptions), and I'm penciling it from that. And then once it's all penciled, then I'll sit down and start the script from the pencils.

MA: Do you find it's more satisfying to be working on your own scripts?

LAYTON: Oh yeah, well of course, because there's a lot of advantages. First, you get a purer product in the sense that I can't crab about the artist because it's me. Also, it

saves a lot of time, I think, for the company too, when y have somebody like a Frank Miller or John Byrne, who c do the whole job themselves. They can cut a lot of corne save a lot of time and a lot of paperwork and a lot of maili and things like that. It's all coming out of one guy.

MA: Yeah, but don't you miss the creative energy of c laboration?

LAYTON: Well, sure. I mean, whenever you have som body you can collaborate with, that's always going to b lot of fun or whatever, but you've got to remember, I that for a *long* time and that was all fine and good, but... good things come to an end. I think it's a finite thing don't think you can just go on forever. I mean, I wanted go on and I couldn't write Iron Man because Dave's writer. So, I had no choice, if I wanted to write, I *had* leave the book. And I really had to pursue my own goa And it wasn't any sort of hassle or anything, I loved wo ing with Dave, I think we did a good job.

MA: Do you enjoy inking more than penciling?

LAYTON: No. The thing is, I've been inking for alm eight years now and I think I get more pure satisfacti from writing. I even considered for a while giving up dra ing and just working as a writer. There is a lot of emjo ment to writing, you know. It's also the fact that it's n and it's like I'm starting from square one again. With i ing I feel there's only so far you can go, and then you ha to work on your drawing, that's the only way your inki gets better. There's a point where penciling, writing and king all become the same thing: that's storytelling. On you understand that, it makes you capable of doing work all by yourself.

But, I think inking is something that I'm going to less and less of in the future. Although, as I said, I s enjoy it. I just did a Spider-Man with John Romita Jr. j because I missed him. You know, I hadn't inked his stuff

Red Wolf

118

Db Layton

o long, and I love his pencils and I love inking them, that 'om offered me an issue to do, so I just said: 'Why not?' or old times sake... He's still my favorite person to ink.

MA: What kind of training have you had?

LAYTON: No actual art schooling. I worked starting out s an assistant to Wally Wood, and Dick Giordano and 'rank McLaughlin.

MA: What was Wood like to work for? Was he a demanding boss?

LAYTON: It was fun. Oh, he knew what he wanted, no loubt about it, but it was a lot of fun because I don't think le ever really took it all that seriously. A lot of times, vorking with Woody was just story after story, you know, about various things. And the thing was, Woody was such n incredible teacher and he didn't realize it. I don't think le really realized how much I got out of him, just in the hort amount of time I worked for him. He never credited limself as really being a teacher, but he worked out a system of explaining things that was so perfect and simple, I hink he could teach anybody how to draw. He really ould. He was amazing.

MA: How about working with Dick Giordano?

LAYTON: Actually, you know, I say I was working with)ick Giordano, it wasn't quite like that. I did a few jobs for lim and so forth, but Dick lived very close to me, when I irst moved out to Connecticut. And I used to ride in and go lack and forth on trains with Dick from New York, coming o work at Continuity Studios. I'd always pin him down nd I got a two hour art lesson going in, and a two hour art esson coming back. And this was like twice a week for a vear, year and a half... so I credit Dick as being a teacher lecause he really is. Dick's an incredible teacher. You :now, most of the guys in this business, half of 'em at east, if they hadn't worked for Woody, they worked for)ick, and I always got a lot of encouragement and a lot of

private lessons from Dick, you know. He was always willing to help me out.

MA: Are there any artists you still look to for influence?

LAYTON: I think you look at everybody, and you're influenced by everybody around you.

When I say influenced, it doesn't mean that I was copying neccessarily from one guy or another, it's just that a lot of what they do, I've been there. With pencilers, I really admire guys like Gil Kane, Jim Starlin. When I was a fan, I really loved Starlin's stuff because it was just right there, straight and simple, you know, and it was powerful. I look at guys like Gil Kane and I think, Wow, that's marvelous. I'm still fascinated with the simplicity. Alex Toth: simplicity at work. Because I think that's what comics comes down to: telling the maximum amount of story with the minimum amount of work involved. You know, it's like the minimum amount of line, the minimum amount of writing. That's why Frank Miller's so good.

MA: Yeah, it's all real spare.

LAYTON: And he gives you everything you need. He realized that it's a visual medium and he gives you that. And, therefore, he doesn't have to weigh it down with a lot of copy. To me, it's good comics.

MA: Are you going to be striving for that kind of simplicity...?

LAYTON: Yeah. well, we all do, I mean, at least we all try, and if you look at a page and you see it's just word heavy, loaded with copy, I think it turns a reader off. It kind of breaks up the visual excitement of reading a comic book, when you just have to wade through balloons and balloons and balloons of dialogue. It also means that it's not there in the pictures, and it should be because, this is a visual medium.

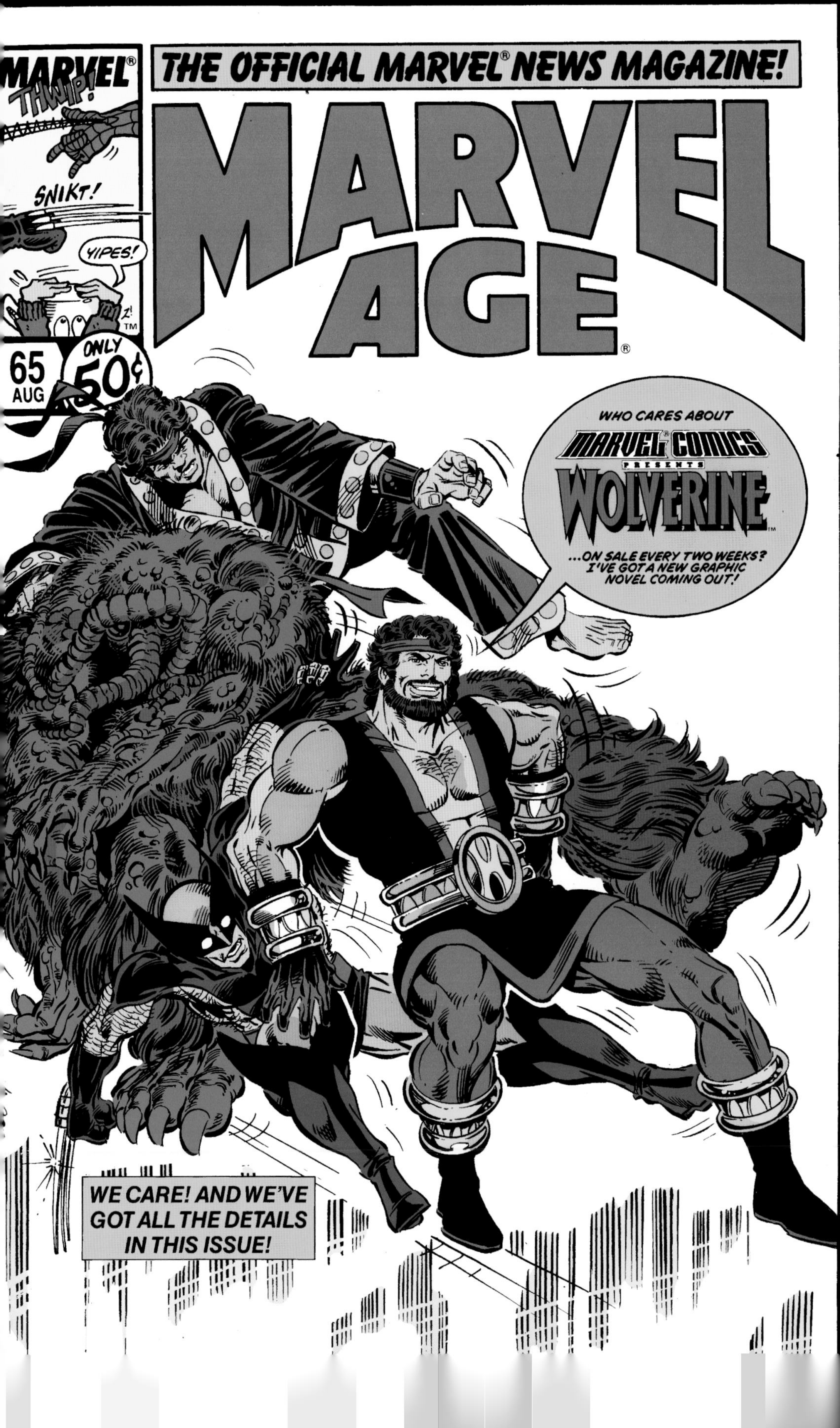

MARVEL®
THWIP!
SNIKT!
YIPES!
™
THE OFFICIAL MARVEL® NEWS MAGAZINE!
MARVEL AGE®
65
AUG
ONLY 50¢
WHO CARES ABOUT
MARVEL® COMICS PRESENTS WOLVERINE™
...ON SALE EVERY TWO WEEKS? I'VE GOT A NEW GRAPHIC NOVEL COMING OUT!
WE CARE! AND WE'VE GOT ALL THE DETAILS IN THIS ISSUE!

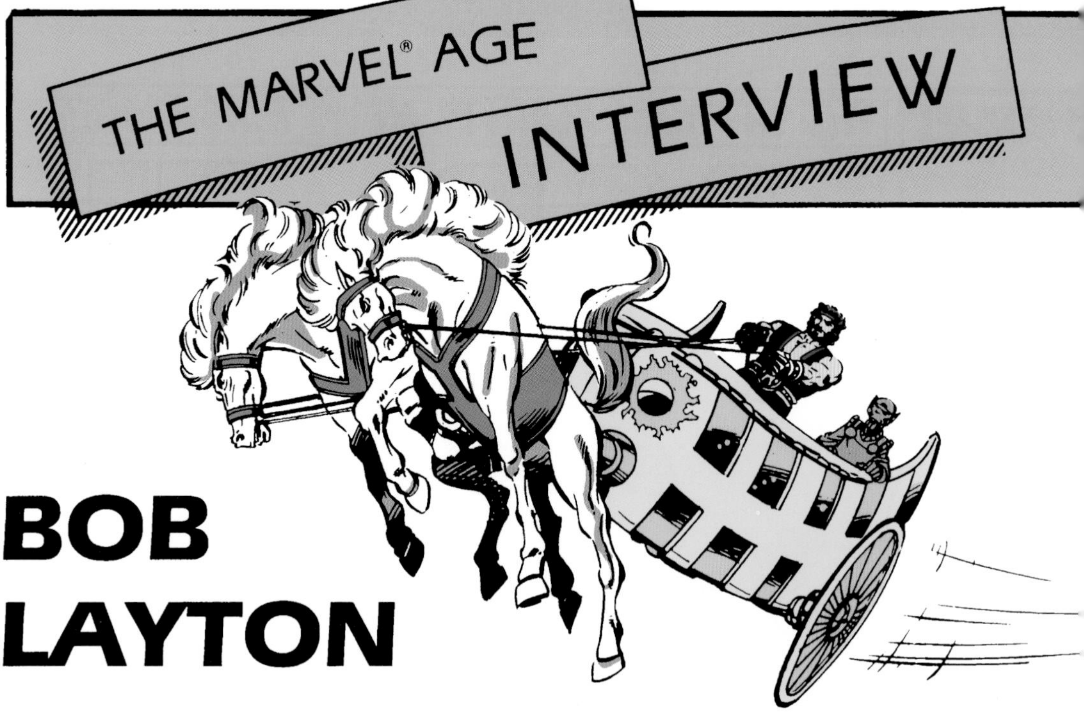
THE MARVEL® AGE
INTERVIEW

BOB LAYTON

Why Bob Layton? Who is he? Well, for starters he is one of the co-creators of X-FACTOR. He's written and drawn *two* Limited Series and worked on many of Marvel's top titles including IRON MAN! And now he has a Graphic Novel coming out, starring the same big guy he did two Limited Series of: HERCULES. I talked with Bob on a rainy Friday while CAPTAIN AMERICA penciler, **Kieron Dwyer**, merely sat there taking up space. This is what I got:

GREG: Okay, Bob. Why **Hercules**?

BOB: You mean originally, years ago?

GREG: Yes, the first Limited Series.

BOB: I had just come off a successful run of IRON MAN (with **David Michelinie** and **John Romita Jr.**), which took place in a more realistic setting. A setting of industrial intrigue and espionage, fast cars and fast living. And, I wanted to do something in the fantasy vein. Something with a more tongue-in-cheek approach. IRON MAN was fairly serious. W dealt with alcoholism and things of th nature. I really wanted to try som thing a little more light-hearted. Som thing that kind of poked fun at the gra diose scale of the Marvel Univers For so long, characters such as **Gala tus** and the **Skrulls** have been take so seriously, and most of the write up here have done their own versic of the Kree-Skrull epic. I wanted say, "Well, they're *all* kind of goof Outer space is a goofy place with a l of strange looking "people" ar "things." Herc seemed to be a prin candidate for all that, being a fiv thousand year old adolescent. H would stand out like a sore thumb in pristine, highly advanced civilization

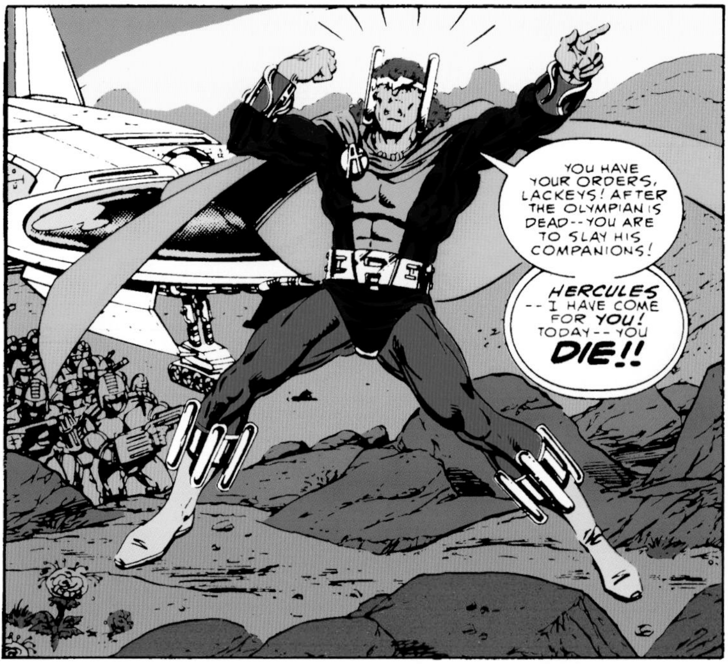
YOU HAVE YOUR ORDERS, LACKEYS! AFTER THE OLYMPIAN IS DEAD--YOU ARE TO SLAY HIS COMPANIONS!
HERCULES --I HAVE COME FOR YOU! TODAY--YOU DIE!!

GREG: What made you decide do the second Limited Series?

BOB: Actually, Marvel decided tha would do a second one. Hercules, well as **Wolverine** were the first tw Limited Series that Marvel did, act ally. Both were very successful. **Ji Shooter**, who was editor in chief at th time, came to me and said "This wa fun and we did real well with this. Ca you do it again? But don't do the sam thing, use Herc." So I did.

GREG: In the first Limited Serie (which is being reprinted in a trac paperback), Herc was sent out to lear humility. What was the basis for th second Limited Series?

BOB: Well, he was humbled a lot the first Limited Series and the secor was . . . what did he learn? Did h learn any thing at all? As you can te from it, not much! But enough. I thir that comics should deal with the mo nportant issues facing our audience, nd that's growing up. Most of us who 'ork in this business are still facing ıose issues. We grew up with the haracters in the Marvel Universe. hey grew as we did. HERCULES is a ın way to present problems faced by dolescents.

KIERON: Being that Herc is a five ıousand year old adolescent.

BOB: Right. Exactly. Had he been orn in the sixties, he'd be hot-roddin' own the boulevard looking for hot ıicks.

GREG: So what we get in the ıraphic Novel is an adult — uh, a ıore mature Hercules. What is left for 'm to learn?

BOB: The thing is, Herc didn't learn ery much. But he learned enough. I ealized, growing up myself, being a ather — you know that old line "When ou hear yourself you sound like your arents"?

GREG: Yeah.

BOB: It occurred to me that some-'here along the line Herc should ound like his father, **Zeus**. He is going) understand what his father was try-ıg to do by making him "grow up so ast." The idea of the Graphic Novel is) bring this "Full Circle," which is the tle of the story. I wanted to put Herc in ıe role of his father and Herc's son in ıe role of Herc. So we're back to the riginal premise, but this time all the haracters have played musical hairs. Herc's son is hovering on the dge of good and evil. And it's a real fe or death situation for Herc. It

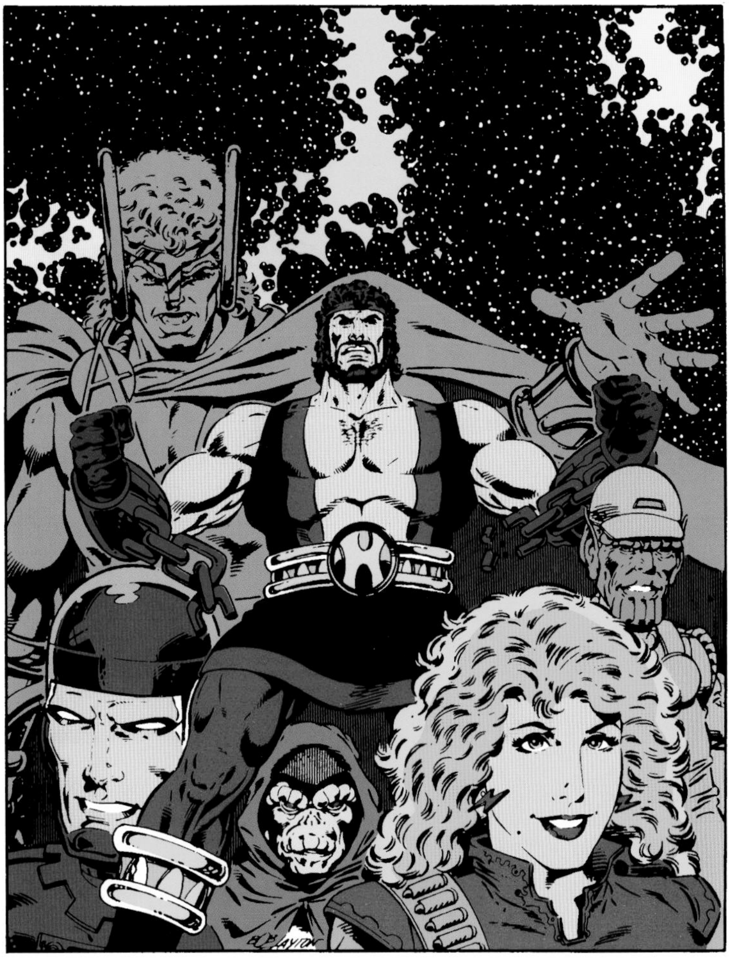

Art is from the HERCULES Graphic Novel

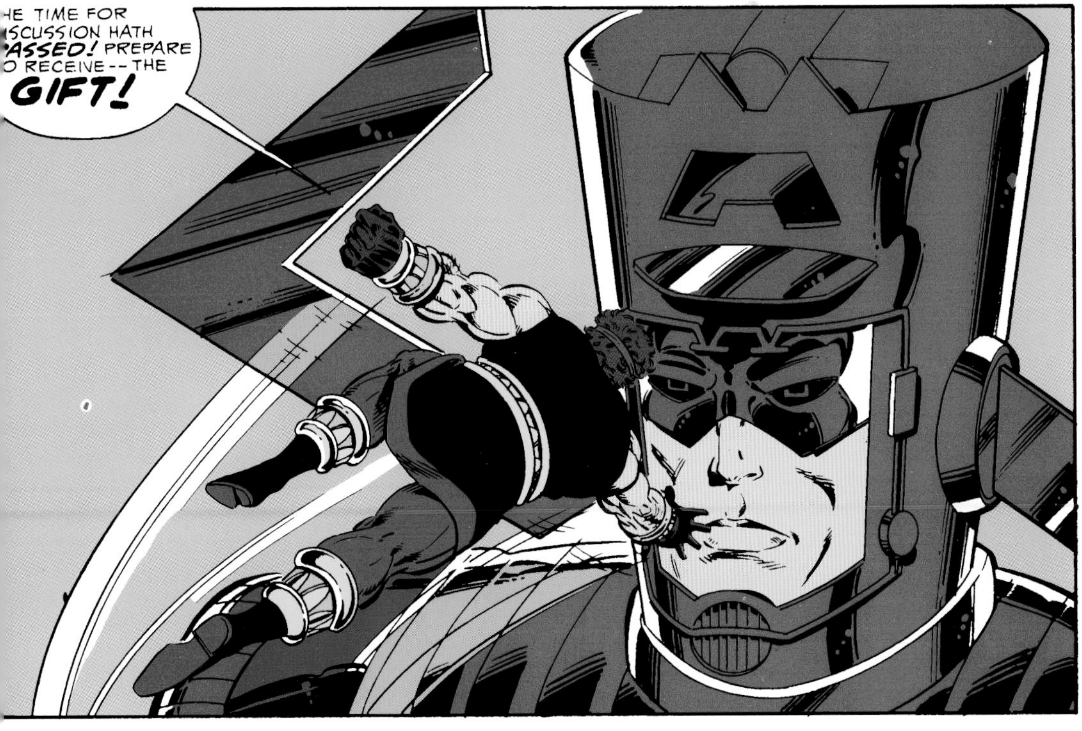
HE TIME FOR
SCUSSION HATH
ASSED! PREPARE
O RECEIVE -- THE
GIFT!

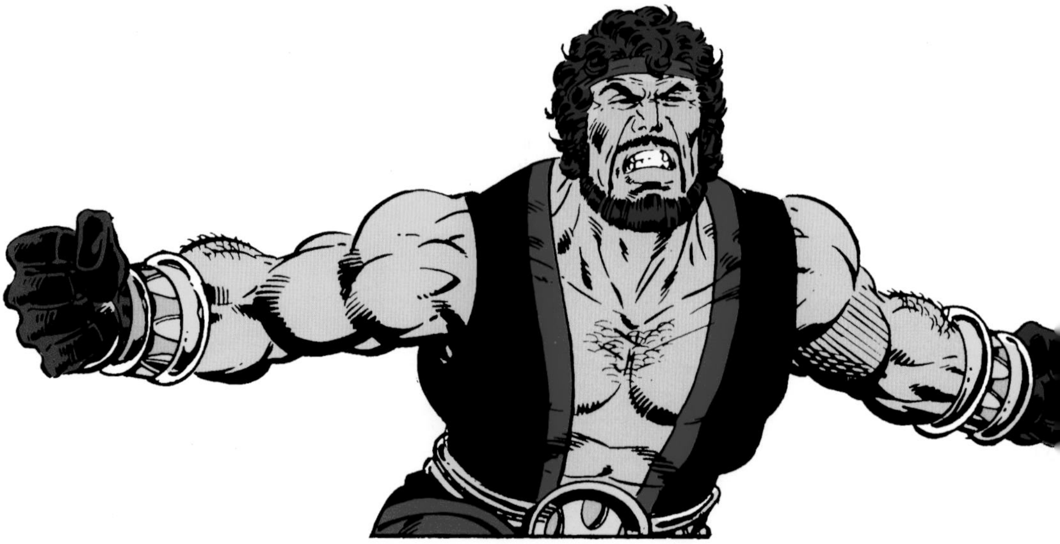

sounds pretty grim, but it is done in the same light-hearted manner as both Limited Series. There's **Skyppi** the Skrull, the **Recorder**, grills and bars (or is that bar and grills?), chases, Herc's bevy of beauties, and of course, a giant inflatable GALACTUS doll, without which, no story is complete.

GREG: On sale in comic shops everywhere?

BOB: Yeah! After the purchase of the Graphic Novel!

GREG: Hey, there's an idea, think Marvel would do it?

BOB: I just want to say that Kieron Dwyer has nothing to do with this Graphic Novel, but he is here.

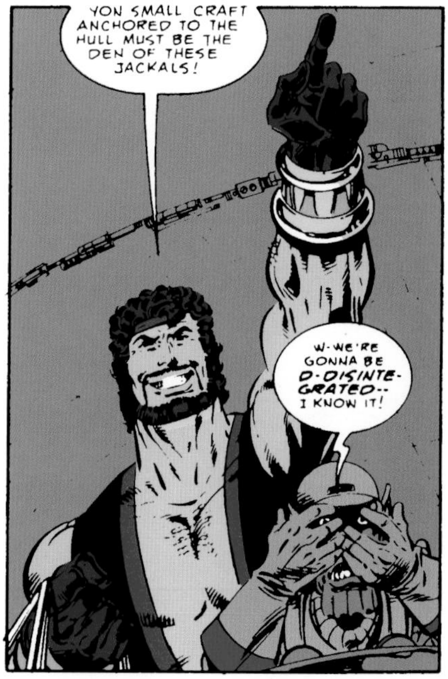
YON SMALL CRAFT ANCHORED TO THE HULL MUST BE THE DEN OF THESE JACKALS!
W-WE'RE GONNA BE D-DISINTE-GRATED-- I KNOW IT!

THE GRAPHIC

"So . . . Onward friends! I have a destiny to fulfill an new race that awaits aborning!" shouted **Hercules** at conclusion of his second Limited Series.

Riding off into the stars, his faithful **Recorder** and t trusted **Skyppi the Skrull** at his side, the scion of Olymp probably wouldn't have been so eager to accomodate Fates had he known what was awaiting him in the pages his first Graphic Novel.

Only moments before Hercules rode away with friends in the second Limited Series, his father, **Zeus**, h briefly explained why he had previously banished his fav ite son from Olympus. As the Fates had long since decre there would come a time when a new race of demi-go would appear to replace Zeus and his immortal clan. W ried that Hercules wasn't maturing fast enough to fulfill preordained role of sire to a new race, his father h prompted him through the maturing process. (It all start in the first HERCULES Limited Series, which if you miss the first time around, is now available in a high-quality tra paperback.) In his zeal to join his fellow immortals in t Olympian equivalent of Heaven, Zeus apparently "forg to tell Hercules he had already inadvertantly fathered first child of this race of new gods — and that was thi years ago!

Imagine Hercules' surprise then, when in the first f pages of "Full Circle," the new 74-page Graphic Novel **Bob Layton**, he discovers he missed out on those tenc years when male-bonding occurs between father and s For that matter, by the time Hercules learns of the existen of young **Arimathes**, his thirty year old son has alrea done quite well for himself by becoming the invincible c queror turned despotic ruler of a good portion of the dromeda Galaxy. And on top of that, Arimathes hates father's immortal guts!

Rather than reveling in his son's dubious accompli ments, an angered and ashamed Hercules ponders wh his son went astray. He has to look no farther than the r power behind the throne, **Layana Sweetwater**! (Hercul spurned lover from the second issue of the first Limi Series.) Still the grand manipulator of men and power t

KIERON: I'll read it.

GREG: Is this the end of the "Herc aga" for you?

BOB: That's a great question. You ow the answer though.

GREG: I'll fake my surprise. No one ll know.

BOB: I just did my first present-day erc story for SOLO AVENGERS, so ere is that. But the future Herc . . . I ended to wrap up the story, but arted asking more questions and . . . n, well, let's put it this way. For now the end of my Herc. But chances e I'll do it again because I love the aracter so much.

GREG: So what else are you work- on these days?

BOB: My sanity. I'm doing IRON AN of course. Kieron doesn't have anything to do with that either, although he has drawn him in CAPTAIN AMERICA! I ink and co-plot IRON MAN with the incredibly talented David Michelinie, who co-plots and scripts the book, and dazzling new penciler **Jackson Guice**. Check it out. I'm having a great time with the book. We have some exciting plans for the future. Look for the return of the **Ghost**, a refurbished version of the **Mandarin**, and a significant tragic event for **Tony Stark**. And of course guest stars such as **Spider-Man** and **Ant Man**.

GREG: Any new projects coming up?

BOB: Well, Dave and I would like to do POWER MAN. The original version of LUKE CAGE — HERO FOR HIRE by **Archie Goodwin** were some of the best comics written. I think the premise got a little lost over time. We'd like to do the book more like the original and call it CAGE — THE LEGEND OF POWER MAN. He would basically be a bounty hunter going after escaped bad guys such as **Doc Ock**. We may do a one-shot and if it does well . . .

GREG: Do you have anything to say to only readers of MARVEL AGE MAGAZINE?

BOB: Yes. I've done more covers than anyone else for MARVEL AGE MAGAZINE.

And there you have it. Thanks to Bob and Maxell tape for this informative look into the . . . into the . . . aw, just thanks.

—Gregory Wright

NOVEL

e was during their first encounter three decades before, y now aged and embittered by memories of her unreted love, she's used her son's inherited godlike strength d other abilities to subjugate the planets in her star sys- of Wilamean.

Whereas a younger, more immature Hercules would ely have come out swinging in his noble attempt to free tyrannically ruled inhabitants of an enslaved galaxy, this re version of the Prince of Power is only slightly more ned as he's inclined to deal with the conflict as a father ead of as a warrior born. Realizing that his estranged is precariously balanced on the precipice of Good and , convinced that misguided Arimathes is capable of at acts of nobility and compassion — Hercules does his t to resolve both the galactic and familial conflicts he ounters.

lthough, as always, Hercules' heart is in the right place, becomes painfully aware that for all his vaunted ngth, he can't keep from suffering the same fate that faced all first-time fathers since time immemorial. That e's forced to stumble through the child-rearing experie in a series of sometimes comical, sometimes poign- trials and errors. Naturally lacking in the grace and macy of such notable fathers as **Mike Brady** and **Cliff table**, Hercules attempts to bridge the communication by imparting Arimathes the ancient wisdom that's ned by being on the receiving end of "The Gift!" (Trans- d, that means the spoiled brat gets a good sound spank- In true Olympian tradition however, this could mean a nking to the Death!)

ong the way there are appearances by Layana's exiled usband, a spy who was on the receiving end of one of ules' legendary drinking bouts (what this spy does to athes' sandals has to be seen to be appreciated!), and Galactus(?)! The core of the story, however, revolves nd Hercules' latest adventure as the hot-headed per- al child grows up to discover he's the father of his own eaded perpetual child and that his life has verily come rcle . . .

—Scott Lobdell

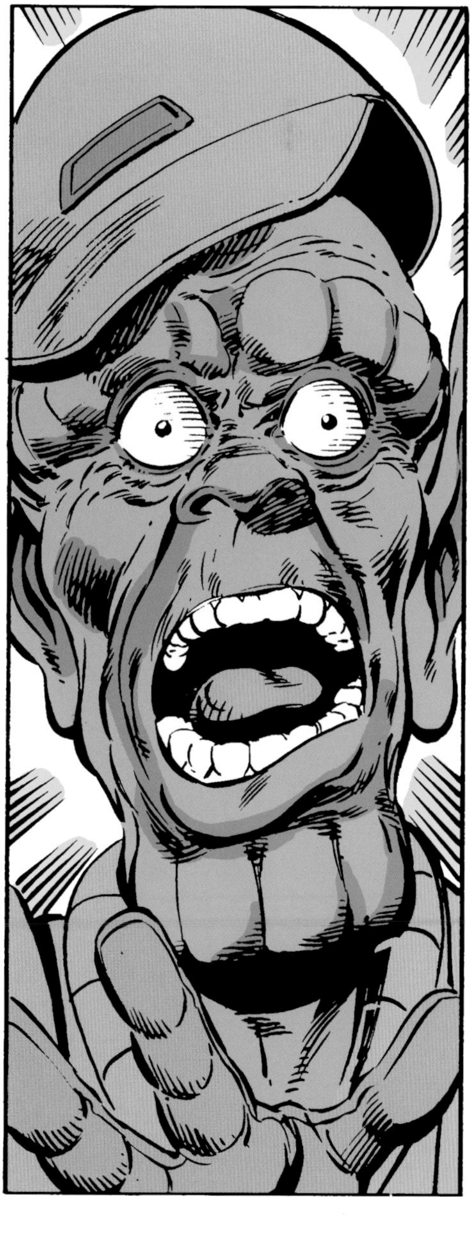

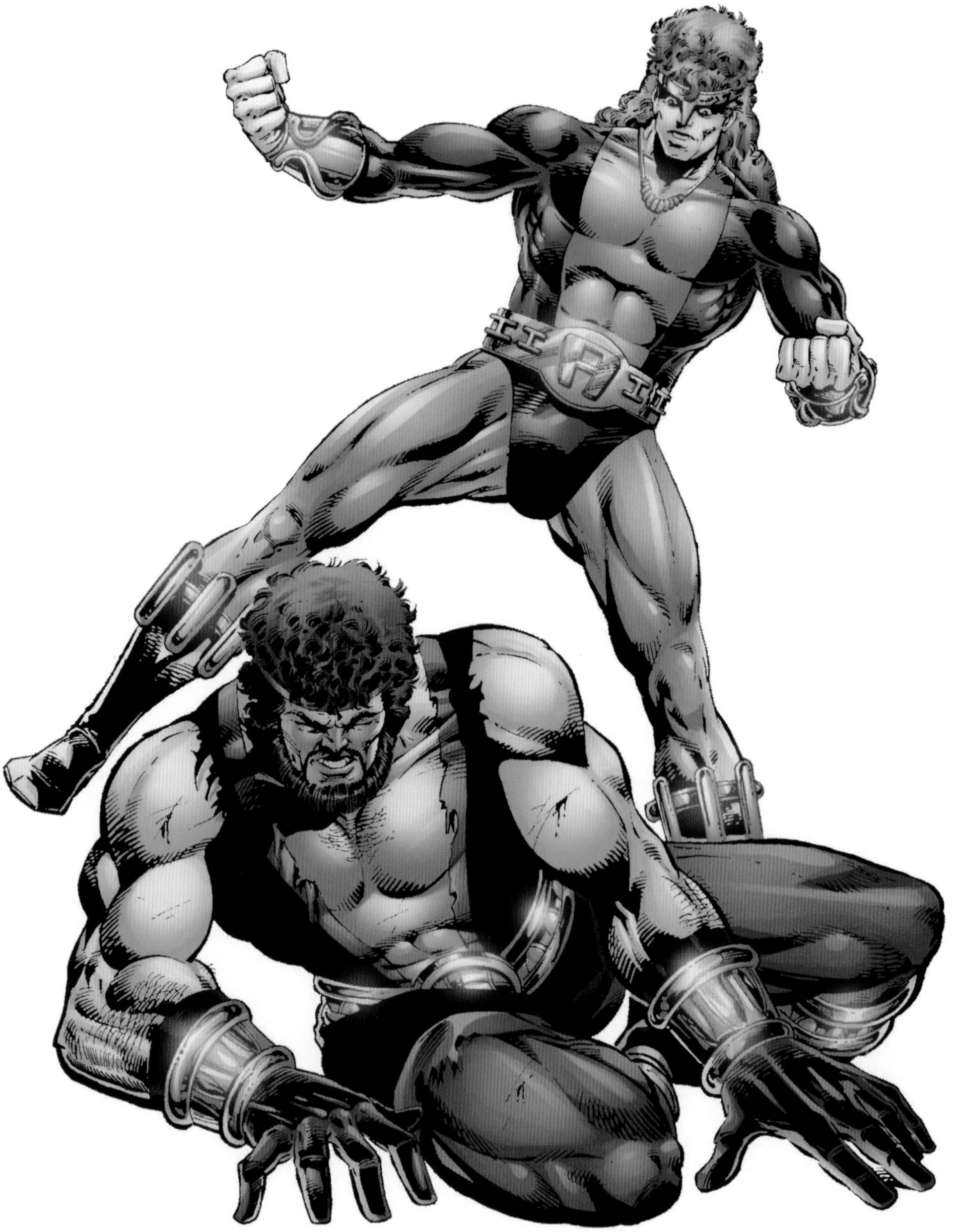

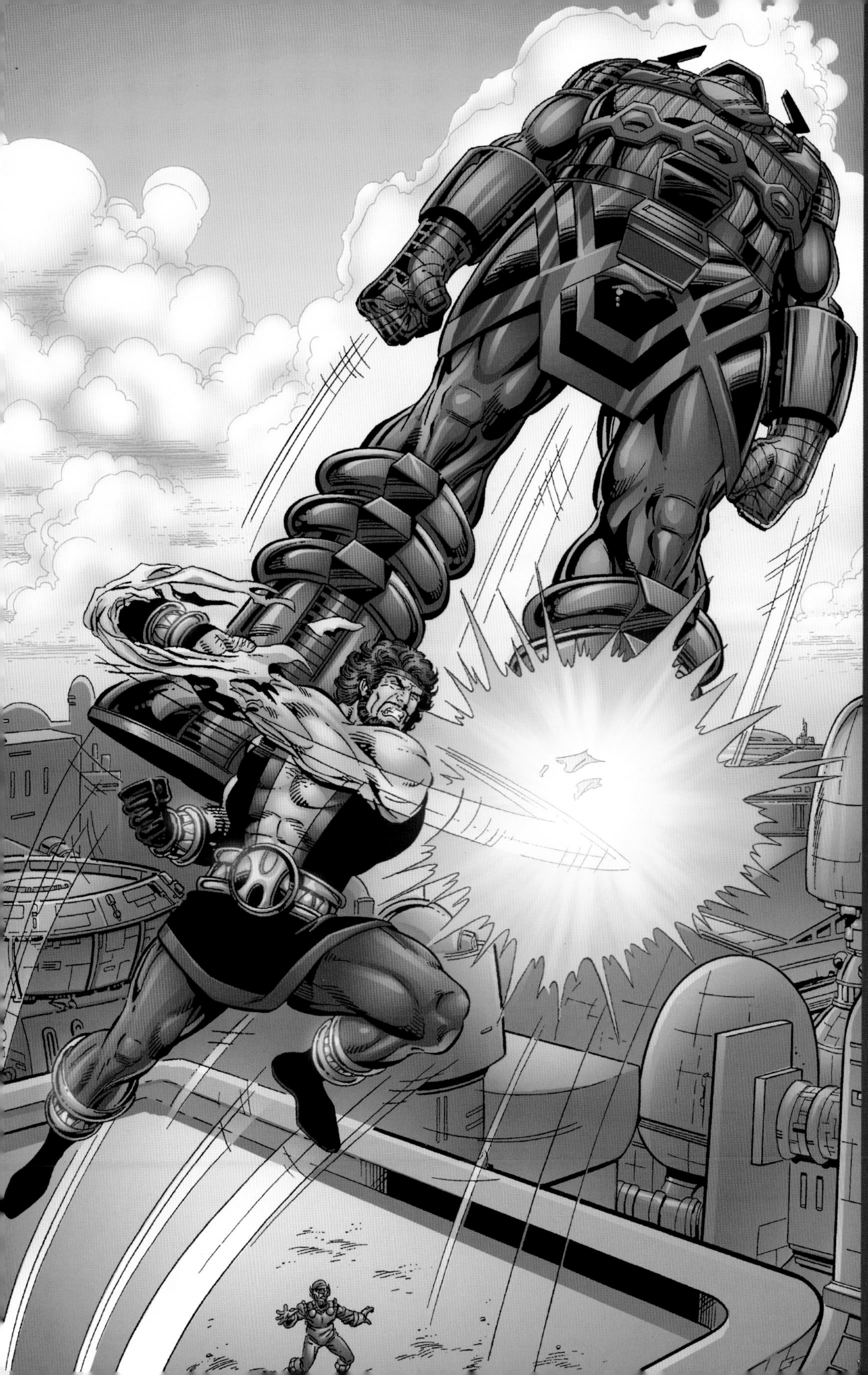